PASSING IT ON

Other Books by Myles Munroe

PASSING IT ON

GROWING YOUR FUTURE LEADERS

Myles Munroe

NEW YORK BOSTON NASHVILLE

FaithWords
Hachette Book Group
237 Park Avenue
New York, NY 10017

www.faithwords.com

Printed in the United States of America

First Edition: May 2011
10 9 8 7 6 5 4 3 2 1

FaithWords is a division of Hachette Book Group, Inc.
The FaithWords name and logo are trademarks of Hachette Book Group, Inc.

Library of Congress Cataloging-in-Publication Data
Munroe, Myles.
  Passing it on : growing your future leaders / Myles Munroe. — 1st ed.
      p. cm.
  ISBN 978-0-446-58047-2
  1. Leadership—Religious aspects—Christianity. 2. Leadership—Biblical teaching. I. Title.
  BV4597.53.L43M855 2011
  253—dc22
                                    2010040142

Contents

Introduction

The Lions

TEN THOUSAND PEOPLE rose to their feet, filling the convention center in the quaint South African city of Bloemfontein with thunderous applause on a beautiful Sunday afternoon. I had just completed three days of motivational and inspirational training sessions with one of the largest multilevel-marketing distribution companies on the continent of Africa. My host, Charlie, the president of the company, hugged me with a deep expression of appreciation as he asked, "Dr. Munroe, how would you like to spend a few extra days here in Africa and go on a safari cruise?" I had no idea what he meant, but I was ready to take a break and experience an adventure.

"Of course I would," I answered. Thus began one of the most memorable vacations I ever could imagine. The next morning a driver picked us up and took us to a marina where we boarded a forty-foot yacht. On board, a pleasant, middle-aged man greeted us and introduced himself as our captain and cook. Just my wife, two other couples, and I would take the journey along a river that ran through five southern African states, including Zambia, Zimbabwe, and South Africa, for a five-day safari through wild country. I was excited as I thought of all the *National Geographic* episodes I had seen on television. I was about to embark on a similar experience in reality.

After settling in, we began cruising up river, astonished by the untouched beauty of nature and the virgin forest filled with birds, reptiles, and other animals in their natural habitat. The captain, perched in his seat high above the cabin, pointed out the many species of animals and plants, warning us of the dangers surrounding us and emphasizing that we must not leave the boat at any time during the trip. The whole setting excited me, waking up the sleeping child inside of me. It was a boyhood dream come true.

Suddenly, I heard a blood-chilling sound coming from the bush on the right side of the river. It was like nothing I had ever heard. Animals and birds became restless and began moving nervously about, responding with their own sounds. We were also uneasy and asked the undisturbed captain what that sound was. He simply responded, "They are going to make a kill tonight." Then he explained that the sound came from a pride of lions organizing for the hunt.

My heart started racing and my palms sweating as I felt the adrenaline rushing through my body. It was as if I were going to join the lions for the kill. I asked the captain if we could observe the action, and he indicated that he would try to position the boat so we could watch the unfolding drama of nature in safety. By now the sleeping child within me was wide-awake! Could you imagine having front-row seats to a lion kill?

The sun was about to set as a family of elephants who were obviously the target of the lions emerged from the bush. These giants of the animal kingdom began to trumpet warnings to each other as they moved like tractors through the trees and grass, which fell like twigs in their wake. Like ghosts, the masters of the wild appeared from nowhere—lions, the majestic cats that rule the world of animals. I had seen them in still pictures, movies, and television documentaries, but here they were in real life, in real time, with real power, about to prove their kingship.

Everyone on board grabbed their cameras and focused on the lions and the elephants, but I noticed something—a lioness holding two cubs in her mouth, gently carrying them to a small mound, and setting them under a tree not far from the action. One by one, she placed them in full sight of the elephants and the rest of the pride. My first reaction to was to think, "What is she doing? She is placing them in danger, exposing them to the force and authority of some of the most powerful creatures on earth."

However, I was about to observe one of the most valuable lessons I would ever learn as I wondered about this aloud to the captain. "Why is she doing that?"

The captain quietly answered, "She wants to make sure they see everything."

I was confused. In the midst of all this danger and power, why would she want to make sure they saw it? The captain, noticing my bewilderment, eased my confused mind, showing me not only why the lion is the king and ruler of the animal kingdom, but also why it has been a successful leader for so long. In fact, the secret to the longevity of the leadership legacy of the king of beasts was in that act of the lioness placing those delicate, little cubs on the mound under the tree to watch. The purpose of this act was to teach the cubs how to hunt by allowing them to observe those who had mastered the art. The lioness teaches by example.

This was the lesson leaders of humankind fail to learn or even consider. This was the lesson of mentoring and the art of preparing for succession. The lions did not leave the continuity of their pride's leadership supremacy up to chance, but rather carried out an intentional, planned, purposeful program for transfer of power and skills to the next generation of leaders.

I sat there in the African bush staring at the solution to most of the leadership challenges of that continent and the world—mentoring and training successors intentionally. I thought of all the coups, dictatorships, infighting, suspicion, and distrust among leaders, especially in developing countries. I saw on the mound under the tree the answer to unstable governments and broken economies. There, staring me in the face, was the least-practiced art of leadership. There, in the wilds of this great continent, was the lesson of leadership that inspired the research that resulted in the birth of this book.

The greatest act of leadership is mentoring. No matter how much you may learn, achieve, accumulate, or accomplish, if it all dies with you, then you are a generational failure. The act and art of mentoring are the manifestations of the highest level of maturity and self-confidence. The spirit of insecurity, low self-esteem, poor self-concept, and devalued self-worth always will focus on self-preservation and self-protection—a defensive perspective in life. This spirit of insecurity breeds the attitude of fear, suspicion, and distrust. These words describe the mind-set of many of the leaders serving in our governments, political parties, corporations, departments, religious organizations, churches, families, and civic organizations.

When many people rise to positions of power, influence, notoriety, and celebrity in our society, because they lack the character and maturity necessary to manage that power effectively, their first order of business is to secure their position, extinguish any opposition, and erect a defense mechanism that others would not dare violate. They see colleagues as enemies and partners as competitors. This creates an atmosphere of schism, friction, suspicion, distrust, and low productivity. Individuals with this attitude toward power and position never will mentor others and actually see the prospect of mentoring as personally unwise and threatening to their own survival.

This lack of willingness, desire, understanding, and interest in mentoring is the greatest curse and weakness of our twenty-first century leaders. The majority of leaders at the controls of our political machinery, economic empires, and massive social or religious structures all seem to be preoccupied with protecting their occupational lives and not their generational legacies. We need leaders who think more of the next generation and not merely of the next position in the organization. We need leaders who feel they owe a debt to the future and who are committed and willing to securing it by intentionally preparing the future stewards of our world. We need leaders who are more dedicated to history than they are to money. We need leaders more interested in investing in people than in pursuing private ambition.

The highest manifestation of true leadership is to identify one's replacement and to begin mentoring him or her. Life is really a generational relay with each succeeding generation responsible for passing the baton safely to the next with all the distilled knowledge, experience, and wisdom intact. All leaders should strive to execute their duties, reach milestones, achieve major progress, and fulfill the vision for their families, businesses, corporations, ministries, and nations. However, they also should work to produce the next generation of leaders who will value, protect, preserve, and build on those achievements.

Too many times we have seen great works, sacrifice, and hard-fought victories squandered and devalued by the irresponsible, insensitive abusive acts of a succeeding generation of leaders who have little or no appreciation for the blood, sweat, and tears expended by those of the former generation. Should the new leaders bear the blame for this abuse of history, or should we place the blame at the feet of the former leaders who failed to prepare, sensitize, and mentor future leaders? Should we consider failure to mentor the next generation of leaders generational suicide? Could it be a divine paradox that the very word *succession* comes from the root *success*?

The most important responsibility of leadership is to prepare for succession. The most valuable goal of leadership is not to succeed in the present, but to secure the future. You are only truly successful in leadership if your accomplishments and achievements are preserved and perpetuated for posterity. It is not what leaders achieve that counts. It is what they transfer. Building people to protect and preserve our institutions is more important than building institutions.

Leading beyond your leadership is the ultimate accomplishment of true leadership. No matter how great your accomplishments may be, if they die with you, then you are a failure.

Therefore, the greatest obligation of true leadership is to transfer your deposit to the next generation. Leadership success is measured by the success of your successor. It takes a lifetime to accumulate the knowledge, wisdom, skills, insights, and experience that make you an outstanding leader. It would be a tragedy to see the wealth of that life deposited in some cemetery and marked only by a tombstone, which can speak to no one.

True leaders must focus on investing in people more than buildings. Their priority should be to make deposits in the banks of human spirits and souls, not just in the financial institutions of Wall Street and Switzerland. Mentoring a successor is the most valuable investment a leader can make because it could guarantee preservation of all the other investments. Losing a lifetime of leadership achievement to an unprepared generation is the highest violation of leadership responsibility. It is imperative that mentoring successors becomes as much of a priority as fulfilling vision. In essence, a vision is only successful if it is durable.

Be ever mindful that you are a link in a long chain of purpose that was designed to fulfill the divine desire of the Creator. Thus, life is not about you, but it is about preparation for the next phase.

History is replete with sad stories of great leaders who accomplished outstanding social, economic, military, political, or spiritual feats only to witness an unprepared succeeding leadership dismantle most of what they spent a lifetime laboring to create. It is a true tragedy to see one generation's work destroyed, ignored, or devalued by the one that followed.

I am certain that every leader throughout history desired to see a vision, work, programs, projects, mission, and passion continued beyond his or her tenure. No generation wants its hard-fought leadership success to be swallowed up in a whirlwind of neglect, insensitivity, and lack of appreciation for the sacrifice expended on that achievement.

We must mentor! No greater measure of leadership success exists than the ability to protect, preserve, and transfer the accomplishments of the present leadership to the next generation. This is the heart of the principle of succession and must be a priority in our twenty-first century leadership challenge. This book is about this challenge, and I invite you to join the adventure and the journey. It is my hope that this book will inspire and equip you to think beyond your own leadership and motivate you to leave a legacy, not in institutions or on tombstones, but in people. May you always remember that your success depends on your successors.

Dr. Myles Munroe

Part 1

The Principles—Success Is to Perpetuate Purpose for Posterity

Chapter 1

The Greatest Leadership Obligation Is Preparing Your Replacement

HUMAN OBSERVERS HAVE designated the lion "king of the wild" or "king of the beasts." Lions are the largest creature in the cat family and of all African carnivores. These large and powerful creatures have the loudest roar and are the leading predators in their ecosystem. The lion is fierce, courageous, and cunning. Yet even the lion knows it will not be "king" forever. The lion is constantly working to prepare its replacement to run the kingdom.

Lions are the only cats that live in groups. Lions travel in prides. A pride is essentially a family of lions and lionesses that live and work together to create an environment in which to "mentor" cubs, the next generation of "kings" and "queens." Before the cub is a year old, the lioness meticulously begins to train her young to hunt and to survive.

Lions are visionary leaders.

First, Get Ready to Leave

Whether you are the head of a family, captain of a football team, chair of a women's organization, president of a company, the CEO of a corporation, the pastor of a church, or the pilot of an aircraft, you are the responsible leader. In your domain, you are king. You are a visionary leader. Your gift has taken you to the top. Congratulations! You have arrived. Now, find your replacement. The first act of a true leader, a visionary leader like you, should be to identify your replacement and begin mentoring that person to eventually succeed you. You might identify several individuals and groom each of them for leadership.

You may ask, "Why? I have other things to do first. I just got here, and I have all these plans. That can wait."

It should not wait. Perhaps if you knew just how long you might remain healthy, active, and effective or how long you might live, it could wait. None of us knows these things. We must prepare someone to follow us. We will have mentored and trained this leader-in-waiting so carefully and thoroughly that he or she could step in at a moment's notice to take our place and run on without stumbling. That person would preserve what we have built and take it to new heights.

> *"The first act of a visionary leader like you should be to identify and begin mentoring your replacement."*

Our successors can do that only if we have groomed and trained them to the best of our abilities for the day they take over. It was our duty to bring them into our inner circle, expose them to our contacts, and instill in them all the wisdom we can offer.

The greatest obligation of true leadership is to transfer the deposit of knowledge, wealth, experience, influence, relationships, and understanding to the next generation. The word *obligation* means a responsibility you have to the future. Perhaps you have been measuring your success by the trappings, as I once did. You see it in terms of the size of a building you built, your salary, a house—or the car. Remember all of those things are decaying daily, and if you built your success on those things, it is eroding daily.

It is not good enough to transfer a title, a facility, or a building to the next generation. It is more important to transfer your knowledge, your experience, and your values—the things that have helped you to succeed. Giving those to the next generation is more important than giving money and wealth. Leadership includes taking what made you who you are and giving it to someone else. That cannot happen without mentoring.

Every leader wants to be successful, but we rarely think about succession as proof of success, the final measure of our own success. We think in terms of projects, products, the bottom line, and profits. We do not think in terms of people. Buildings do not succeed you. Equipment does not succeed you. Only people can succeed you and carry on your vision. People will remember your name and perpetuate your legacy. As we age and consider our frailties and our mortality, it is time to start doubling up on the time spent on mentoring and preparing for a smooth succession.

The first act of true leadership is to identify, train, and develop a replacement. To put it another way, the first act is to begin mentoring this new leader. If I can get this point across, I could help save many organizations, departments, ministries, and countries.

The first thing that many leaders do when they enter a position of power is to get rid of opposition. They try to annihilate threats. You see this in Third-World countries and leading industrial nations. It is the spirit of "kill or be killed." You see it in businesses, where those who are threats to corporate power are fired. I am recommending the opposite. Your first act should be to begin surveying the horizon, looking around you to identify the potential replacement/successor, and mentoring this prospect.

What Is a Leader?

Before we go on, it might be helpful to share with you (or to review for those who have read my previous books) my philosophies about what leadership is. You have to understand and appreciate what you have before you can pass it on. You have to be the right kind of leader to produce leaders for the future.

I have spent decades studying the issue of leadership from the time I was an undergraduate at Oral Roberts University and a graduate student in leadership administration at the University of Tulsa. I have studied the theories of many business leaders, economists, and scholars on leadership. The many theories and perspectives offered by the early and contemporary leadership gurus addressed multiple issues and principles on the subject of leadership. However, I was still unsatisfied in my pursuit of understanding the essence of true leadership, and I continued my search and research. It was not until I discovered the leadership philosophy and school of thought of t⟋ rabbi Jesus Christ that I felt I had found the answer to ⟋ dilemma. It was His introduction and demonstration of the ph⟋ of "servant leadership" that provided the context for the type and s⟋ of leadership that brings value, worth, and dignity to all humankind. After many years of study and implementing this philosophy of leadership in my life and organization, I have seen the superior advantage and benefits to both the individual and the corporate effort. This "servant leadership" philosophy forms the foundation of all the content of the leadership training programs, seminars, and consulting projects that I have facilitated around the world. I have written dozens of books and spoken hundreds of times on this leadership philosophy and model exemplified by Jesus Christ.

His standard for leadership was that of serving your gift and energy to the followers for their benefit. He modeled the behavior of a servant leader and urged His protégés to do likewise. In His final "working dinner" with them, He demonstrated and later explained the concept.

> **Matthew 20:25–27** Jesus called them together and said, "You know that the rulers of the Gentiles lord it over them, and their high officials exercise authority over them. Not so with you. Instead, **whoever wants to become great among you must be your servant,** and whoever wants to be first must be your slave—"

Then He goes on to say:

> **Matthew 20:28** "Just as the Son of Man **did not come to be served, but to serve,** and to give his life as a ransom for many."

Jesus' concept of the leader as servant and not as one to be served was demonstrated by Jesus Himself, and He urged students (the disciples) to achieve greatness through the same spirit of leading through service, not by controlling or oppressing others. Servant leadership, as I define it, is the discovery of one's purpose, gifts, and talents with a commitment to offer them in service to humankind. In other words, servant leadership is the discovery of what you are supposed to serve to the world.

Servant leadership is being prepared to serve one's gift at every opportunity. Now, I want to emphasize the last part of the statement: *every opportunity*. To become an effective leader, you have to take advantage of each chance to serve. Do not wait until you are great to be great, or you will never be great.

If the bathroom needs cleaning, that is an opportunity to exercise your gift for attention to detail and high standards to those in your organization. If they need help with the youth organization, that is an opportunity to demonstrate your gift for empathizing with and commanding respect from young people. If the leaders need someone to clean the building after every session, volunteer and display your gift for organization by recruiting and supervising a team to do it quickly and efficiently. That is an opportunity to serve. If the organization needs someone to type and you can do that, then submit yourself. While serving, you can show off your speed, devotion to accuracy, and mastery of computer skills.

Maybe your vision is to become a great speaker, teacher, pastor, or CEO. That opportunity has not come yet, but the opportunity to park the cars presents itself. Park the cars. If nothing else, you can demonstrate your loyalty and your people skills in handling the owners. Servant leadership is serving at every opportunity.

In a previous book *In Charge: Finding the Leader Within You*, I summarized my thinking about servant leadership. These are the key points:

- **Every human being was created to lead.** Your desire and disposition to lead is inborn.
- **Every human possesses leadership potential.** You have the ability to lead in an area of gifting.
- **Trapped in every follower is a hidden leader.** If you accept false

ideas about who can or cannot become a leader, it can smother your potential.

- **Though everyone was born to lead, most will die as followers.** If you do not identify and tap into your giftedness, it will be wasted and buried with you.
- **Leadership is your history and your destiny.** You were created to be a leader and designed to fulfill your assignment.
- **The world needs your leadership.** You exist to meet a specific need on earth that no one else can meet.

What Is Succession?

Succession is an amazing word. It begins with the very concept of success. Success has to do with movement. It has to do with continuity. **Successful succession guarantees continuity.** Succession means to "follow after," but the definitions of "succeed" in some dictionaries even put the sense of "following" before the idea of doing well. Etymologists tell us that the word *succeed* comes from ancient terms that mean to "follow" or "go under."

Success itself has to do with advancing toward something, and for the most part, people think of success as "I establish a goal. I move toward the goal, and I accomplish the goal. I am finished." In a very simplistic sense, that is true; you decide you want to build a house, and you start the design, you build it, and now that it is finished, you receive the key. You could call that success, but succession preserves success.

We normally think of success as having to do with pursuing, achieving, and concluding something, but success implies moving, advancing, continuing. Succession is the perpetuation of purpose. Purpose is your assignment. Succession is protecting your assignment beyond your lifetime. Succession preserves all of your hard work after you retire or die. Succession is the transition of the leader's purpose, content, character, standards, values, morals, and qualities to succeeding generations. Succession first involves transferring your vision to another generation of leaders. That is a hard thing to do.

It means you must transfer your way of thinking to another person. That requires a lot of intimate time together. To effect the vision transfer, the mentor must devote time to the potential successor.

The vision must live on even if you die. If your vision dies with you, you failed. I have seen unfinished churches overgrown with grass. Why? Because the leader failed. Crowds came to his services and people shouted at his sermons, but no one carried on and completed his tabernacle. The weeds that choke the unfinished dreams will always expose failure. Unfinished monuments are a sign of failure, telltale signs that you did not mentor and invest in the right thing, the people for whom you were responsible.

Success is not what happens while you are alive. Success is what happens after you leave. This is why the word *successive* is so important. The terms *successive* or *succeeding* generations suggest continuity. We want to be successful, so we accomplish a project. We are proud that we did it and want everyone to remember what we produced in our lifetime. That is not success. Success is knowing someone will continue the work after you leave.

You are successful if your vision outlives you through another person. If we forget you after you die, no matter how great your accomplishments were, you are a failure. You measure your success by the people you leave behind. Someone who comes after you can destroy every goal that you achieved. If you are sixty, seventy, or eighty years old and you have done wonderful things, will they outlast you? The only way to guarantee they will is through succession. **True leadership is about continuity.**

Succession is not just achieving success. Succession is preserving success. What you achieve, you need someone to preserve. Can you imagine building your family business all your life and then some untrained son sells it after you die for half the price, just so he can buy some golf clubs? All your life you worked hard, invested and built a building, built a business, or built this massive empire. Then a son, daughter, cousin, or your wife's next husband sells it on the market for half the price to buy something that provides immediate gratification. We have seen this happen very often.

When it is time for leaders to transition, many have not prepared a successor, so there is a conflict, a fight, or a scuffle for leadership. When a new leader emerges from that, the winner may be committed to destroying everything you have built to prove that he is different or better. This has been the modus operandi of most leaders. If you have studied developing countries, you know that in most cases when a leadership transition occurs, a coup breaks out. Often people are killed and the country experiences tremendous turmoil. A similar thing happens in corporate board rooms, political parties, and church organizations when it is time for these transitions, generally without the violence though.

This is why succession is so critical. It preserves success. Greatness in leadership is measured by its continuity. It is not about you. It is about the next generation. You do not want anyone to destroy, misuse, or redirect your organization from its original intent. You want it to advance and develop beyond what you have done. You keep your purpose alive through a successor. You do not want all your dreams, plans, and ideas to go into the casket with you. Keep them alive in someone you mentor.

My definition of succession is the effective transfer, conveyance, and transition of the leader's vision, passion, purpose, intent, dreams, character, standards, values, morals, and qualities to succeeding generations of leaders.

Succession perpetuates purpose.

Chapter 2

Preserving Your Legacy

THE MAJORITY OF the experiences that most of us have had with leadership transfer came after somebody died. What follows usually is not a smooth transfer, but a conflict, a fight, a struggle. Many times brokenness, frustration, and, worst of all, a split will cripple or destroy the organization the leader built. How many of us have seen this in our families, churches, governments, or businesses?

When the "president for life" of the African nation of Gabon died recently after more than forty years in office, government leaders at first denied he was even ill and continued to dispute reports that he was in ill health only hours before announcing his demise. Due to fear of a coup as news of his death spread, national officials immediately shut airports, closed borders, blocked Internet service, and stationed guards in government buildings and at the utilities. Traffic was in gridlock as people sped home from work and rushed out to buy groceries, fearing stores would close.

That may be the extreme, but chaos is very common when a leader dies. Anyone who has lived long enough to experience leadership transition will agree that confusion, fear, uncertainty, and insecurity accompanied the change. All of these can be very debilitating, immobilizing, and dangerous to the organization, country, family, or business. They are a direct result of the leader's failure to prepare for transition, products of the inability or unwillingness to mentor and prepare others to succeed him.

When the head of the family dies, children fight among themselves for the spoils. Jealousy and hatred destroy the love they might have shared in the past. Look at the infighting over the custody of Michael Jackson's children and the disposition of his assets. To some, he was just a successful entertainer, to others an oddity, but he was also the head of a family and the leader of a billion-dollar entertainment enterprise generated by his music and rights to the music of the Beatles and others. The legal battles could go on for years and destroy what he left. Even in ordinary families, children, stepchildren, wives, ex-wives, and coinhabitants may fight so bitterly over petty issues and things of little worth that kinfolk do not associate with each other generations later.

"Measure leadership success by the success of the successor."

I have seen the chaos of transition in corporations, churches, and other organizations as well. When one strong leader passes on, fighting takes hold. Followers resort to deception, deceit, and destruction. These are indicators of the failure to prepare and mentor successors. How does one leader transfer leadership to the next without destroying the organization and losing everything?

Beyond the Horizon

The greatest act of leadership is mentoring. It took me forty years to write this one sentence. I thought a great leader is one who built a big building or organized a massive campaign. I thought leadership was about building a corporation worth millions. This is not the measure of greatness. Greatness must be measured by the transfer of success to future generations. In this book, I want to talk about how to transfer leadership from one generation to another, from one leader to another.

I find it very intriguing that the first-century, young rabbi Jesus Christ built an organization at thirty years old that is now more than two thousand years old. It is the largest company on earth with upward of two billion clients. I happen to work for the company. He started the company with just eleven investors, to whom he gave shares. They did not have to buy them.

The greatest leader of all time gave these shares to the partners by passing on knowledge, by mentoring. He told them they were no longer servants because a servant does not know what his master is doing. He had shared everything with them, so they were "friends."

> **John 15:15** "I no longer call you servants, because a servant does not know his master's business. Instead, I have called you friends, for everything that I learned from my Father I have made known to you."

Jesus was a secure leader. "I am going to give you everything," He essentially said. "Why? Because I don't plan to stay."

That is not an attitude that we often see in leaders today. Jesus never built a building, never opened a bank account, and never established a physical institution, yet His company is still expanding after two thousand years. That means greatness and leadership is not in buildings. It is in building people. We are so stuck on wanting our names on buildings, which can decay and fall down, that we forget the greatest investment any leader can make is in people.

Some leaders have their names engraved in their office chairs. They have that chair chained to the floor, and they have a seat belt on the chair. Every Monday they click it on and say, "No one is taking this. This is my position, my company, my church…"

True leaders do not hold on to the knowledge, experience, achievements, opportunities, or relationships they accrue in their positions. True leaders transfer knowledge. They cultivate the inquisitiveness of their mentees. Like the lioness, they encourage the mentees to observe them in action. The leader encourages them to ask questions. "Ask me how I did this and why I did this. I want you to know what I know. Because the sooner you learn this, the more quickly I can move on to my next position." **The greatest accomplishment of leadership is succession.** Failure to mentor a successor is the cancellation of leadership legacy. Failure to mentor a successor is the cancellation of your own legacy.

Transfer of Ownership

Your influence will not continue in buildings or bank accounts. Your influence will continue in people. This is why the greatest leader of all time invested three and a half years in people—in a training program for people. He had this idea of living forever through them. Buildings are perishable. People live on. You last in those who remember your name. You last in those you mentor. You last in the leaders you left in your place and in the leaders that those leaders train to replace them and so forth.

I do not want my name on a building because a hurricane, a terrorist act, or an earthquake could wipe it out. I want people to remember my name by the continuing leadership of those I mentored and by the successor that I molded.

So we need to consider: what are our priorities?

Four principles summarize my concept of succession in leadership:

1. Visionary leadership is generational.
2. Vision is greater than the visionary.
3. Mentoring is the highest responsibility of leadership.
4. Succession is the greatest measure of leadership success.

Leaders must focus not so much on fulfilling their vision as on preparing new leaders to carry it forward. Many leaders have great vision, but they think they should fulfill it in their lifetime. They do not think much about posterity. When a leader does not prepare the successor, the result is always chaos and destruction. Two major mistakes leaders make are to believe that they are the only ones who could and should fulfill the vision and to think that they should fulfill it in their lifetime.

Visionary leaders always possess a sense of destiny. Destiny forces one to think beyond a lifetime. Destiny is bigger than all of us. It is that massive, uncompromising eternalness of life. Visionary leaders always think of their mortality. They are not afraid of it. They interpret destiny as the privilege to paint in a small piece of history. This is why visionary leaders communicate the vision of the future effectively. They are able to paint pictures and give conceptual vision to the future of others. Visionary leaders transfer ownership of the vision to the next generation. Visionary leaders focus on training others to fulfill the vision even beyond their lifetime. Leaders lead beyond their own leadership. They go beyond what they are supposed to do. They are constantly thinking about what remains after death. These are true leaders.

Measure leadership success by the success of the successor. This means that true leadership does not use achievements or goals, programs and projects as measures of success, but looks to the quality, character, competence, and passion of people around the leader who can fulfill the vision. Leaders are not in the business of focusing on projects. To a true leader, people are more important than projects. People are more important than paper, personal ambitions, or pride. Leaders do not manage people. Leaders develop people.

Mentoring is the greatest and highest responsibility of leadership. It is not just a necessity for the operation. It is obligatory. Yet the responsibility for mentoring is usually not in the forefront of leaders' minds. Most people we consider leaders focus mainly on themselves, their own achievements, and their successes. They focus on what they want to do, what they want to be known for, and what they want to build as a legacy. Most leaders build their legacy in their work and not in people. I encourage you to shift that paradigm. Your greatest legacy is not a product or an institution that you left behind, but rather a person or people. This approach is different from anything else I have read on succession and leadership.

Leaving your child a building or a house is not succession. That is inheritance. Whatever a person inherits, he can lose, but if you mentor a person, he cannot lose what you gave him. Mentoring is a transfer of things that are durable: vision, passion, intent, and character.

The average leader today has no interest in mentoring. He or she is preoccupied with defending a position and protecting turf. These are insecure, false leaders with titles.

You know people in your company who have been there for forty years, and you still cannot get rid of them. They do not even want promotions. They just want that position. How do you break that spirit? You teach them about mentoring. Teach this to your staff, those you are mentoring, because if they understand this early, they will not hold on to jobs too tightly. They will not develop the spirit of entitlement. That spirit of "this is my space" will be broken if they study and embrace mentorship.

Mentored to Lead

Mentoring involves encouraging another to serve in that person's area of gifting. Through the opportunities for service that you provide, the mentee can discover, practice, and refine a gift. By serving that gift to others, the mentee discerns and fulfills purpose. At the same time, seeing you serve so willingly and joyfully influences the mentee. The mentee helps you carry out your vision and fulfill your purpose.

I have come to define true leadership as **the capacity to influence others through inspiration, generated by a passion, motivated by a vision, brought by a conviction, produced by a purpose.**

To lead people anywhere, you have to influence them. Your influence inspires the mentee to carry out your vision. No one will buy into your vision if you do not have passion for it. Your passion grows out of conviction that your vision is worth pursuing. That conviction grows out of finding your purpose. The mentee finds purpose in your passion for your vision. He or she catches the vision.

The secret to leadership is not the pursuit of power. Leadership is a pursuit of self. While you may delegate some authority and confer a position on your mentee, you demonstrate that leadership is not a pursuit of those things. You show your mentee that when you discover what you were born to do, your leadership is born. Thus, leadership has very little to do with people. It is about self-discovery. It is finding your passion and pursuing it, and then people will find you. This is why leadership really cannot be taught. It can only be mentored. You can teach people the principles for discovering themselves, and when they find their purpose, the leader is born.

Purpose is the beginning. Purpose is having a sense of destiny. Your purpose then fuels your conviction. Your conviction is a sense of significance. In other words, a leader is someone who discovered that he or she is important to the world. Your mentoring must endow your mentee with a sense of purpose.

That happened to me. I had an argument with my Creator.

I said, "I cannot be that important."

He said, "Yes, you are."

I said, "No, I can't be that important. Don't you know where I was born? Who my relatives are?"

He said, "Look, you are that important."

Do you know that the attitude I had is common to all the leaders that I have studied? When God spoke to Abraham, He got an argument (see Genesis 17:17). When God spoke to Moses, they argued (see Exodus 3:11–14). When God first spoke to Gideon, He had to argue with Gideon just to make him believe (see Judges 6:13–24). In other words, we never believe the truth about ourselves.

You must help your mentees see they are that important, and the sooner they accept that, the sooner the third step develops, and that is vision. They begin to see how to fulfill their purpose. Vision is a concept of the future, and when the vision comes, passion comes. Passion is a deep desire and commitment to achieve the vision. That passion inspires other people. In other words, passion becomes what I call "contagious energy," and that breathes air into people.

When your mentees become so passionate about something that they are willing to strive for it, it breathes life into them. You have become contagious. Think about great leaders. Most of them went to prison or in other ways demonstrated they were willing to die for their passion: Jesus, the Apostle Paul, Martin Luther King Jr., and Mohandas Gandhi. They inspired people. Once you inspire people, you can influence them and attract support. You do not demand it. You attract it. People are attracted to passion.

Therefore, if you want people to follow you, find your passion, and if your passion takes over your life, people will run after you. A leader does not look for followers. Followers are attracted to the leader's passion. If you say you are a leader, but no one is following you, you are simply taking a walk.

Your mentee must see from your example that following is a privilege that people do not have to give you. They can leave your church or resign from your company at any time. To keep people submitted to your passion, never let them see your passion waning. Keep your passion. Share it with your mentee. You can become tired, but you must maintain and renew your passion.

New and Improved!

If you are going to be successful in producing a successor, you must make mentoring your priority. Mentoring is hard work. You serve as a model, an advisor, a counselor, a guide, a tutor, an example for another. Your goal is to produce one greater than yourself. That may come as a shock. When you are mentoring someone, you are not trying to produce a person who is *like you*. You are mentoring to develop someone *better than you*. Mentoring is about replacement with a better product. Always leave in place someone who is better than you were. A true leader is always training a replacement, and the goal is to make that person better than the mentor is.

The greatest leadership challenge is establishing the priority of self-replacement. Leaders do not clone others in their own image. They help others discover themselves, deploy their own abilities, reach the height of their own capacities and refine their unique personalities. Mentoring is not about making a person you—making someone talk like you, act like you, or dress in a suit like you. That is not leadership. That is personality worship.

The greatest leader of all time taught me so much by His attitude. He would say something like this: "If I do not leave you, you will not be able to do greater works. But if I leave you, knowing how well I trained you, then you will do greater works than I have done." In other words, a successor should achieve more.

> **John 14:12** "I tell you the truth, anyone who has faith in me will do what I have been doing. **He will do even greater things than these**, because I am going to the Father."

Succession is the greatest measure of true leadership. Most leaders define success in leadership as what they achieve, but if everything dies with them, they are failures. If everything you achieve stops when you stop, you are a failure. We have many examples in the world where we can visit relics of old organizations, the building projects that died with the leader. Thus, the challenge of true leadership success is to ask, "What will die with you?" The goal of leadership should be to answer confidently the question, "What will live after I die?"

Succession protects the value of history. Succession uses the foundation of history to make history. Succession guarantees the value of effort. For example, you work for twenty years building something. If you have a good successor, they will protect all the work that you put in. In the absence of proper planning for succession, someone else can tear down something that you built for twenty years in twenty minutes. Your successor can just wipe it out.

Effective succession is the only way to secure desires from the grave. What did that dead person desire? Only succession can secure that. Succession is the only way for a leader to live beyond the cemetery. The bottom line is that it does not matter how great your leadership was in your lifetime. Will it survive beyond your lifetime is the greater question. The answer lies in how well you have prepared the heirs to your domain.

Chapter 3

Secrets of Successful Succession

THIRTY YEARS AGO I began the global organization through which I now enjoy the pleasure of helping millions of people around the world to improve their lives. I knew from its inception, however, that becoming tied to any position, title, or privilege would hinder my ability to move beyond the boundaries of the original organization and ministry. I had to be willing to wear the titles, power, benefits, and privileges of my position loosely. I had to remind myself daily that this position could either become a trap, tying me to the past, or a springboard, leading to a greater future. I am aware that my pilgrimage on this planet is a series of roles, assignments, and responsibilities that are transitional and must never be possessed but passed on.

This sense of transitional responsibility motivated me to appoint my leadership team at the start of this global vision in 1980 and to begin to identify the person I could mentor to become my successor. From the beginning, I emphasized that everyone had leadership potential and that we were building for the next generation. I constantly kept the future before our staff and the organization's members. I knew that to realize my vision for global reach through the organization that I had the privilege to birth and develop, I would need to establish an intentional succession process. This would release me to continue building our international structure. Fifteen years after starting the organization and after securing the foundation, mission, and vision,

I knew the time would come for me to relinquish the power, privilege, and authority I enjoyed and to share them with my mentee. In 1995, I made an official decision to appoint from among the team the leader who understood my heart and vision, the one who would be willing to sacrifice. Today, that leader has principle responsibility for the core organization and is doing an outstanding job. This critical move of putting a successor in place has allowed me the ability to expand the organization worldwide. I could not have done that if I had remained strapped to the first seat of power. My conclusion is that mentoring and succession is the only way to extend yourself beyond your limited position.

True leaders must:

- Find the courage to mentor.
- Secure a legacy for the next generation.
- Transfer their deposit to the next generation.
- Measure success by the success of their successors.

Jesus Builds a Transition Team

The historic leader Jesus Christ began organizing and building His organization at age thirty and appointed His first few leadership team members from among common village folks who were also business owners involved in the fishing industry. As soon as He gathered His first leadership students, He began to speak of His inevitable destiny—to be arrested, tried, tortured, crucified, and resurrected from the dead. He constantly reminded them of His need to leave them and urged them to prepare for this inevitability. Early in His ministry one day after the mentees had failed to exorcise a demon from a little boy, He asked them a revealing question.

> **Matthew 17:17** "O unbelieving and perverse generation," Jesus replied, "how long shall I stay with you? How long shall I put up with you?"

The implications of these questions are profound. His words reveal the frustration of a teacher or mentor who expected His students to learn enough to allow Him to turn His work over to them with confidence. It also indicates His deep desire for them to learn what He knew and to perform at His level.

Here are the most important considerations for succession planning, using the mentoring style of Jesus Christ, the greatest leader who ever lived, as our model and standard:

"The secret to succession begins with the leader's acceptance of his mortality."

Plan your departure the day you begin. You are dispensable, mortal, and temporary. Start with the attitude, "I am temporary, and my greatest job is to leave someone greater than myself in this position." You start planning immediately to leave this position. The secret to succession begins with the leader's acceptance of his mortality. It begins with a consciousness—"I am temporary"—that allows confident leaders to begin planning their departure. "I am aware that I must quickly find a replacement, train and develop someone quickly in case my departure is soon." You must "begin with the end in mind," as the best-selling author and business trainer Stephen R. Covey put it in his classic guide *The 7 Habits of Highly Effective People*. That was Habit 2. He meant it for normal, daily tasks or projects. In this case, the logical "end" is the end of your tenure, your working life, or the end of life itself. Recall how Jesus reminded His team that His departure was inevitable and should be an incentive for them to apply themselves to the lessons at hand:

> **Matthew 17:22–24** When they came together in Galilee, he said to them, "The Son of Man is going to be betrayed into the hands of men. They will kill him, and on the third day he will be raised to life." And the disciples were filled with grief.

True leaders should always lead with their departure in view, being ever mindful that their priority is to work themselves out of a job.

As a leader, you cannot buckle yourself in and strap yourself to the seat of power with the hope that no one can or will try to move you. To do so works to your disadvantage because it restricts you from progressing beyond your current position.

Finishing well is more important than starting well. It is how a leader completes tenure. Finishing well depends on what and whom you left in your place. Many leaders start with great momentum, passion, and lofty goals. Then they let it all die with them. One of the greatest secrets of finishing is not with a project but with a person, finishing not with success but with a successor.

The organizational ministry of Jesus Chris after two thousand years of continued growth, expansion, and progressive movements is a stellar example and prototype of a leader who finished well. When the time came for transition, He spent the final months of His life focusing on refining and developing His successors, as revealed in many of His instructions, prayers, and mentoring sessions with His students. He was constantly aware that all the work He had done was not as important as finishing His tenure well. In His aspiration to complete and transfer His work and vision to His successor, He made the following statements:

> **Luke 14:28–30** "Suppose one of you wants to build a tower. Will he not first sit down and estimate the cost to see if he has enough money to complete it? For if he lays the foundation and is not able to finish it, everyone who sees it will ridicule him, saying, 'This fellow began to build and was not able to finish.'"

In our lifetime an example of one who finished well was John Osteen, the charismatic pastor who founded Lakewood Church. He started his ministry in an abandoned feed store in Houston, Texas, in 1959 and built up a multiracial, interdenominational congregation of six thousand or more. He had a worldwide teleministry and a thriving missionary outreach when he died with little warning forty years later. Osteen's son Joel had worked with his father for seventeen years producing his television program but had never preached until the week before John Osteen's death. The young man did so at his ailing father's insistence and, he believes, at the urging of God to accept the assignment. To boost his courage, Joel said, he wore his father's shoes in the pulpit. At that point, his father was expected to survive his illness, but he died within days. Reluctant and feeling unprepared, the younger Osteen stepped in and not only kept his father's legacy alive but grew it into a ministry that meets in a former arena and fills stadiums all over the world.

Now Lakewood Church boasts the largest congregation in the United States with more than 43,000 worshipers a week, according to its website. Joel Osteen's television ministry goes out to listeners in one hundred countries, and his books are *New York Times* best sellers, reaching millions of readers. The media have called him one of the most fascinating people and one of the most influential Christians in America. His father finished well because he had the foresight to choose a successor. John Osteen saw his son as the one to fill his shoes, and before he passed, he had wanted others to see Joel in that role.

Mentoring a successor is not negotiable. The leader accepts the responsibility of identifying and mentoring his or her successor. It is not a matter of "Should I?" but, "When do I start?" It is not a matter of whether I should. It is an acceptance of "I must do this." A study of the leadership philosophy of Jesus Christ reveals his conscious commitment to identify and mentor His student and His successor, Simon Peter, son of John. Consider His words:

> **John 16:4–7** "I have told you this, so that when the time comes you will remember that I warned you. I did not tell you this at first because I was with you. Now I am going to him who sent me, yet none of you asks me, 'Where are you going?' Because I have said these things, you are filled with grief. But I tell you the truth: It is for your good that I am going away. Unless I go away, the Counselor will not come to you; but if I go, I will send him to you."

These words reveal not only Jesus' keen awareness of the transitional nature of His earthly assignment, but His commitment to His mentees and to the preparation necessary for them to succeed Him. He also saw His departure as a trigger for greater success and progress for His mentees, and He was determined to leave them for the sake of the organization's success.

This spirit of sacrifice is exemplified in the story of Pablo Picasso's father, who accepted his destiny to nurture the boy who became one of the best-known artists of all time. Picasso was mentored to greatness by his father, Don José Ruiz y Blasco. A curator and art teacher, Don José recognized the genius in the little boy, giving him lessons at home and in the fine-arts academies where the father taught. As the young man flourished under this careful tutelage, the mentor realized his protégé's talent so outshined his own that he had no more to teach him. Legend says that Picasso's father was so in awe of the youth's talent that he gave the boy his brushes and palette, vowing never to paint again himself. Don José sent his son away to study with greater teachers but often used his influence with journalists and jurists in competitions to promote Pablo's work.

He recognized the need to mentor intentionally, to prepare and promote a successor. It is essential that leaders not leave the future stability, durability, and longevity of their organizations or families to chance. Leaders must see mentoring as a necessity and requirement. Mentoring a successor must be as natural as leading and must become the motivator for leading.

Know when it is time to leave a position. Leaders do not want to think about moving on to another life beyond their current position. Retirement or death should not be the reason for leaving a position. Leaders should leave because they are moving on to the next phase of their life. One of the secrets of successful transition is preparing your successor while preparing your own succession. To what do you succeed? That is as important as who succeeds you. Some leaders have thought this through. At the age of 71, Howard Dodson Jr., the director of the New York City Public Library's Schomburg Center for Research in Black Culture, was looking toward the next phase. Dodson, who has been credited with visionary leadership in historic preservation, announced nearly a year ahead of time that he planned to retire in 2011 so the search for a successor could begin. While others focused on his long list of accomplishments after a quarter century at the helm of a prestigious institution he had steered to greatness, he already had an agenda for future discoveries and learning expeditions. In an interview for *The New Yorker* magazine, he said he would soon be heading off to Xi'an, China, Machu Picchu, Peru, and Ethiopia to see some of the world's treasures for himself. This was his time, not only to leave but also to do other things.

Perhaps as a historian, he was aware that ancient and contemporary history is replete with leaders who became so possessed by their own sense of importance, power, and influence that they wanted to be buried in their office, have their title as their tombstone and the accolades of their admirers as their wreaths. Nothing is as addictive and intoxicating as power, authority, and influence. One of the most difficult decisions most leaders have to make is to surrender the reins of power to another. True leaders must be secure enough to leave and fearless enough to face their own future.

Knowing when to leave a position is essential and critical to leadership, and any mismanagement of delicate process can dismantle and destroy years of hard work and investment of resources and human capital. This principle is so vital to the success of the organization that it is better for the leader to leave too early than to stay too late.

Could you imagine a championship basketball or football player extending play on the team well after retirement age, attempting to run the court or field with young firebrands itching for fame and glory? That champion would become the source of ridicule and disgrace for the whole organization. This is why great players leave at the height of their game. Great CEOs depart at the apex of their success. Great spiritual leaders leave when they are celebrated, not merely tolerated. True leaders do not see death as the ultimate signal to leave a position, but rather they see the sense of completion of their phase and contribution to the ongoing advancement of a vision bigger and nobler than their own existence.

One of the greatest examples we have of knowing when to leave is the former President of South Africa, Nelson Mandela. After achieving the highest position in his nation and reaching a goal he had desired for decades—one that demanded the sacrifice of his personal freedom, he decided to let it go after only one term. His sense of transitional leadership and the need to mentor a successor was stronger than his desire for power, influence, and control. Mandela is the prototype of the true leadership spirit. He handed his successor, Thabo Mbeki, all the power and influence of thirty years of struggle in a thirty-minute ceremony.

Do not overstay your time. Leaders who stay in a position too long do more damage than those who leave too soon. It is better to leave early than to stay too late and retard the development of the next generation of leaders. By the time Fidel Castro stepped aside as the leader of Cuba in 2008 at the age of 82, he was the focus of much criticism and ridicule, including from members of his own family, as well as of allegations of corruption. His rare appearances in public seemed to serve merely as reminders that in his weakened form he bore little resemblance to the striking, brash figure recalled from his earlier feats as the leader of a revolution.

This is in sharp contrast to Jesus, who knew when His time had come and was prepared to hand over the reins. Consider His prayer to the Father:

John 17:1–18 "Father, the time has come. Glorify your Son, that your Son may glorify you. For you granted him authority over all people that he might give eternal life to all those you have given him. Now this is eternal life: that they may know you, the only true God, and Jesus Christ, whom you have sent. I have brought you glory on earth by completing the work you gave me to do. And now, Father, glorify me in your presence with the glory I had with you before the world began. "I have revealed you to those whom you gave me out of the world. They were yours; you gave them to me and they have obeyed your word. Now they know that everything you have given me comes from you. For I gave them the words you gave me and they accepted them. They knew with certainty that I came from you, and they believed that you sent me. I pray for them. I am not praying for the world, but for those you have given me, for they are yours. All I have is yours, and all you have is mine. And glory has come to me through them. I will remain in the world no longer, but they are still in the world, and I am coming to you. Holy Father, protect them by the power of your name—the name you gave me—so that they may be one as we are one. While I was with them, I protected them and kept them safe by that name you gave me. None has been lost except the one doomed to destruction so that Scripture would be fulfilled. "I am coming to you now, but I say these things while I am still in the world, so that they may have the full measure of my joy within them. I have given them your word and the world has hated them, for they are not of the world any more than I am of the world. My prayer is not that you take them out of the world but that you protect them from the evil one. They are not of the world, even as I am not of it. Sanctify them by the truth; your word is truth. As you sent me into the world, I have sent them into the world."

These words express the emotional and psychological state of Jesus Christ during the final days of His life on earth, as well as His deep awareness of the transitional nature of His assignment. He not only communicates His inevitable departure but also His confidence in the disciples' ability to continue His work through their personal relationship with His Heavenly Father. In essence, He delegated not only the vision and mission of His assignment, but He also delegated His relationship with His father.

Understand that your greatest contribution to the future is your successor. People usually miss this great secret. I am convinced that your successor should succeed you in your lifetime. Do not wait to make succession decisions on your deathbed or leave it to others by failing to mentor, prepare, or designate a replacement. The secret is to understand that when your successor is successful, you have made your greatest contribution.

Jesus set a leadership priority and kept a conscious focus not just on starting a project, but also on finishing effectively, expressing deep dedication to completing His phase as a visionary leader. Note the following statements:

John 4:34 "My food," said Jesus, "is to do the will of him who sent me and to finish his work."

John 4:37–38 "Thus the saying 'One sows and another reaps' is true. I sent you to reap what you have not worked for. Others have done the hard work, and you have reaped the benefits of their labor."

The principle of one sowing and another reaping implies that true leaders are always aware that they were not called to finish the race alone but to prepare successors to pick up their portion of history and complete their phase. It is obvious that the chosen successor of Jesus Christ, Simon Peter, did not have to create the vision of the kingdom of God. It was laid down by his leader. He reaped the benefits of Jesus' hard labor even unto death.

John 17:4 "I have brought you glory on earth by completing the work you gave me to do."

In an example from our day, the Dalai Lama, considered the spiritual and temporal leader of Tibetan Buddhists, shocked some of his followers when he started talking about a succession plan because tradition holds that succession of the Dalai Lama is by reincarnation from a long line of predecessors. In recent years, however, the reigning Dalai Lama has spoken publicly of the possibility of referendum before his death, allowing the Tibetan people a voice in the choice of a successor.

"When my physical condition becomes weak, and there are serious preparations for death, then the (referendum) should happen," he told a crowd of world religious leaders gathered in India, as quoted on freeTibet.com.

Some people attacked this idea as heresy, but the Dalai Lama insisted it was in keeping with the Buddhist tradition and that the reincarnation or succession of the institution of the Dalai Lama was not necessarily automatic but subject to the people's approval. This greatly admired leader referred to himself on his website, www.dalailama.com, as a simple "Buddhist monk" and even joked in an interview on his website, that he was already in "semiretirement" after the selection of an administrator to handle the temporal affairs of Tibet in 2001.

He had made his greatest contribution to the future by paving the way for succession and choosing someone to handle the day-to-day operations while he was still around to guide the way, just as Jesus began to prepare Peter.

As an inspiring leader with passion, vision, and purpose, you are unique. The world has benefited from your gift. You have reached the pinnacle of success. Nevertheless, you are a mortal. If you are thinking about succession, you probably hold a responsible position. You know you need to move on to greater things.

Look around. Size up your colleagues. Who could replace you?

Point to remember:

Measure success by the success of the successors.

Chapter 4

Vision and Succession

I STOOD AMONG hundreds of wide-eyed visitors, young and old, from many different nations, in the center of a room filled with towering statues of men and women who were the architects of a nation that has influenced the world as no other has since the Roman Empire ruled the known world. Many of these images were well-known, and others were new to me as a tourist from the Bahamas standing among the statues in the rotunda of the United States Capitol. The sculptures had one thing in common. They were evidence of a legacy of the preservation, maintenance, protection, and, most importantly, the successful transfer of a vision of a nation and governing ideology that still stands as a testimony to the reality of succession.

Hanging on one of the walls was a large painting that drew me in as the inscription on the plate below indicated it was a picture of the "Founding Fathers" of the United States of America. As I stood in amazement with an overwhelming impression of what these few men had done, I could almost hear their silent voices rising from the work of art—exchanging, debating, and agreeing on a vision that would lay the foundation of a nation that would outlast all modern nations and set a standard for many to follow. These men birthed the vision and charted the course of a democracy that would rival any great empire in history. However, the deepest impact all this had on my inquiring mind was the realization that after nearly two hundred and fifty years, the fundamentals of the great social and political document the Founders wrote is still as alive as when they first penned it and added their signatures to validate it. This to me was one of the greatest acts of successful succession.

The ability to conceive and to document a vision is not as difficult as passing on that vision to the succeeding generations. In this chapter, I want to address this most important aspect of mentoring and succession—passing on the vision for the future.

> *"To understand the need for succession, a leader must have a vision of the future."*

Very young children often find it difficult to understand that once upon a time, they did not exist. At such a tender age, they have no vision of the past, and family pictures or stories that do not include them can confuse them. "Where was I?" a preschool child might ask. Similarly, older people struggle with envisioning a future without them in it—a time when they will be absent from the family portrait.

Yet they must know the time will come when they will be out of the picture, and life will go on for others. It is never too early to think about what will happen to your family, your organization, and your legacy when you are merely a memory and an image in the photograph on the mantle.

In the lion kingdom, the mother has the vision to know that the cubs will grow up and have to feed themselves one day. The lioness knows this long before her babies have the concept of a time when she will not be there to hunt for their food while they rest and observe from a safe place.

The most important aspect of the lionesses' behavior is that they allow the young cubs to *watch* the action. This is critical, as it goes beyond communication through sound, or speech in the case of humans, to provide *visual images of the future* for the young lions. In essence, the adult lions transfer the *vision of the future* to their posterity. Mentoring is about training and preparation for the future; succession is about transferring and transitioning to the future. If your vision dies with you, you are a failure. As I stated earlier, success is about succession. You are truly successful when the next and succeeding generations preserve and embrace the future.

The Role of Vision in Succession

Where there is no vision, mentoring and succession are unnecessary. Vision *is* the purpose for mentoring and the motivation for succession. Any attempt to discuss the subject of vision is like dipping a cup in the ocean in an effort to explain the expanse of the water. However, let us try to understand the basic principle of vision and the vital role it plays in the process of mentoring and succession. For thirty years I have studied and explored this comprehensive subject of vision, and its many facets and perspectives still intrigue me. However, for our purposes in this book, I would simplify the definition as follows:

- True vision is a human cause worthy of self-sacrifice.
- True vision is a view of the future more noble than self-preservation.
- True vision is destiny in pictures.
- True vision is divine purpose in Technicolor.
- True vision is a concept of a future more preferable than the past and present.
- True vision always benefits succeeding generations.

What Vision Is Not

In these past thirty years, I have spoken to millions of leaders and aspiring leaders about the subject of vision and its vital role in leadership. When I ask leaders if they have a vision and if they can describe or define it, I am amazed that many fail the test. The way some leaders describe vision explains why they fail to achieve their desired results. They convey to me a general mission statement with vague notions of changing the whole world, but with no specific perception of the future.

Here are some criteria for framing what is not a true vision:

- Vision is not a human concoction of the future.
- Vision is not a conception of your private view of the future.
- Vision is not personal, private, or selfish ambition.
- Vision is not a goal, but it produces goals.

- Vision is not a complicated list of programs, but it produces programs.
- Vision is not mere physical sight, but perception of the unseen future.
- Vision is not ambition, but it inspires self-service.
- True vision is not for self-promotion, but it promotes others.
- True vision never destroys humanity, but it builds and preserves human value and dignity.
- True vision can never be fulfilled in your lifetime, but it extends to generations.

It is this last point that makes mentoring and succession necessary. True vision is generational. To understand the need for succession, a leader must have a vision of the future—a future in which that leader will have no active role. That is hard for many people to imagine, but such a vision is crucial to planning for succession. Who will follow you? Who will provide for the others? Who will perpetuate the legacy?

Vision is the essence of leadership and the purpose for mentoring for succession. Therefore, a visionary leader is one who sees beyond his phase and perceives the need to incorporate others into the process of his journey. Leaders must see more, see farther, and see before others see. This visionary spirit separates true leaders and statesmen who have a mentoring spirit from mere politicians and managers focused on today's needs or wants. This is what separates them:

- The politician focuses on programs. The leader focuses on vision.
- The politician's priority is securing the next election. The leader's priority is securing the next generation.
- The politician is preoccupied with *promises*. The leader is preoccupied with pursuing *purpose*.
- The politician thinks of protecting his political seat. The leader thinks about preparing a replacement to take his seat.
- The politician seeks power over his generation. The leader seeks to empower the next generation.

Vision and the Visionary

A leader is born when an individual is awakened to a human need that becomes a personal obsession and a driving passion, igniting a commitment and dedication that becomes more important than self-preservation, cultivating a will for personal sacrifice. This obsession eventually will manifest itself in perceptions and images that we call a vision. True vision will always produce sacrifice and require sacrifice. However, true vision is also of a magnitude that breaches the boundaries of our short existence on Planet Earth.

You as a leader in any category must understand this expansive nature of vision if you are to achieve true success. Look at a few important principles of vision and the visionary demand for embracing mentoring and succession principles:

Vision is always greater than the visionary. This principle underscores the fact that true vision will always be more comprehensive than the one who conceived it. The visionary must accept the reality that he or she will not and should not expect to fulfill or complete the vision within a term of leadership service or in a lifetime on earth.

The visionary is the catalyst for the vision. The vision is greater than the catalyst. The visionary is the channel for delivery of the generational assignment. The visionary is responsible for receiving, defining, clarifying, simplifying, communicating, and transferring the vision to others and for attracting and inspiring them to the cause of corporate effort. This principle implies that the visionary must never believe he or she *is* the vision or the center or source of the vision.

Vision is generational. This principle is important for all leaders to understand and should become the foundation of the leader's obligation to prepare the future leaders. Vision is never given for one generation, but is transferred as a trust to the leadership of the day. True vision is dynamic, fluid, and flexible. Every generation of leaders owes the debt of vision to the next generation. Ignoring this principle has been the source of great failure for leaders throughout history.

Vision is transferable. This principle means that true vision can serve any generation in history and therefore must be capable of movement from one generation, culture, social environment, and age group to another. In essence, true vision can be picked up by a new generation and continued.

Vision is fulfilled in phases. This principle emphasizes that all true vision is transgenerational and extends beyond the lifetime of the visionary. This precept frees the visionary from the pressure of completing the vision in his or her lifetime or leadership service time. This concept makes him or her responsible for identifying the specific *phase* for which he or she carries the baton and for being willing to release the next phase to his or her mentored successor.

Vision is personal but never private. This principle highlights the reality that true visionaries receive the vision personally but always are conscious that their vision is a trust to be delivered to their community, their nation, and the next generation. The visionary is a trustee. Vision is never for private consumption but for public service. A true vision is a debt owed to the present and future world.

Vision is seasonal. This vision underscores the principle that all true visions are designed to be fulfilled within the timing of God's divine calendar. Every divine vision and purpose has a divine timing attached to it. ("There is a time for everything, and a season for every activity under the heavens": Ecc. 3:1) The visionary must be sensitive not only to his *phase* but also to the *seasons* of the vision. Therefore, it is possible to attempt to fulfill a vision prematurely and sabotage its potential.

Another crucial aspect of vision is that it is more important than the visionary. This statement may sound simple, but many leaders have made the mistake of believing that the vision was about *them* and that they were the source and foundation of the vision. They live under the notion that the vision cannot exist or cannot be fulfilled without them. This dangerous and serious misconception, or delusion, can cause a multitude of mistakes and negative results, including depression, overwork, frustration, impatience, and internal conflict. Many leaders have found themselves dethroned, impeached, indicted, fired, or voted out because of such thinking. The words of King Solomon give great insight into this danger and could protect us from a misguided sense of self-importance. "Where there is no vision, the people perish: but he that keepeth the law, happy is he" (Prov. 29:18 KJV).

These time-tested words of Solomon are full of wise counsel for all visionary leaders. They remind us of the following:

Vision is the source of personal and corporate discipline. The word *perish* used in this context is derived from a concept of "throwing off self-control" or losing self-discipline. Vision creates the spirit of personal and corporate discipline that keeps a group or organization focused.

Vision is more important than the leader. Please note in the statement above by King Solomon that he does not say, "Without a leader the people perish," but rather "Without a *vision*, the people will perish"—lose discipline. The principle highlighted here is that the visionary leader may present and share the vision, but the vision becomes more important than the leader. The leader is dispensable, but the vision is indispensable. The leader is temporary, but the vision is permanent. The leader is for his generation. The vision is transgenerational. The leader is for a phase. The vision is forever.

People do not follow leaders, they follow *vision*. The statement also teaches the principle that people may be attracted to the visionary, but they must and will be committed to the vision. The leader's greatest responsibility is not to attract people to follow, but rather to transfer allegiance to the vision. True leadership transfers people from personality to purpose.

When the leader dies, the *vision* **must live on.** This principle is inherent in the wise declaration of King Solomon and draws attention to the principle that the vision must and will outlast the visionary and extend beyond his or her influence. It is my conclusion that the greatest gift a leader can give his followers is a vision (of the future).

These important principles form the motive and foundation of this book. Only when a leader understands, appreciates, and embraces the reality that true leadership is always transitional and progressive will he or she intentionally commit to the crucial task of mentoring successors.

First, true leaders must see more in the people in their arena than those individuals can see in themselves. As a leader, you must be conscious of the people around you who are worthy of being mentored even when they do not see themselves in that light. Second, leaders see farther than others can see. As a leader, look at life after your death and design it. You can fashion your future beyond your grave by mentoring. Third, leaders are able to see things long before others see them.

Leaders are very conscious of and sensitive to everything that affects their mission and vision. They are quick to interpret signs and events and to discern their effects on the leaders' priorities. They are always thinking about how the present will affect the future. They think, "Ah, I had better put that in place in case I am not here. I should fix this before I leave. I need to provide for this before I go."

There is a tremendous example of successful mentoring and succession in the Old Testament account of the great King David and his demonstrated commitment to mentoring and transferring his vision and plans for the future temple of worship for his people. What an interesting character!

King David, who was perhaps Israel's greatest king, had a vision of a peaceful and prosperous nation, free from war and strife. King David also carried in his heart a vision of constructing a permanent place of worship for God so that the people could settle and have a central venue. What is amazing was that David did accomplish his phase of this great vision. He subdued all the enemies of the nation and confirmed it by building his kingdom's capital, calling it Jerusalem, which means "city of peace."

However, being a true leader, and perhaps remembering the failure of his predecessor, King Saul, King David had a keen awareness that he was dispensable and that he could not complete the vision he held in his heart. It was this awareness that motivated David to begin mentoring his son Solomon. David did not leave the mentoring of his son to chance. He was intentional, spending hours and days teaching, instructing, and modeling leadership—wisdom—to his posterity. Proof of this mentoring program is the content of one of the most important books in the biblical text, the book of Proverbs. Note how Solomon opens his book:

Proverbs 1:1–5

The proverbs of Solomon son of David, king of Israel:
for attaining wisdom and discipline;
for understanding words of insight;

for acquiring a disciplined and prudent life,
doing what is right and just and fair;

for giving prudence to the simple,
knowledge and discretion to the young—

let the wise listen and add to their learning,
and let the discerning get guidance—

King Solomon repeatedly stressed the need to listen to the instructions of
your father and the commands of your mother:

Proverbs 1:8–10

Listen, my son, to your father's instruction
and do not forsake your mother's teaching.

They will be a garland to grace your head
and a chain to adorn your neck.

My son, if sinners entice you,
do not give in to them.

Proverbs 3:1–3

My son, do not forget my teaching,
but keep my commands in your heart,

for they will prolong your life many years
and bring you prosperity.

Let love and faithfulness never leave you;
bind them around your neck,
write them on the tablet of your heart.

These words indicate that King David mentored Solomon and that the son
understood the value of mentoring for succession.

A Successful Mentorship and Succession Example

King David's vision of building the temple of worship for the God of Israel
was a project he once thought he was to accomplish himself. However, he

learned, as I have said, that the vision is always bigger, greater, and longer than the lifespan of the visionary. King David is one of the most successful examples of leadership, mentoring, and succession in history. Here is one account of the success of his process:

> **1 Chronicles 28:10–13** "Consider now, for the LORD has chosen you to build a temple as a sanctuary. Be strong and do the work." Then David gave his son Solomon the plans for the portico of the temple, its buildings, its storerooms, its upper parts, its inner rooms and the place of atonement. He gave him the plans of all that the Spirit had put in his mind for the courts of the temple of the LORD and all the surrounding rooms, for the treasuries of the temple of God and for the treasuries for the dedicated things. He gave him instructions for the divisions of the priests and Levites, and for all the work of serving in the temple of the LORD, as well as for all the articles to be used in its service.

The process of mentoring and succession from King David to Solomon is an inspiring case study for our focus in this book. Follow the progression of this account:

> **1 Kings 5:1–7** When Hiram king of Tyre heard that Solomon had been anointed king to succeed his father David, he sent his envoys to Solomon, because he had always been on friendly terms with David. Solomon sent back this message to Hiram: "You know that because of the wars waged against my father David from all sides, he could not build a temple for the Name of the LORD his God until the LORD put his enemies under his feet. But now the LORD my God has given me rest on every side, and there is no adversary or disaster. I intend, therefore, to build a temple for the Name of the LORD my God, as the LORD told my father David, when he said, 'Your son whom I will put on the throne in your place will build the temple for my Name.' "So give orders that cedars of Lebanon be cut for me. My men will work with yours, and I will pay you for your men whatever wages you set. You know that we have no one so skilled in felling tim-

ber as the Sidonians." When Hiram heard Solomon's message, he was greatly pleased and said, "Praise be to the LORD today, for he has given David a wise son to rule over this great nation."

> **1 Kings 8:17–21** "My father David had it in his heart to build a temple for the Name of the LORD, the God of Israel. But the LORD said to my father David, 'Because it was in your heart to build a temple for my Name, you did well to have this in your heart. Nevertheless, you are not the one to build the temple, but your son, who is your own flesh and blood—he is the one who will build the temple for my Name.' "The LORD has kept the promise he made: I have succeeded David my father and now I sit on the throne of Israel, just as the LORD promised, and I have built the temple for the Name of the LORD, the God of Israel. I have provided a place there for the ark, in which is the covenant of the LORD that he made with our fathers when he brought them out of Egypt."

This account is one that we need to study carefully to learn the principles and process implemented by King David to achieve such a successful leadership transition. King David not only transferred the vision and mentored his successor, but he also put aside resources and materials to help the next generation succeed. Those resources included the financial means, equipment, and building materials, as well as the collective wisdom and experience of his leadership team to complete the project he knew he could not build. He was able to see beyond the span of his life.

Solomon carried out David's vision, and when he had completed the edifice, he brought the objects David set aside into the temple as his father envisioned.

> **1 Kings 7:51** When all the work King Solomon had done for the temple of the LORD was finished, he brought in the things his father David had dedicated—the silver and gold and the furnishings—and he placed them in the treasuries of the LORD's temple.

King David saw more than others saw; he saw farther than others and saw things before others saw them. It took a visionary leader to "see" the temple and plan the construction. It took a visionary leader to know what should go into the temple. It took a visionary leader to mentor a successor who would take up the vision and do the work necessary to carry it out. A visionary leader sees the plans the Spirit puts in his or her mind.

Are you thinking and seeing beyond what others see? The decisions that you make will secure the future if you are a visionary leader. Your interest should be in the future because that is where you are going to spend the rest of your life. David's vision of the future of his nation motivated his actions in his time and became the incentive for mentoring his son Solomon and providing resources for his future success. Vision is the purpose and motivation for mentoring your successor.

Leadership is born when vision is captured. When a person captures the vision of the future that is worth sacrifice, he is a leader. The leader's tenure ends when the vision is accomplished or is achieved, which could be a lifetime or two lifetimes, but vision is what provides the motivation for mentoring and choosing a successor. Vision provides the blueprint for a future that extends beyond a mere lifetime. Vision allows you to see someone else completing the temple. Vision shows you what the portrait will look like when you are no longer around to pose for it. Vision motivates you to see that your "cubs" know how to stalk their prey to feed themselves. Leadership without vision is simply management of goals. Vision gives meaning to leadership. It provides the direction and the force for leadership. Leadership exists for the purpose of vision. Leadership begins and ends with vision.

Leadership is a corporate investment in hope. A leader is a dealer in hope. Your job as a leader requires you to mentor people. By mentoring, you give them the incentive to invest their time, energy, resources, and ambitions in a hope for a future that they believe is better than the present. This hope fuels their desire to carry out your vision and protect your legacy.

To a leader, vision is reality. Leaders normally live in another world. This is why people think visionary leaders are naïve or consider them unrealistic. However, the unrealistic nature of leaders is what makes them important to you. The world needs people who believe in things that others cannot see so they can stop being victims of what they can see. The world needs people who can "see" the temple when it is merely an idea or a pile of raw material.

The most important component in leadership is not power, but vision. People want to get positions of power—politicians, preachers, and corporate executives all fall victim to this very dangerous pursuit. They yearn for power when in fact vision is more important because power is supposed to be used to serve and fulfill vision. Vision provides momentum for leadership.

Vision is also the measure of leadership. How do you measure your leadership? Measure it by the vision that you want to achieve. Measure it by the vision of the future without you around to continue achieving. If I wanted to determine how well a leader is doing, I would measure her against what she intended to do, what she claims she desired to do, and what she did to see that it continued beyond a lifetime.

People also ask me, "What keeps you inspired?" I tell them I'm inspired by what I see that has not happened yet. Doing something that no one has done before is my inspiration. I think this vision allows the leader to endure criticism, opposition, detractors, and discomfort. It allows the leader to delay gratification. Vision is so powerful that it allows leaders to bear hardship, distress, and imprisonment. Vision is such a powerful thing that it can even allow the leader to welcome death. Dr. Martin Luther King Jr. planned to go to jail and accepted that he might die to achieve his vision. Jesus intended to die to fulfill His vision of a new world.

The Bible says of Jesus that "for the joy set before him [he] endured the cross, scorning its shame, and sat down at the right hand of the throne of God" (Heb. 12:2). This tells us that vision allows you to see a future and beyond the suffering to a worthy end goal.

Thinking in Pictures

Vision is always bigger and nobler than the visionary. That is what leadership is about. Someone asked me some years ago, "What is vision?" Vision is the capacity to see beyond your eyes. Vision is the capacity to see the invisible and believe the impossible. Vision is purpose in pictures. Vision is the ability to see the future in Technicolor. Vision is documenting details of a preferred life.

Visionaries can amazingly capture the future in detail. Recently, a made-for-television movie depicted the life of Temple Grandin, Ph.D., an extraordinary woman who has autism and excels in part *because* of it. What others would see as a limitation informs her vision and allows her to maximize her gifts. She uses some of the traits of a condition that others consider a disability as strengths to help her see how to engineer systems for containing and handling animals. Grandin is a professor of animal science whose revolutionary systems handle half the livestock in the United States.

She explains how the heightened sensitivities, compulsiveness, and focus that can nearly cripple many other people with autism allow her to feel what the animals feel, see what they see, and map out her vision of the solutions in her head in such detail that she can direct others to build them. As a professor, she mentors others to do the same. As a lecturer, she helps others understand the animals and the people who share her condition. She credits the fact that she "thinks in pictures" for her amazing skill. She is a visionary.

I live as a visionary. One becomes a leader when you see the unseen. Vision is a conceptual view of the future. Vision is a glimpse of the reason for your existence. Vision is the perception of your divine assignment for your life and beyond. Vision inspires you to mentor the temple builder and "see" the finished work, a space you will never enter, filled with the treasures you stored up for that day.

Points to remember:

Vision is always greater than the visionary.
Vision is purpose in pictures.

Chapter 5

Are You Brave Enough to Mentor?

WHILE THE LION'S reputation for courage comes from its dominance of other animals in the wild, perhaps the bravest thing it does is to prepare its young to stand on their own. In our lives, we deem it a courageous act even to consider giving up power. Mentoring requires courage in multiple ways.

- It takes courage to train your replacement.
- It takes courage to make yourself unnecessary.
- It takes courage to work yourself out of a job.
- It takes courage to train the person who will make sure you do not stay.

The last thing any of us wants is to be replaced. We want to protect our position, and none of us wants to feel we are not significant. Yet true leaders seek to replace themselves. Successful succession requires working yourself out of a job and making room for the next phase of leadership. Jesus Christ addressed this with His disciples:

> John 16:7 "But I tell you the truth: It is for your good that I am going away. Unless I go away, the Counselor will not come to you; but if I go, I will send him to you."

All leaders should have this attitude. In other words, "It is expedient that I go away. It is necessary that I leave you. It is in your best interest that I vacate this position."

What kind of philosophy of leadership is that? It is maturity. It is self-confidence. It is awareness of your own value. It is a sense of self—of knowing who you are and what your value is.

> *"Be willing to relinquish power.*
> *It is the sign of greatness."*

If your value comes from being a manager, then you had better not lose that position. If your significance comes from having people call you pastor, bishop, or doctor, you had better not lose that job. However, if your value is not in the title, the position, or the paycheck, then wherever you go, your value goes with you. Do not become synonymous with your title. Do not become synonymous with your position. Be willing to relinquish power. This is the sign of greatness. Great leaders train their replacements to produce more leaders.

The measures of true leadership are not how well we maintain followers but how well we:

- Produce leaders.
- Judge success by the diminishing dependency of the followers.
- Make ourselves increasingly unnecessary.
- Prove we are able to leave.
- Produce replacements who can lead others.

Leaders Produce Leaders

Visionary leaders are already preparing for the time their leadership will end because they can see what lies ahead. They are preparing new leaders to rise up and take their place.

The ultimate goal of true leadership is not to maintain followers but to produce leaders.

I have taught this to thousands of leaders around the world. The conventional concept of leadership is that leaders need followers and the number or caliber of one's followers defines one's leadership. This is a very dangerous notion because if one believes having followers defines leadership, then in order to be a leader, you will always need to have people following you.

"Following" is normally defined as lesser, subordinate, or ordinary, less intelligent, less valuable, less significant. That too is dangerous because if you believe that your leadership depends on having people around you who are less intelligent, then the temptation to oppress increases. The temptation to impede the advancement of others increases. Your staff's confidence in their potential and hope for the future will wither.

The first measure of true leadership is in the production of leaders, the idea that every person under your influence has the capacity to replace you and that you are committed to mentoring them to do that. That is the most wonderful attitude that any leader can have. If the leader is dedicated to that idea, the spirit of hope, inspiration, motivation, and passion among those around him or her is unlimited. That mentoring spirit makes the leader successful. When people dedicate themselves to achieving the goal of another person who believes in them and regards them as potential replacements, as equals, productivity is limitless.

Jesus conveyed this attitude toward His assistants and passed the mantle to them after His resurrection and reappearance to them.

> **Matthew 28:18–20** Then Jesus came to them and said, "All authority in heaven and on earth has been given to me. **Therefore go** and make disciples of all nations, baptizing them in the name of the Father and of the Son and of the Holy Spirit, and teaching them to obey everything I have commanded you. And surely I am with you always, to the very end of the age."

Here is a man who just accomplished the greatest victory in history, achieving authority over death and life. He achieved authority over everything in existence. He said all authority has been "given to me," or essentially, "I am in control of everything." Normally when you give people this type of power, they would use it to protect and defend their positions, to preserve and protect their turfs. For that reason, His use of power shocks me. He takes the authority that He was given and He delegates it, gives it away to others, and He says, "Therefore (you) go." He told them to go and spread the power.

If you give a human all of that power, he would be tempted to take on all of the responsibility and not practice the mature leadership principle of sharing power. Yet Jesus did the reverse. He distributes the power to activate other people's dreams, goals, visions, energy, potential, gifts, and talents. He uses authority to create authority. This exemplifies the greatest act of leadership. He is showing us that the purpose of power is to release others and empower them.

This is the shining light of true leadership. Leadership is empowerment. Leaders do not seek power. They seek to empower. Insecure people with leadership titles pursue power. Secure leaders empower people. They mentor people to make them powerful. My job is to make everyone around me powerful. Your job is to make everyone around you powerful. A true leader mentors to make sure others succeed. True leaders are not concerned with their own success. They achieve success through the success of the people they mentor. Empowerment is more important than power in the mind of a leader.

True leadership measures its success by the diminishing dependency of its followers. This explains why many leaders do not mentor and why they do not produce successors. They believe in some strange way that the more people depend on and need them, the greater they are as leaders. In fact, the opposite is true.

Mentees should not become parasites to a leader. They should be like a child in the womb. A parasite feeds on the host, not giving back. It can even destroy the host. A child is not a parasite. A baby dolphin is not a parasite. A fruit on a tree is not a parasite. While a fetus is entirely dependent on its mother, that is but only for a season. Eventually the offspring—whether human, dolphin, or tree—emerges, grows, and becomes independent. The child is capable of giving back, even of becoming a parent. Even the fruit pit can become a tree. Likewise, the mentee draws knowledge from the mentor, but eventually matures and is able to function independently, contribute value, and eventually lead the organization.

True leaders do not measure success by how many people depend on them. They mentor people to make them independent. They work for the independence of their mentees. They invest in the independence of their mentees. They want to see their people become independent, and they take pride in that.

Leaders often become insecure when people no longer call on them for help or advice. They feel as though they are no longer valuable. In reality, that should be the greatest evidence that the successor is able to lead. Under the leadership philosophy of the young rabbi Jesus Christ, the emphasis should be on reproducing leaders and making yourself increasingly unnecessary. Leadership is not about holding on, but rather about letting go of a position.

In the Scriptures, Matthew tells of a time when Jesus went to the mountain to pray. His students went to a village where they met a man who had a demon-possessed son. The father brought the child to them, but the disciples could not cast out the demon. People gathered around. Then Jesus came down from the mountain and asked what was causing so much commotion.

The man said to Him basically, "I brought my son who has a problem to your students, and they could not help him." Jesus did not attack the man for complaining or His disciples for their failure. He asked His disciples a question that reveals a lot about His mentoring style.

> **Matthew 17:14–17** When they came to the crowd, a man approached Jesus and knelt before him. "LORD, have mercy on my son," he said. "He has seizures and is suffering greatly. He often falls into the fire or into the water. I brought him to your disciples, but they could not heal him." "O unbelieving and perverse generation," Jesus replied, "**how long shall I stay with you? How long shall I put up with you?** Bring the boy here to me."

How long should I be with you?

This is a very powerful question. This is a leadership question, a mentoring question, a leadership succession question. He was saying in a way, "Look, I am not here forever. I want you to learn from me. I want you to understand me. I want you to know that I will not be with you long. I will not be with you forever."

How long must I be with you? What a beautiful question! To me this is the most awesome question about leadership succession. This question should become a part of the vocabulary of leaders. It communicates the spirit of mentorship and succession—the desire of true leadership to produce leaders. He expected them to handle this, so He was saying, "Look, did you not learn anything from me? I want you all to replace me."

He also took the time to tell them where they went wrong and how to do better next time, as the rest of the passage indicates.

Matthew 17:18–20 Jesus rebuked the demon, and it came out of the boy, and he was healed from that moment. Then the disciples came to Jesus in private and asked, "Why couldn't we drive it out?" He replied, **"Because you have so little faith. I tell you the truth, if you have faith as small as a mustard seed, you can say to this mountain, 'Move from here to there' and it will move. Nothing will be impossible for you."**

Jesus knew He would not be with them long, and He wanted them to face the reality. He was preparing them to take over. Immediately after that, He tells them.

Matthew 17:22–23 When they came together in Galilee, he said to them, "The Son of Man is going to be betrayed into the hands of men. They will kill him, and on the third day he will be raised to life." And the disciples were filled with grief.

Protecting the Turf

The last thing that many leaders—whether religious, corporate, educational, or political—want today is a replacement. They protect their turf. The leaders are more concerned about protecting their position than about replicating and replacing themselves through mentoring.

The measure of true leadership, however, is the ability to leave. True leadership makes itself unnecessary through mentoring. Leaders must begin to accept that they are not as "irreplaceable" as they think. Somehow we think that if we do not do something, no one will do it, or that if we cannot do it, no one can. This too is a very dangerous fallacy. We must lead with the consciousness that we have to become unnecessary to the organization. The more we think that way, the easier it is to mentor others, develop our successors, and invest in our replacements.

When our enterprise no longer needs us, this is the most telling evidence of success, not failure. When it is not necessary for me to be in a board meeting to know that it will run smoothly and productively, that is a good sign. When I am absent from a marketing meeting and the team produces great promotional campaigns that I could not conceive, this reveals a good sign that my leadership has been effective. I am not in the pulpit preaching every Sunday morning. Yet the church continues to fill up with people, and the congregation is inspired and exalted. That is evidence that the positive results and impact of mentoring those in the environment of the ministry are experiencing a measure of success.

True leadership makes itself increasingly unnecessary. Gradually the leader can leave because he did such a great job. The greatest example of this is Jesus Christ. He sat with the disciples in the upper room, and He talked about leaving. After He died and rose from the grave, He lingered with them for a while and then finally left. To a degree, they were still dependent on Him. We can tell because they stayed, looking up and staring after He ascended into heaven.

> **Acts 1:6–11** So when they met together, they asked him, "Lord, are you at this time going to restore the kingdom to Israel?" He said to them: "It is not for you to know the times or dates the Father has set by his own authority. But you will receive power when the Holy Spirit comes on you; and you will be my witnesses in Jerusalem, and in all Judea and Samaria, and to the ends of the earth." After he said this, he was taken up before their very eyes, and a cloud hid him from their sight. They were looking intently up into the sky as he was going, when suddenly two men dressed in white stood beside them. "Men of Galilee," they said, **"why do you stand here looking into the sky?** This same Jesus, who has been taken from you into heaven, will come back in the same way you have seen him go into heaven."

I believe the angels that came gave us one of the greatest leadership lessons. The angels essentially said to them, "Why do you stand here gazing?" Many people do that when a leader leaves. They gaze at the chair the CEO sat in. They tiptoe past the office the last president used. They encase the pastor's robe in glass. They keep the family homestead just as Mama left it. They keep their deceased husband's ashes in plain sight on the living room mantle even if they remarry. They remain immobilized because of their dependency.

The angels motivated the disciples to get off the mountain, go back to Jerusalem, find the other disciples, and get back to work. "The same Jesus you see leaving will come again, but in the meantime, you go and be empowered to do your own work." They were prepared and able to do it because Jesus had mentored them. The idea of making yourself unnecessary, of being able to leave, is critical.

The final measure of true leadership is when your mentees can lead others. Measure your success as a leader and mentor by how many people are following the leaders you trained. When they can mentor effectively, you are an effective leader. In a family, it works like this. If you are a parent, you do not measure your success by the behavior of your children. That is not the tool. You measure your success as a parent by the behavior of your grandchildren. In other words, if you were a great parent, it will show up in your grandchildren because your children will parent their children the way you parented them or even do it better than you did. So study your grandchildren. Have you produced children who can produce leaders?

If you have mentored effectively, then your mentees will mentor effectively. Leadership is reproducing leadership. Mentoring and developing successors takes far more courage than protecting your turf does.

The Mentor's Job

Mentoring is the commitment of a mentor to develop someone else through a practical relationship. Mentors offer:

Timely advice. The mentee has to accept the fact that the mentor will offer advice and opinions. "Timely" means at the moment the mentor thinks will provide the best learning experience—a teaching moment. He will turn to the mentee and give instruction. Lessons delivered on the spot, in real time instead of after the fact, are best. That is even preferable to lecturing about things that could happen in the future.

Resources. The mentor shares such resources as letters, articles, and books for the mentee's benefit. If you are a good mentor, you expose the mentee to the things that helped you. Those in my mentoring program know that nearly every month they will get a list of books from me that I am reading. If I find an article that is very helpful to me, I will send that article to the people in my mentoring program. If I find a CD or a program that is helping me, I expose the mentee to that. I want them to know what I know.

Financial help/guidance. The mentor might assist the mentee financially but has no obligation to do so. The mentor might buy a book, help with travel costs, or cover the registration fees for an event. If there is a commitment on the part of the mentee, the mentor will be encouraged to help.

Freedom for the mentee to emerge as a leader even beyond the level of the mentor. The mentor wants the mentee to become greater. That is the purpose of mentoring. If you want the mentee to excel beyond your accomplishments, you have to provide opportunities for that to happen. Many times when I have a mentee with me, I put him in front of my audience to speak. I will give him my microphone, saying, "You go ahead and talk to the people. Let me expose you to my market." I am helping the mentee to emerge. What took me thirty years to gain, I can give to my protégé in thirty seconds. This is the power of a mentor. A mentor can change the mentee's life in a day, saving that person a lifetime of trial and error.

A role model for leadership functions. A mentor shows how to lead in many different settings. You allow the mentee to see how you handle pressure, criticism, disappointment, and abuse of yourself or others. They see you leading in the various settings of life.

Direct access and opportunities for development. I might say to my mentee, "You should go to that seminar." I do this because I know that he or she needs to learn something in that particular environment. Or I might say, "Buy this book," or "Subscribe to that magazine." I know what they need to learn. Sometimes I call a mentee to say, "I want you to go on this trip with me," and the mentee asks, "Why?" I explain, "Because on this trip, I will be exposed to certain environments that I want you to see." My invitation gives the mentee access to events or places that he or she normally would not have the chance to experience.

Coleadership to build confidence. The mentor allows the mentee to share the work. I provide access for others to benefit from the platform that I have built. I do not have to do that, but I do not want to hog everything. If you are going to mentor people, you have to "colead." You want the mentees to have the privilege to share in your market, your exposure, and your influence. Give them opportunities to be in charge of things. Let them run a meeting or present the new marketing plan. You can watch, comment, and make sure they learn through the process but allow them to share leadership. Build up the confidence of that person.

Mentors can give a mentee instant credibility and recognition. They can give the mentee their name, which may be worth a lot. When I wrote my first book, I was reluctant as an author, fearing that no one would read my book. The publisher said to me, "Do you know someone—maybe a mentor—who would be willing to put his name on the book?"

My number one mentor was Oral Roberts. I spent five years being mentored by him personally as an undergraduate at Oral Roberts University. As a student I was appointed to the world national committee. He met with us every Tuesday at noon, just five of us. He would talk to us in a little room in the chapel. What a privilege! Later he appointed me as a mission director to test me. Then I became director of missions for the whole school. He told me to mentor someone to take my place, and I did.

Years later I was an unknown author. I sent him the manuscript and asked him to read it and consider writing the foreword, which meant lending his name to my book. I was so afraid. I was asking him to give me his fifty years of successful ministry in fifty seconds. I was humbled by his response. He read the entire manuscript, sent back the beautiful foreword, and told me, "I am proud of you, son, and you can have my name."

That first book is called *Single, Married, Separated, and Life after Divorce*. It has sold more than a million copies—because of his name. By the way, his name was larger than mine because he had the credibility, not me. He was giving his whole life. Suppose there were errors in that book. He was taking a risk because he knew me. He was my mentor. He still was until his death in late 2009. He was more than ninety years old, and he still called me his son.

When you mentor, you can open doors for others in one second that could take years for them to get through alone. Oral Roberts never asked me for anything in exchange for giving his name. He simply gave me the gift of fifty years of his life.

Another time I wrote John Maxwell, a highly respected authority on leadership who has sold nearly twenty million books himself, and said, "Look, I have a book on men…" I sent it to him. He wrote a foreword. I wrote another book and sent it to Dr. Fred Price, founder of Crenshaw Christian Center/Ever Increasing Faith Ministries in California, one of the largest and most-influential churches in the United States. I said, "Look if you think it is worthy of your name, would you write a foreword?" Now, I do the same thing for many people. My name has become valuable. I am willing to share it as a mentor to others. Many of my mentees have written books now, and they are always asking, "Will you do a foreword for my book?" When I say, "Absolutely, yes!" I am sharing my creditability, my influence with them. People who trust me will trust them. You are mentored so you can mentor other people. It is not about you. It is about the people you develop.

The Mentor's Mind-set

In all these ways, the mentor invests in the mentee and allows that person to flourish. Mentors allow budding leaders to see the processes involved in leadership—the issues, responsibilities, and obligations. As the lioness does with her cubs, they model decision making so the young leaders can see it, allowing them to share privileged experiences. They accept the responsibility of being role models. They direct the developing leader to resources and opportunities for growth.

All of this requires the effective mentor to keep the following principles in mind:

Understand that leadership is "caught" more than taught. That means mentoring your understudy for leadership is not limited to verbal instruction, but includes allowing them to experience things through your life. The mentee has to observe and catch on to what you are teaching.

See potential in each person. Mentors must understand basic human nature. The mentor understands that human potential is always present, but not necessarily manifested. He or she can see more potential in the protégé than the person sees in himself. The mentor does not judge based on what the mentee does or has done, but rather on what that person could do. The mentor looks at what the mentee can be. Mentors can accept and overlook errors because they believe more in potential than they do past behavior. They tolerate the poor judgment and the miscalculations of a mentee because they believe in potential.

Tolerate mistakes. The mentor allows for error. If you are going to reproduce leaders, learn from your own experience. You were not *all that* all the time. You had your own problems. Someone tolerated you for a long time.

Allow people to make some errors. The mentor also understands that mistakes are a part of the educational process. In many cases mentorship requires that you set up the mentee to fail, not to do harm but to teach, because failure is also an important classroom for leadership development. Do not trust a person who never fails. Failure is the incubator for character development. Character development is more important than skill development. The mentor allows for the mistakes because others have done it for him or her. All of us are "in process." We are works in progress. We are all under construction, and everybody is at a different stage of life. A mentor never judges from the standpoint of where the mentor is, but rather from where the mentee is. That allows for mistakes and makes room for improvement.

Demonstrate patience. This is related to tolerance. Patience is knowing the value of time and experience. It requires patience to give the mentee time to experience different environments, emotions, and situations as part of the learning process. It requires patience to mentor them on the path to acquiring competence and eventually independence. It requires patience to watch your children grow up to become mature adults. It takes patience to grow a successor. Jesus displayed patience many times. After Peter denied Him, Jesus sent word through the angel, saying in effect, "Tell Peter he can come back to the meeting. I know what he did. It's okay. Tell him to come back. He's in charge."

> **Mark 16:7** "But go, tell his disciples **and Peter,** 'He is going ahead of you into Galilee. There you will see him, just as he told you.'"

After the resurrected Jesus appeared to the disciples on the shores of the Sea of Galilee and fed them breakfast, He handed Peter the responsibility for His flock, but first He tested him.

> **John 21:17** The third time he said to him, "Simon son of John, do you love me?" Peter was hurt because Jesus asked him the third time, "Do you love me?" He said, "Lord, you know all things; you know that I love you." Jesus said, "Feed my sheep."

Great leaders have endless patience. They have the wisdom to know that you will go through trials and learn from them. Be patient.

Make time to spend with your mentee. I reserve time for the people I mentor through our program at Bahamas Faith Ministries International (BFMI). Anyone who is in my program can come to my house at least twice a year, spend the day with me, meet my family, and see how I live. They can observe how I work in different environments. In the examples the Bible gives us, the mentors—Moses with Joshua; Elijah with Elisha; Jesus with Peter, James, and John—each gave their time.

Provide opportunities to learn. Mentoring has more to do with providing opportunities to *experience* leadership than it does with merely teaching leadership. The mentor creates situations for the mentee to learn. This can happen in many different ways. For instance, the mentor can expose the mentee to his or her programs, projects, and events as I do when I use my platform for my mentees, allowing them to speak, letting them run a meeting, or lending my name to their book. A mentor shares space with the mentee. The mentor shares his exposure with the mentee.

Be honest with correction and generous with praise. If someone needs correction, give it. If they did well, tell them. From time to time, the mentor will confront the difficult task of addressing the weaknesses, idiosyncrasies, mistakes, moral failings, or poor judgment of those under his guidance. You must be honest with the person you are trying to develop. If you want that person to grow, you have to be frank and not appease them or accommodate anything that can retard development. The mentor should also be lavish with encouragement and praise when deserved because people need affirmation. The mentor should be able to praise generously because someone did it for him or her. Praise is a great source of comfort and stability for those we mentor.

Provide recognition. Tell the mentee how well she is doing. Let others know how well she is doing too. Recognition is a little different from just praising someone. Praise might be done in private. Recognition is generally in front of others. A mentor can instill confidence in a mentee by introducing a mentee to your audience, presenting the mentee to those in your environment, or sharing your platform. This is a powerful force. It shows belief and faith in that person when you introduce her to your market. You have given that person high recognition and honor. Recognition also means giving your mentees access to your relationships, introducing them to people you know and letting others know their value.

Keep a long-term perspective. This has to do with seeing the future, believing in it, and then working to make it a reality. Mentorship is working with the future. When you begin to mentor a person, you mentor with vision. The mentor anticipates what is up ahead or what is coming because you know the vision. You expose your mentee to things that are relative to your field. For example, you are a bank executive, and you want to mentor a young officer. You do not mentor that person to become a mechanic. You offer mentoring related to banking. If you are a priest, you mentor a future priest. You mentor with the perspective of your vision of what they will become.

Focus on developing people, not managing them. You cannot manage a human. Individuals have a will. Even God cannot manage humans. He paid the price for their salvation, but He still cannot save them. He said, "Whoever is thirsty, let him come; and whoever wishes, let him take the free gift of the water of life" (Rev. 22:17). Even though Jesus prepared the way, we still can refuse Him. Jesus does not impose salvation on us. We have to choose. We have free will. You can manage a copier, a printer, or a computer, but not people. We should develop people. I am an equipment manager and a people developer. A mentor is more concerned about human development than about technology. The mentor does not allow things to become more important than people. Equipment can never compete with the potential, intellect, emotions, and physical development of a person.

Understand that transformation comes only through association. Mentoring can take place only through close association. You produce leaders by allowing them to come into your space. Allow people to enjoy the glow of your light. Let people feel the power. Let them taste it. Let them see the power. Like the lioness that places her cubs nearby, you have to allow the mentee to come close enough to observe how you work and think.

View people as opportunities, not interruptions. If you are a mentor, you probably are a busy person. Most people qualified to be mentors are deeply engrossed in activities with great responsibility, perhaps running a country, organization, or business. Mentors are very busy people. That makes mentoring very challenging. Remember, however, not to consider people who want to learn from you as nuisances. If you have a mentoring agreement (see chapter 20, "Mentorship Is by Agreement"), the mentor cannot view the mentee as a bother. Any time my office tells me that a mentee wants to see me, I stop doing whatever I am doing because we have an agreement. If I am in a foreign country working with a group or government and someone I am mentoring leaves a message that he needs to talk to me, I respond at the first opportunity. It is not an interruption. That individual knows he must respect my time, but I also know that I promised to give my time.

People are opportunities. I will never forget how that lesson took on special meaning for me one day when a group came to my office in Nassau. My secretary, who is also my sister, called me to say that some people were there to see me. I thought, "This is not a good time for this." People often come to see me unscheduled, but this day I was working on a deadline to finish our annual report. I told my sister that I could not see anybody right then.

She said, "I know you are busy, but they said that they *must* see you. They have been reading your books and watching your TV shows. They came to the Bahamas on a cruise, and they took a taxi all the way over to our center. They just want to see you for three minutes. Just to shake your hand and tell you thanks for helping them."

I said, "Ah, man!" Then I heard a voice in my head say, "People are not interruptions. They are opportunities. They are people."

Right then I closed my folder, shut my computer, and said, "Bring them up." They came up to my office, a couple dressed in their casual clothes, sandals, straw hats, short pants, and T-shirts.

They were so happy to see me. We hugged and greeted, and I said, "Sit down."

They said, "No, we did not come to stay long."

I said, "Sit down."

They said, "Why?"

I said, "Because you are people."

"You would actually take time to see us?" they asked.

"Sure, you are people."

That is what I heard the voice say.

Then we sat down and chatted a little bit as they told me how much my work had blessed them and changed their lives. Their young son had started a business from reading one of my books, and they were so excited. Listening to them, I was deeply encouraged. When I said, "Thank you so much for coming," I meant it from my heart.

They stood up and asked, "May we take a picture?"

"Sure," I said.

We took a picture, and we were walking to the door when the man turned around and said, "By the way, we brought you something." He gave me an envelope, and they left.

I quickly went back to work on my report. When I opened the envelope later, I found a check for ten thousand dollars, and I prayed, "Lord, send me more people."

Never consider people interruptions. In some of the circles in which I travel, other leaders and presenters have entourages, security, and people with microphones who follow them. I show up with my wife, and people ask, "Where are your security guards?" I respond, "My wife is my security." I do not want to protect myself from the people I came to serve. People are not interruptions.

What are you missing out on when you tell people, "Oh, I have no time for you. I'm a man of the church. I have a vast ministry to run"? Jesus took time for children. His disciples wanted to act as security guards, but Jesus said He came to serve. He did not need protection from the people, especially not the young. Neither do you if you are going to mentor effectively.

> **Matthew 19:13–14** Then little children were brought to Jesus for him to place his hands on them and pray for them. But the disciples rebuked those who brought them. Jesus said, "Let the little children come to me, and do not hinder them, for the kingdom of heaven belongs to such as these."

Jesus blessed the little ones on the spot and used it as a teaching moment for His grown-up mentees. You cannot train people if you avoid them. Leadership is about people.

A Time to Rejoice

I use seven key points to summarize the marks of a courageous leader.
Courageous leaders:

1. Free others to be leaders.
2. Provide opportunities for others to find and fulfill their God-given po-

tential and purpose.

3. Mentor successors willingly.
4. Think in generational terms.
5. Embrace the chance to be absent.
6. Refuse to see the success of mentees as a threat.
7. Rejoice when mentees become greater and more effective than you were.

Jesus once sent out seventy-two followers deputized to heal and preach, and He rejoiced when they came back reporting their successes.

> **Luke 10:17–24** The seventy-two returned with joy and said, "Lord, even the demons submit to us in your name." He replied, "I saw Satan fall like lightning from heaven. I have given you authority to trample on snakes and scorpions and to overcome all the power of the enemy; nothing will harm you. However, do not rejoice that the spirits submit to you, but rejoice that your names are written in heaven." At that time **Jesus, full of joy through the Holy Spirit**, said, "I praise you, Father, Lord of heaven and earth, because you have hidden these things from the wise and learned, and revealed them to little children. Yes, Father, for this was your good pleasure. "All things have been committed to me by my Father. No one knows who the Son is except the Father, and no one knows who the Father is except the Son and those to whom the Son chooses to reveal him." Then he turned to his disciples and said privately, "Blessed are the eyes that see what you see. For I tell you that many prophets and kings wanted to see what you see but did not see it, and to hear what you hear but did not hear it."

Often when leaders hear good reports about their staff, they become threatened. However, Jesus rejoiced in their accomplishments, as we should rejoice when our mentees are leading others.

Points to remember:

It takes courage to mentor.
Make yourself increasingly unnecessary.
Produce leaders who can lead others.

Chapter 6

Leading Beyond Your Lifetime

MANY HAVE COME to me and said, "I have read your book." Others might have seen my television show, listened to a CD, or come to a conference, and they tell me that something I said changed their lives. They built a business or started a ministry of their own. To me, that is leadership success. Your legacy is what you do for the people around you that will make them better than you are.

My greatest joy comes when I see people around me starting their own businesses, believing in their dreams, pursuing their passions, and developing their ideals and ideas. I take pleasure in making them leaders of others.

The measure of true leadership optimally is your ability to leave. You are successful when your organization grows after you leave. When the greatest leader of all time left the earth, He had eleven devotees, and then one hundred twenty showed up in the room. Then in one week, there were three thousand, and the rest is history. The church grew in His absence.

The only memory people have of you might be the old picture in the lobby. Instead, paint your face on the hearts of people. If they never put up a photograph of you, will people still speak your name in the halls? Would you hear them talk about you? Would you hear things like this?

"She did this for me."

"Yes, I was discouraged, but one day she spoke to me."

"Yes, I started this business because one day he gave me this idea."

In other words, will your name be on lips rather than walls? Legacy is about giving life, not photographs, to people. Therefore, your greatest contribution is to outlive yourself. How do you outlive yourself? By transferring yourself to other people. Succession is about living beyond your grave, and the only way to do that is to reproduce yourself in the next generation. If you seek power because you need power, you will never mentor. But if you seek to serve the next generation and leave a legacy, you will always desire to mentor.

The good leader is:

- Thinking beyond his leadership.
- Thinking generationally.
- Aware of his mortality.
- Aware of his dispensability.
- Responsible for the organization's future.
- Very secure in the position.
- Not afraid of the success of others.
- Acting as a visionary.
- Preparing to leave, not to stay.
- Securing his legacy.

How Long Do You Have?

I think it is very important and critical that people learn quickly as they rise in the ranks of leadership that they are dispensable. I am always in touch with my death. Become friendly with your demise. Always think of yourself as a flower that fades and turns to dust. You could be here today and gone tomorrow. Think that way, and you will work harder on the right things, things like investing in people.

Have you noticed that no one lives forever? Most of us probably have a good seventy years, if we are blessed with good health. If we are very, very blessed with grace, we may make it to seventy-five or eighty years old. After that, most of us are unable to contribute effectively to our generation. A few people are blessed to live to see a hundred years or more, but all will eventually die. We have to prepare for that.

A true leader is always preparing to leave. Every day I live, I write my obituary. Every day, I decide what people will say over my dead body. I am writing that myself, and I hope you are writing yours. What will they say about you when you die?

"Success without a successor is failure."

Leadership success is not measured by what you have done, but by what you can successfully transfer to the next generation: the vision, the passion, the ideals, and the dreams that you will not live long enough to finish. Can you give them to someone else? That is your leadership success. That is how you measure it—by living forever through people.

You know you are going to die, so you might as well make it worth it. Do something that is going to make you live beyond the cemetery. Do not live just for yourself. Leadership is about transfer—the intentional release of power.

If we are good leaders or good parents, we want to leave something of what we have accumulated to those we left behind. Whether we want to or not, we have to leave all our material assets behind, as Job, the long-suffering Old Testament servant of God, reminds us.

> **Job 1:21** "Naked I came from my mother's womb, and naked I will depart. The LORD gave and the LORD has taken away; may the name of the LORD be praised."

We may prepare by writing a will or buying insurance and designating a beneficiary. We may name a guardian for our dependent children or direct that our pets go to a good home. We may leave our business to our widows, widowers, or children. Yet some people give no thought to these matters or die before they have had a chance to express their wishes for the future. None of us knows when our time will be up, as Jesus said:

> **Matthew 25:13** "Therefore keep watch, because you do not know the day or the hour."

Perhaps all you have to bequeath are the things you have taught your children, the loving memories you shared with your husband, the goodwill that your company has built up, or the unselfish works you performed through your ministry. These are your legacy.

What Do You Bequeath?

A true leader wants to leave something in place. If you come to the end of your journey and leave nothing to show for it, that is a tragedy. You might have founded a company that is now on the Fortune 500 list or a ministry that has so many members that it has to meet in a stadium and hold six worship services on Sunday. If your heir destroys it all within months because of poor preparation and bad judgment, your legacy is nil. It does not matter how great you are or think you are, nor what monuments you have created, if it dies with you, you fail.

"Why blame me?" you might ask. "I was a successful entrepreneur. I built an empire here. I was a master of commerce in my lifetime..."

True, you might have made millions or converted thousands, but you failed. You neglected to choose and mentor a successor who could preserve your legacy. In your lifetime, you were responsible for training the next generation. It was your obligation to preserve your legacy beyond that lifetime. The transfer of leadership is the greatest obligation for a leader.

Moses was a successful leader. Joshua was a miserable failure in the end. If you read the story of Joshua and Moses, you learn how he mentored Joshua, trained him from a young age, and gave him the company when he was too weak to go on. Joshua ended up with three million people, a lot of money, and a mobile tabernacle that was mortgage-free. He had everything going for him, and when he died, he left it to no one.

Joshua might have been a hero to many because he marched his people across the Jordan and into the Promised Land, but he failed as a leader. He did not leave a successor. Most of the leaders I have known failed because their work died with them. The next generation had to start all over again to rebuild what they could. That is a waste of a whole generation.

I have watched leaders come and go, taking their vision with them. Then someone else comes and takes their spot on earth, bringing a fresh vision. This to me is sad because I do not believe that God intended for any of us to bring a new vision to the earth. He intended for us to make a link in the chain, to connect our visions, our perspectives in life, from generation to generation, continually building on the vision.

We have to transfer the vision of our time and connect it to someone else to continue in his or her time. That heir to the vision in turn will do something in the next generation, essentially assuring that we never die. You could say that a leader with a successor never dies. A leader without a successor dies twice: with the physical death and with the death of the vision that ends.

You are not successful because of what you have done. You are successful because of what you can transfer to the next generation. **The generation that follows you proves your greatness. Measure your greatness by what you are able to preserve for the next generation.** A true leader is always preparing to leave. Protect, preserve, and perpetuate your leadership by making sure others will carry out your legacy and build on your success.

Principles for Legacy Preservation

If you hope to see your vision continue, bear in mind these principles for legacy preservation, leadership that extends beyond your lifetime:

Leadership is never given to one generation. Most leaders inherited a trust from the previous generation to give to the next generation. True leadership is never just for your time. Always think, "What am I supposed to contribute to the future? What am I supposed to prepare for the generation that is coming? What am I supposed to give them? What did I take from the previous generation and improve on that I can hand to the next generation for its leaders to improve on?" Leadership is not just for you, it is always for your successor—a succeeding generation.

Leadership that serves only its generation is destined to failure. If you do not think beyond your generation, everything you achieve will die with you. You will be remembered only in your time. Your name will be forgotten, unspoken by future generations. This is the worst thing that could happen to a human. Never lead with only your generation on your mind. Whether you are a Sunday-school teacher in a megachurch, department manager in a major corporation, or president of a large country, your leadership exists not only for your generation but also for future generations.

God is a generational God. When I say that God is "generational," I mean that He thinks beyond this generation. He is mindful of all generations. God never speaks just to you. He speaks to your loins. God always speaks to the generation trapped underneath you. If you ever think God is speaking to you, you are going to lose your legacy. If you study Scripture very carefully, God always reminds the person to whom He is talking that He is not really addressing them. God always speaks to the unborn because He thinks generationally. So leadership that is genuine, that is from God, always thinks generationally. Do you know how long it took the Israelites to get the land that God promised Abraham? It was so long that Abraham never got there. God was thinking in generations.

> **Genesis 26:3** Stay in this land for a while, and I will be with you and will bless you. For to you and your descendants I will give all these lands and will confirm the oath I swore to your father Abraham.

A vision that is genuinely from God will always be bigger than your lifetime. People think they should complete their vision in their lifetime, but God is too big for that. He will always give you a vision that will outlive you. Part of your responsibility as a visionary is to prepare your replacement to continue the work. Many leaders that people admire were, in my view, failures because they took to the cemetery everything they were supposed to leave with us. Their work died. I believe that is not God's plan.

God will never give you an assignment that you can complete in your lifetime because he is a generational God. He will not allow you to complete the vision. He will allow you to finish your phase of it. You can always tell when a dream is from God: You can never finish it. You can only finish your part of it, the part assigned to you in your lifetime.

I think one of the greatest statements made by Jesus Christ on Earth, whom I consider the greatest leader ever, was, "It is finished."

> **John 19:30** When he had received the drink, Jesus said, **"It is finished."** With that, he bowed his head and gave up his spirit.

What is important is that He did not say, "I am finished." There is a big difference between saying, "I am finished" and "It is finished." The latter refers to a phase. Why? He is still working, is He not? Yes, but He went to another phase that required relocation to another place. The first phase was finished. He completed an assignment. What is He doing now? Interceding. He is in the intercession phase.

Your next phase may require relocation. However, if you are stuck—hanging on to that old phase, God cannot get you to do greater work. You can be so in love with what you are doing that it blocks you from your greatness. Never think that what you are doing now is so great you cannot see beyond that. It is a phase. What can be better than resurrection? Simple. Going to Heaven to sit on a throne and pray. Jesus is on a throne. To get there, He had to finish the first phase.

What you think is so great now may not be the pinnacle of your life. The dream in your heart will always be bigger than your lifetime, and your assignment is to complete your phase of it. It is important to know when your phase is over. The length of life does not determine completion of one's phase, but completion of the assignment measures one's fulfillment of life. Jesus Christ finished the earthly phase of His assignment at the age of thirty-three.

Your assignment might be for only a few months, maybe a few years, or even a decade. Do not remain tied to it because life is much bigger than your job. Stop planning to grow old where you are. You are blocking the next generation. Your life is bigger than your job, so do not remain stuck in it.

If the spirit of mentoring and succession comes upon you, you will always be progressive. You will always be free to move. If you capture that spirit, you will never be depressed when the company fires you because your interpretation of that would be, "It is time to move on." You were not fired. You were released to your next phase.

God of All Generations

I am intrigued when I read in the Scriptures about the relationship between God and man. As I noted in the preceding principles, whenever God deals with humans, He deals with them in terms of the future. He told Adam and

Eve to multiply, subdue, and fill the earth. That instruction has to do with the future.

> **Genesis 1:28** God blessed them and said to them, "Be fruitful and increase in number; fill the earth and subdue it. Rule over the fish of the sea and the birds of the air and over every living creature that moves on the ground."

Then He called Abram and told him that he would have a seed, the seed would have a nation, and the nation would be blessed—nation after nation. He was not talking to Abram. God said that the nations would be blessed through him. God was always referring to generations.

> **Genesis 12:1–3** The LORD had said to Abram, "Leave your country, your people and your father's household and go to the land I will show you. I will make you into a great nation and I will bless you; I will make your name great, and you will be a blessing. I will bless those who bless you, and whoever curses you I will curse; and all peoples on earth will be blessed through you."

When God talked about the salvation of humankind, He promised a Messiah would come and save the whole world, which means His promise to the prophets about the Messiah was not for the prophets but for nations and the world beyond that (see Genesis 12:1).

Everything God does is generational. He is the ultimate leader. If He thought generationally, we must think generationally. The older I get, the more I realize this is just a brief moment in history. The eighty years that a long life might last is so short compared to a thousand years beyond when your name will not even be remembered. We must think in terms of generational leadership.

Whether a person is CEO of a company or minister for a youth group, leadership is never given to one generation. If you are the elected head of a country, your leadership is not given to one generation. If you settle on that concept, you will realize that every leader is temporary.

Often our temptation as leaders is to think the world begins and ends with us. It clearly does not. Leadership is always transitional. Any leader who thinks he or she is permanent must remember the Creator has one neutral-izing agent for that: death. No matter how terrorizing or how wonderful a leader may be, death will eventually terminate that individual's phase.

From Womb to Tomb

Once you accept that you will not be here forever and that planning for suc-cession might be a good idea, it might help to understand how we develop as humans. Life has three phases: dependence, independence, and interdepen-dence.

Phase 1

Dependence

Everything that has life begins as a dependent, whether a child or a fruit. Dependence is not a sign of weakness, but rather a sign of wisdom. The child remains in the womb because it needs a host. That is wisdom. I think that whenever we attempt to avoid the dependent stage, we place ourselves in danger of premature death. That is true of the human being, the animal, and the fruit tree. If we detach fruit before it is developed, it may never ripen. The same thing is true of humans.

You must understand that you were not conceived alone. You will never develop alone. You need to begin your journey submitting to, learning from, depending on, and cooperating with a host. In leadership, we call these peo-ple coaches or mentors.

Mentoring is critical. Mentoring protects the emerging leader from pre-mature destruction. Mentoring nurtures. Just as a mother nurtures a child in the womb, a mentor provides incubation for development and advancement of a person. The placenta in the mother's womb is vital to transferring food, vitamins, and sustenance into the child. The mentoring environment is crit-ical for the transferring and transmitting of vital information. The root and branches of a tree nurture the fruit by giving it what it needs, and so it is with all of life. Mentoring is imperative.

The tree must keep the fruit attached until it ripens. When the time is right, it will fall from the tree on its own. The mother needs to know how important it is to keep the baby in good health and to take care of herself for the sake of the child until it is mature enough to function outside the womb. Many leaders do not understand that the people around them are green fruit, buds they need to develop.

Phase 2

Independence

Eventually the child will mature and gradually outgrow the need to depend on the mother for everything. The fruit will ripen and drop away from the tree. Every living thing reaches a stage of independence. Independence is maturity itself. For the mentor, it is the second-greatest evidence of success. Independence involves being able to function apart from the host, but it does not mean abandoning the host. It means that you focus on maturing. Independence requires communicating back to the mentor or the host how successful they were in helping to develop you. Independence is not walking off saying, "I don't need you anymore." Independence is telling the host, "Thank you. You successfully developed me to where I am now—mature enough to express my individual identity, to manifest my uniqueness, and to show my distinct value to you my host/mentor and the world."

Phase 3

Interdependence

Interdependence is the ultimate measure of success. At this stage, the mentored one is now required to mentor. The new mentor contributes back to the ongoing development of the species, of the organization, and of the succeeding generation. Independence is leadership fulfilling the promise of succession. Interdependence is reproducing after your kind. It is giving back something better to what produced you. Every succeeding generation of leaders will be better than the proceeding generations. Interdependence is the perpetuation of future leaders. At this stage, the leader can say:

- I am obligated to mentor.
- I am responsible for reporting back to my mentor.

- I am going to mentor.

The ultimate goal is not independence but interdependence—not just separating from the host or parent but also giving back to and accepting help from others. Generations are interdependent. Leaders help assure that the next generation is ready to step up to the plate.

A Dependency-Reduction Plan

I have heard leaders say that they could not take a vacation because their enterprise would fall apart while they were away. If that is the case, they should be fired! The ultimate measure of true leadership is your ability to leave. You can always tell a poor manager, an ineffective supervisor, or a weak leader by what happens when they are out of the office. Every time the poor manager leaves the office, the staff has a coffee break and water-fountain party. Remember those times when you could not wait for the manager to leave so you could sit around with everyone else and talk for two to three hours? When the manager comes back, everybody runs back to his or her desks. That is a sign of a poor leader.

What happens in your organization when you leave? Could you stay away for more than two weeks for a great vacation? Why do you need to call every hour when you are away? Because you are not a leader. If the staff keeps calling you while you are on vacation to ask you questions or get directions, then you are a weak leader. You should be able to go on vacation and say, "I am not going to call you. Do not call me every day. I will not be checking my BlackBerry. Do not text me. Just do what you know how to do. Whatever comes up, just remember what I have taught you."

What happens in your absence will be the measure of your greatness. Your ability to leave is the measure of your leadership. People ask me, "How do you get to travel two hundred thousand miles every year, all over the world, and still have an organization that is so massive and yet runs by itself?" I tell them it is because I spent the first ten years focusing on developing people in my organization to take responsibility and to fulfill their leadership potential. In other words, I intentionally created the environment where the need for my direct supervision decreased.

Have you started planning your departure? No? Maybe you are thinking something like this: "Man, you must be crazy! This is my job, and no one is going to take it. I worked hard to get to this position. God gave me this job, and I am protecting my territory. My plan is to retire from this job and collect my pension."

If this is your perspective, then you will never achieve the legacy of leadership you deserve. You are not exhibiting the character and nature of a true leader. True leaders do not plan to live on pension, but on purpose. They are more interested in contributing to humanity than in seeking gain from humanity.

The ultimate goal of true leadership is not to maintain followers but to maintain leaders. Your goal is to produce leaders.

True leadership is measured by the diminishing dependency of your followers. You can tell how effective you are as a leader by how much less people seem to need you. They have grown to the independence level.

Your greatest contribution is to outlive yourself. The only way to outlive yourself is to reproduce yourself. That is why Jesus Christ is still alive today. He lives through the millions of "little Christs"—or Christians—in the world.

Insecure leaders need people to need them. That dependence props up the weak leader. An insecure leader to me is a paradox. The two words do not go together. They contradict each other, but some people parade around as leaders. If you are insecure and you have a title, you are dangerous because you will always want to protect and defend yourself. People like that would kill their opposition. They do not just fight against competitors. They destroy their rivals. Insecurity breeds contempt for those who threaten the leader's position. That is a defect. It is a failure.

One of the greatest failings of leaders is fear. The greatest fear of leadership is the success of the followers. Have you ever heard this? "You can be good, but don't ever be better than me." The moment the followers begin to outshine the leader, the leader finds reasons to send them on vacation, to relocate them in another part of the organization, fire them, or put them on involuntary early retirement—anything to get rid of them.

In other words, we become insecure when people around us start succeeding. Some of us feel threatened when no one comes to us for help. How sad. When the people around you are more successful than you have been, it is a compliment to your leadership. Always remember this: If you hold a man down, you have to stay down with him to keep him there. Fear of success of others is a great failing of leaders. It is a sign that they are weak leaders. It takes courage to mentor your successor. Diminishing dependency is the measure of effective leadership. It is like a parent bringing up children. If your son is fifty years old and still asks you to cook for him on a daily basis, you need to be fired as a parent. You failed. Your child should be cooking for you sometimes and be teaching his children to cook.

If you are a very successful pastor, for example, you will find the line of people coming up for your prayer call gets shorter and shorter until no one comes forward to the altar for prayer. Now, that frightens a pastor.

One pastor said to me, "Dr. Munroe, something is wrong in my church. Years ago, when I called people to come up for healing and consolation, they filled the altar. No one comes anymore."

I said, "What are you depressed about?"

He said, "Well, maybe I'm doing something wrong."

I said, "No, that's a sign that it's working. They do not need you to pray anymore. They are praying for themselves. If you say everybody who is poor come forward, and no one comes forward, that means everybody is rich. You should be rejoicing as a pastor."

You have done your job well. Whatever you have been training them to do, they have been doing, and their prayers have been answered. They have an effective prayer life, and their needs have been met. Everyone has been saved. Everyone has been healed. They have fewer needs to bring to the altar. They need you less.

The ultimate measure of true leadership is the ability to leave. Can you take what you are building and give it to someone else? If you understand that it is not yours and that you are just a steward, then it is easy to leave. If you think it is yours or your family's property, you will not want to leave it.

If you find it difficult to take time to rejuvenate yourself and enjoy the things you worked so hard to achieve, you may be exhibiting signs of failed leadership. If you are insecure about your own leadership position as a pastor, manager, or supervisor, then you might not be the leader you should be. If you are afraid to leave your pulpit for a vacation because you think your youth pastor might take over the church, you are a failure. Perhaps this sense of insecurity could be evidence that you have not focused your efforts on

mentoring and producing potential leaders who could carry on in your absence.

Leaders who show these signs of insecurity have not helped the next
generation of leaders to move from a state of dependence to a state of independence and finally to a stage of interdependence. I spend a lot of time
away from my organization. My greatest joy is when they do not miss me
when I am gone. When I return, they often do not know that I am back. I
do get a little nervous though. From time to time, I have to tell the staff,
"Hey, I am back. Hi, y'all! Hey, you remember me?" Still, it is a joy when
things keep going in my absence.

Points to remember:

If your vision dies with you, you have failed.
Every leader is temporary.
Measure leadership by the diminishing dependency of followers.
Interdependence is the ultimate measure of success.

Part 2

The Pitfalls—Prepare for When You Are Not Around

Chapter 7

Provide a Model

"I KNOW THAT you are inexperienced—green, wet behind the ears. I know that you have not been with me for more than a couple of weeks, but let me tell you what I am going to do. I am going to send you out two by two. I want you to go out. I am going to give you authority. I am going to authorize you to do some things. You are not mature yet. You are not experienced yet, but I am going to trust you with a little bit of power."

That is essentially what Jesus told His followers in Luke 9 and 10. The Scriptures say that they cast out demons, healed the sick, raised the dead, and cleansed the lepers. When they came back to Him, they could not wait to report what had happened. They said something like this: "Master, you would not believe that demons trembled when we showed up and the sick were healed. We really showed them. Boy, were they sorry to see us."

> **Luke 10:17** The seventy-two returned with joy and said, "Lord, even the demons submit to us in your name."

Jesus rejoiced in their success.

Since the greatest responsibility of leadership is to reproduce leaders, it is vital to explore fully why leaders should focus on developing leadership under their care. Many pitfalls await us on the way to establishing an effective succession plan that will assure a solid legacy of success. Succession succeeds when the successor lands in the position with proper preparation. He or she is prepared because the former leader was an effective mentor, delegator, trainer, or role model.

Now consider the pastor who goes on vacation and leaves the assistant in charge for a couple of Sundays. When he gets back, all the members are talking about how well the assistant preached. "He was better than the pastor!" If the pastor overhears the conversation, what should he do? He should leave again and find excuses to let the assistant preach more regularly.

"Leadership reproduces leadership." Let us say that you leave your assistant manager in charge and go on vacation for a month. When you get back, all the employees say the productivity was up and sales are through the roof. "Best profits we have ever had!" What would you do with that assistant? If you are smart, you will go back on vacation.

True leaders do not let the success of their followers threaten them or make them jealous. They expect success. They welcome it. They train people to make sure that day will come. They mentor.

"No one helped me, so I am not helping anybody." That is often the attitude we have. "I got here by my own hard work. I'm a self-made man. I did it the hard way—pulled myself up by my bootstraps. Let them get there the best way they can." If those are your words, you are replicating the selfish habits of the leaders who were in your life.

Leaders must learn how to transfer power. They should not be afraid to let go of any authority. Leaders cannot remain snared in a trap of not wanting to make necessary choices. Do not postpone decisions about succession out of concern that this will create antagonism, jealousy, or hatred within the staff, congregation, constituency, or family. Transition is not hazardous to your survival and legacy. It is a greater hazard, however, not to have an effective transfer of power. To transfer power intentionally and in a timely, well-thought-out fashion risks creating discomfort in the organization for a short time, but failure to transfer power effectively is like throwing a pack of meat to hungry dogs and hoping one of them emerges as a leader before they all kill each other and become prey for other animals.

We must assure that leaders—be it in government, religion, corporate, civic, or family life—arrive at positions of authority and power with the bene-fit of intentional, objective, strategic training and mentorship. It is incredible how many leaders came into their positions because they won some type of battle, not because somebody handed them a baton. Often we consider gain-ing our leadership position a victory over someone else. "I won the election. I won the senate race. I won the bishop's title." We act as if we achieved something at the expense of others. This is not leadership. This is conquering human souls. Leadership is supposed to be power passed from one person to another.

Remember that any power that you have is a gift. If you received some-thing, it was not yours originally. You were not born with authority. You are given authority. If you take authority, you are illegitimate. True leaders emerge. They do not conquer. When a leader emerges naturally, that is le-gitimate power. True leaders do not decide to be leaders. They are victims of destiny. Just as children who have not had effective parents often fail to be good parents, leaders who have not had good mentors will have difficulty mentoring and preparing future leaders.

This book is designed to break that pattern. Let us examine some of the ways we can provide a model to mentor and train others to replicate good leadership.

Understand leadership. As "servant leaders," we lead without control-ling, managing, or oppressing people. Our leadership has very little to do with other people. It has more to do with self-discovery. It involves finding our personal sense of purpose, discovering our true gift, and cultivating and developing our gift to pursue that purpose. It is sacrifice, paying the price to fulfill that purpose and vision. When we discover our purpose and our gift, we develop the confidence, security, self-worth, self-esteem, and self-signifi-cance that protect us from threat of competition, comparison, and jealousy. These strengths allow us to develop other successful leaders. True leadership creates the environment for others to discover themselves.

Reject the poor leadership habits of our predecessors. Even if no one trained us, we must train others. As true leaders reproducing leaders, we must be the model. Others will replicate what they see in us. If our boss held key information close to the vest, failed to delegate, and pushed out poten-tial rivals, we should do the opposite. If our boss or pastor did not mentor and encourage new leadership, we must do those things. It is time to break the cycle. Someone has to stop this. We should not do to others what people did to us. Those who did not have formal mentoring must take the lead to mentor others. Identify potential leaders and set up a program to train them. Tell someone, "I am going to mentor you. I am going to make you great! I'm going to develop you and make you better than I am! I am going to help you. I'll train you. I will be an example to you." Why not?

Seek good models and mentors. If you have a leader who is a good role model, you can become one. We have to look for ways to be good models for someone else. We have to break the cycle. This is why fathering is so important. A good father will produce a good son, who will produce another good son. Your models become your life lessons that you can teach other people. Produce leaders by setting an example. When Jesus washed the feet of the disciples, He modeled the behavior for them. He did not just tell the disciples what to do. He usually demonstrated and let them watch. It is more important for the leader to show than it is for the leader to say something. The mentor will do things and then ask if you learned anything from it. "Did you see what I did? Did you see how I handled that situation?" You are supposed to learn from the experience. Jesus says in essence, "I am your master, and I washed your feet. Therefore, from now on you should wash each other's feet."

He was not establishing a church ritual; He was saying whenever there is a need, fill it. If you are present and you are capable, then you do it. Leadership needs to be modeled. He could have fussed at them, attacked them, and told them how disappointed He was that they had not already washed one another's feet when they found no servant available. These are grown men. But He did not say a word. He just picked up a basin. In some cases, it is more important to *do* as a leader, than to speak as a leader. I would prefer you talk about what I did than about what I said. In that way, I model behavior I would like to see in you. That is what a role model does.

Provide formal training. We should not leave others to learn on the job just because we might have had to do that. Leaders must be trained to train. That is the reason my organization exists and why I share this information in my books—so you can train others to use their resources, money, and time with precision and skill. We need to be trained so that we can train. If I train you, you are going to be better than I am, and I expect that. That is what I want because if I train you properly, you will train other people better. Leadership reproduces leadership. We cannot leave leadership to chance. Many leaders are not products of formal training, and they think on-the-job training is good enough for others. Somehow they have stumbled their way into the positions they hold. Circumstances opened a door for them, or history destined them for a position. They happened to be there when the person above them left or died, and no one else volunteered or was available. Maybe they had some haphazard training to do a specific job, but no formal training in the principles of leadership. To reproduce leaders, they have to provide that training for others.

Have the confidence to delegate. Summon the courage to share authority, influence, and knowledge. Learn to trust others by sharing control and information. Delegating presents risks. You may feel that if others learn what you know, they might not need you. Each time you delegate a task, you have to teach a little bit of what you know. You have to share wisdom and power. Give others opportunities to exercise their gifts and to grow as leaders. Good leaders reproduce leaders. The successes of those coming behind are not a threat to them. They are not jealous of the gifts others have, and they do not try to suppress or oppress future leaders. Leadership is about sharing power. In other words, true leaders empower. They do not hog the power. The only way you can share power is to be confident in yourself. You are unique. No one can steal you. So give yourself away.

Find the power to let go. Adopt the attitude that you are in the business of being a chief maker. Surround yourself with potential leaders. Your value does not come from your position. Your sense of worth does not come from your title. Your sense of self-esteem does not come from how much authority you have. You cannot be the chief and have everyone else be your subjects. If you feel that way, it is time to let go. Those of us who have made our positions synonymous with our value should understand that is akin to suicide. If you are strapped to your seat, it is time to take off the seat belt. Rid yourself of any sense of entitlement—one of the greatest weaknesses of leadership. Often we think, "This position belongs to me. I've been here for forty years. How dare you come and take my position? I've been the director of this department for years. I've been the prayer-warrior leader for decades. I've been the deacon. I've been in charge of the ushers." Let it go. It is time to let go. We are not entitled to these things. Wise leaders are happy to train people so they can move on to the next spot. They are not afraid to let go. Reproduce leaders who can take your place.

Put "people work" before paperwork. Prioritize people over policies, projects, and paper. Instead of producing memos, reports, five-year projections, and spreadsheets, produce leaders. Mentoring is about people, not memos. "I have a lot of work to do today. I cannot see anyone." Have you ever said that? Do not look now, but that is you. To reproduce leaders, you must spend time with people. Paperwork has its place. For me, it is from 11 p.m. to 3 a.m. That is what I do. The days belong to people. The greatest work of a leader is developing people, not hiding from them. The leader does not spend his days behind closed doors in an office on the tenth floor, eight to nine hours alone with a landline, "smart" phone, computer, fax machine, and remote control for the big-screen television. To reproduce leaders, you have to get out and work with the raw materials, the people who work with you. I walk around my entire organization very often. I go into every department, and I touch base with everybody. Why do I do this? The ivory tower lifestyle is demonic. Take time to train people. Training happens when you come down from the tower and get with the people. You touch and you talk. "How's your family? How are you doing? What's your challenge right now?" When I do this, I see things that need doing that no one else sees. "Oh, that needs changing. Why is this like this?" Get away from paper and find the people. Leadership is about serving people. Instead of leaving behind an excellent final report, leave us a good person to follow you. Make some changes now. Restructure your priorities from this day forward. Let this be the year that you become a people developer. Be a true leader.

Affirm others. When you affirm people, it builds their confidence. "That was a good job you did. You are so good at this. You have really found your calling." We must learn to affirm others. It is not hard to do. Affirmation produces functional humans. We all need affirmation to develop healthy self-concepts, self-esteem, self-worth, and a sense of value and significance. Learn to say positive and encouraging things to those around you. To mentor, you have to affirm, praise, and lift them up. We need to say, "That was great. I want you to do this again for me. Actually, why don't you take over the entire project and run with it because you are very good at what you do. I am so proud of you." Say that to the people who work for you. Walk through the entire company and affirm people. Secure leaders affirm everybody. They do not need to threaten or scare people. They are not afraid someone will take their job or think they are soft. Confident people affirm others. I challenge you to be leaders who produce leaders. Affirm people and then let go. Get rid of the attitude that says, "No one helped me, so why should I help you? I am not going to mentor you. No one mentored me. I had to work hard to get what I have." That is the wrong spirit. We should want to mentor so that the next person does not have to work so hard to get ahead. Mentor to prevent the other person from going through the stress you encountered and to grow leaders who will be better than you were. Help them start where you left off and take your dream to the next level.

Make room for mavericks. Resist the urge to discourage and smother them. Allow the maverick to develop. Stifle the temptation to fire him, discredit him, or ship him off to another department. If you tolerate the maverick, you can produce leaders. You know what a maverick is, right? It is somebody who is full of energy, new ideas, and big dreams. That should energize you too, not irritate you or make your feel old, dumb, and inadequate. Mavericks will question outmoded systems and methods that no longer work. The maverick will offer new facts and innovative theories. This rebel comes bearing new ideas to break up your old traditions. You, of course, feel protected by those traditions. A maverick challenges the old thinking. When this happens, stop clinging to traditions and shed those preconceived notions about how to do things. New ideas are not a threat. Break away from the familiar. Do not cling to programs, projects, policies, and people just because they feel familiar and make you feel secure. When a new breed of individuals enters that circle pushing fresh ideas or untested concepts, we should not be resentful. "Who do they think they are?" They are mavericks. Embrace them. A leader who accepts and encourages those young, fresh, aspiring leaders and gives them opportunities to grow will guarantee his legacy. Welcome the mavericks.

Share decision making, rather than dictate. Give opportunities to explore new ideas instead of just giving instructions. Learn to achieve consensus, not merely give directions. We need to trust the collective vision of the people around us instead of relying only on our own judgments. Encourage debate, give consent, and share ideas. Allow people to solve problems by themselves as part of an organization of leaders. The dictator says, "You listen to what I say. I'm the boss here. Do as I say. I am the bishop. I am God's anointed. I am the pastor. Do you know how long I have been chairman of the board?" The courageous mentor says, "What do you think? Use your own judgment. Come back to me with your ideas, or work it out among yourselves. I trust you to come up with a solution. I like the creative and innovative concepts you have brought to the organization." As courageous leaders, we are secure and self-confident enough to withstand those who might question our authority. The traditional concept of leaders is that we have an organization with *a* leader. That is not God's concept. God wants an organization *of* leaders. Dictatorships are outmoded and unworkable. Allow people to make decisions. As mentors we must look beyond our own perspectives to embrace the multiplicity of good decisions that can come from our team. Leadership is not dictatorship. Release people. Reproduce them.

In the United States, President Barack Obama is a good example of a leader who has welcomed debate. He encouraged discussion. I think one of his greatest strengths is the ability to listen. Perhaps Winston Churchill may serve as an inspiring model of a leader who was able not only to galvanize the resilience of the British people against the dictatorial regime of Hitler's Germany, but he was also able to unify the Western allies in a successful military front to defeat the fascists. Churchill's ability, through his effective communication skills and his willingness to listen and value the aspirations of others, contributed to his success as a leader.

The willingness to listen is a sign that you are secure where you are. You are not afraid of challenges and questions, even disagreements. You are comfortable in your capacity to navigate through all of that and make good decisions in which everyone shares.

True leaders open the doors for people to walk through, create opportunities for people to develop, and give incentives for others to achieve their own greatness. They provide a model.

Points to remember:

Good leaders reproduce leaders.
Mentor others to break the cycle of inadequate preparation of leaders.
Affirm others and make room for mavericks.

Chapter 8

Be an Authentic Authority

LEADERS HAVE AUTHORITY. They are authorized to use their gifts. Authority is related to the word *authorize*. It is also from the root word *author*. This word means one who is the founder or creator of something. Author refers to the creator. Leaders are born when they find their authority. They find their authority when they find their gift. Another word that attaches itself to authority is authentic. A leader is a person who has found the thing that is so natural for him, so authentic, that when he is doing it, he is simply being himself. A real person will become a leader. Being real—just being your-self—makes you a leader.

That is why true leaders do not work for money. They work for fun. Money follows. Authenticity will always find prosperity. When you are au-thentic, the money and the people seek after you.

Study the great people in the world today, the people we call great. They are simply having fun. When the television interviewer Charlie Rose asked the actor Morgan Freeman if he would ever tire of acting, he said, "No, I am just having fun."

The greatest leader of all time, the ultimate leader Jesus Christ, showed us the purpose of authority is to release authority. I recalled earlier that Jesus informed His students that He had been granted "all authority in heaven and earth." Then He turned around and delegated it to them (see Matt. 28:18–20). One of the greatest challenges to human nature is the management of power. You got that promotion so you could release other people's authority.

Authentic authority releases the authority of other people.

Let me put it another way. Good leaders employ people. Great leaders *deploy* people. Ordinary leaders gather people around them. Great leaders distribute them. Go into the world. Go. Great leaders love to delegate.

Authentic leaders are not afraid of the success and growing authority of their protégés.

The apostle Paul understood this. He said,

> **Philippians 2:22** But you know that Timothy has proved himself, because as a son with his father he has served with me in the work of the gospel.

The apostle John understood this too. He charged Timothy to continue the work:

> **1 Timothy 6:13–14, 20** In the sight of God, who gives life to everything, and of Christ Jesus, who while testifying before Pontius Pilate made the good confession, I charge you to keep this command without spot or blame until the appearing of our Lord Jesus Christ . . . Timothy, guard what has been entrusted to your care.

In 3 John 2–4, he says:

> Beloved, I wish above all things that thou mayest prosper and be in health, even as thy soul prospereth. For I rejoiced greatly, when the brethren came and testified of the truth that is in thee, even as thou walkest in the truth. I have no greater joy than to hear that my children walk in truth. (KJV)

Jesus Himself told the disciples they would do "even greater things" than the works He had been doing (John 14:12).

The purpose of authority is to transfer it, release it, and empower others. Most of us become nervous when people who have been under our influence begin to prosper. It exposes our insecurities. Others might see our deficits. If the success of others makes you insecure, you have not yet achieved the level of authentic leadership.

When Jesus spoke to His team after they failed to cast out the boy's demons, the questions He asked were intriguing ones. "How long shall I stay with you? How long shall I put up with you?" (Matt. 17:17). He was really saying, "Look, problems will be coming your way many times. Do not depend on me." He was training them to stop depending on Him. It was as if He said, "I am working on you. I am training you. I am developing you, but I am not going to do it forever."

Insecure leaders become nervous when people around them are becoming better, but authentic, secure leaders are always training those around them to be better than they are. I challenge you to do that. Imagine that I run this department. I am the manager. I am in charge, and I tell the folks in my department, "Look, I do not want to be with you too much longer, so learn quickly." I think that is what Jesus meant.

> *"The purpose of authority is to transfer it, release it, and empower others."*

Now the average insecure leader today has a different attitude. The attitude is, "I am not going anywhere. You might as well just forget this spot. You are not taking this away from me. I've been trying to get here for twenty years. I'm finally here, and I'm staying here. How long are you willing to wait for this? Do not hold your breath." The secure leaders turn the questions around: "How soon can you be ready? What would it take to get you up to speed to take over? I want to shift more of the responsibility to you. I need to move on to something else. I want you to take my place." If you think that way, you are an authentic leader—a leader who has found value within. True leaders bring value to the position, and when they leave, their colleagues may miss them but they can accept the successor. If you bring value to the job, you are going to be the last one anyone would want to leave.

Jesus, the ultimate leader, told His students that it was better for them that He left (see John 16:7). True leaders fully understand that they are transitional. True leaders are aware of their dispensability and make an intentional exit to their next assignment. It is emotionally and psychologically healthy for leaders to accept that leadership is a temporary privilege. The leadership perspective of Jesus Christ and His transitional thinking is a model for leaders of our day. He stands out as the standard for the mentality of authentic leadership that elevates the debate for succession thinking.

True leaders are not married to their titles or positions and are fully conscious of the temporary nature of their leadership role. Imagine our contemporary leaders selling the idea that their goal is to leave their position of authority and pass it on to their followers. This is a foreign thought to most of our leaders today, and I hope the example of Jesus inspires future leaders to adjust their philosophy.

The greatest example of leadership in history, Jesus Christ, constantly reminded His followers that He intended to leave and pass on all of His responsibilities to them. What a way to think! When you start your next staff meeting, try saying, "Today I want to start the agenda by talking about my departure. Let me just say that this place will become better when I leave. It will be better for all of you when I leave here."

Let Me Try That

Jesus, the great leader, was walking on the water one day when one of His followers asked, "Can I come?" That is a dangerous question.

> **Matthew 14:28** "Lord, if it's you," Peter replied, "tell me to come to you on the water."

Here you are in the president's office, at the top of the company, and one of the trainees comes in the door and says, "Mrs. President, can I sit there? Teach me how to do your job."

The implications of this request from a student of Jesus to attempt the very act that the teacher was performing was the heart of a mentee to experience how the leader did things. In essence, this was the only student from among the twelve who responded as an effective mentee. He also further defined the relationship with their mentor. The responsibility is upon the mentee to pursue the mentor in order to benefit from the relationship, but an authentic leader will engender that response.

This desire and hunger to learn and to make a demand on the wealth of knowledge, experience, and wisdom of the mentor encourages the mentor to expose the mentee to resources that can assist in his or her further personal development. It is important to note that the response of the mentor was positive, immediate, and daring. He simply said, "Come" (see Matt. 14:29). Mentors will always invite the mentee who pursues them to experience their world. Mentors will teach only what mentees want to learn.

The statement, "Tell me to come," also indicates Peter's (mentee in this instance) willingness to enter the world, the knowledge, and the experience of the mentor. However, this question will always challenge and expose the level of maturity, self-confidence, and security of the leader. As a business leader, a consultant, and a pastor, I have had this question asked of me many times, including by individuals within my own organization. My response is a feeling of excitement, confidence, and relief. The more I am able to share my knowledge, experience, and environment, the more I am set free to progress to greater heights and into uncharted territories for my own life. If I teach the mentee to walk on water, I can move on to walk on air. As a pastor, I want to gather around me those to whom I can delegate and eventually transfer my responsibilities. My call may be permanent, but my position is not.

Tomorrow's leaders are already around me. Every chance I get, I push them and keep testing everybody. People around you can always do more than you are allowing them to do. True leaders rejoice when their trainees become more effective than they are. That is the heart of authentic leadership. We become happy when our staff members are doing things that we do and are doing it even better than we could.

When you are a leader who knows who you are, why you were born, and what you came here to do, you know that no one can replace you. Other people's success is proof of your success in leading them.

Point to remember:

The purpose of authority is to release authority.

If you are an authentic leader, you will:

Think beyond your leadership. This is imperative. If you are going to be a leader who mentors your successor, you must think beyond your leadership. You are not an end in yourself, this is not about you, and you are not the star. You are simply an extra on stage.

Think generationally. Think about the unborn and what you will provide for them and how you will prepare this place for those who come behind you.

Be aware of your mortality. Great leaders always think about their death. Foolish leaders believe they are never going to die. You are a great leader if you are constantly conscious of your mortality. "I could die tomorrow."

Be aware of your dispensability. You are dispensable. A leader always knows the board can fire him or her in the morning. They know they must always secure life after that job. Think always in terms of leaving. You are dispensable. Leaders occasionally need a revelation. We get this idea that if the Lord called me, no one can replace me. No. You are dispensable. We can actually do without you. Can you imagine that? We might even be better off without you. I made a decision that in the next few years of my life, I am going to empty myself of my vision. I am going to identify some people, and I am going to empty myself because I am dispensable. Vision is not dispensable, but visionaries are. It is a privilege to be leading, not a right.

Understand that you are responsible for the organization's future. This is very important. Most of the time people in leadership positions and organizations, whether it is a political party, a church, a business, or a family, get this idea that we are in that position to secure ourselves. We try to win promotions, earn a big salary, enjoy a private parking space with our name on it, get the corner office, and revel in a title, the bishop, Dr. So-and-So. In effect, God says, "No, this is about the organization. Leadership is about securing the company, and the only way to do that is succession. You want a human to protect this place."

Be secure in yourself. Authentic leaders' security is in themselves.

They do not get security from what they do, what they are called to do, or what position they have. Their security is inherent in their value to God. They know they are important to the world because they were sent to fulfill an assignment. That is their security. No matter where they are, they are still confident.

Rejoice in other people's success. That is a big one. I have never seen so much jealousy as I have witnessed in the Christian environment. Jealousy is a sign of insecurity and a lack of vision. Jealousy means you do not know who you are and so you do not want anyone one else to be themselves. Jealousy means you are insecure in your own self. A confident person will always encourage other people's success. The confident leader rejoices when other people succeed. When you train people and they succeed, that goes to your credit. Therefore, you help them succeed.

Act as a visionary. Secure leaders do not act as owners. I do not own a company. I do not own this ministry. I am just a visionary. I am a delivery boy. I come to deliver you something from the eternal. I came to take the invisible, make it visible, and then leave. I am not here to own this. I am just the delivery channel. That is leadership.

Always be preparing to leave, not to stay. I was intrigued when I observed this concept among the first meetings Jesus Christ, the greatest leader, had with His team, His mentees. Do you know what was on the agenda? One word: death. Why is that important? He wants to set the atmosphere from the beginning. He basically says, "I called you here today to make an announcement. I am going to die. Now, let us start the organization." That is what He did. He began by announcing His departure. I dare you. I dare you to do it. Prepare others for your departure. Jesus began it that way, saying essentially: "I will be crucified, and they will bury me, and I will come back the third day, but I want you to know up front I am going to die. Now, let us begin. I am not going to be here, so you all must learn quickly." What a way to begin. Can you make that announcement to your organization? Call a big staff meeting and say, "All right. I want you all to know that I am going to die, um, not immediately but eventually. I want you all to know that while I am with you, I will teach you everything I know."

That should be your attitude. I guarantee that you will get more productivity after that meeting from your people because they will finally believe you care. It is not about you. You are temporary. Once you make that announcement, it generates a spirit of obligation for you to mentor. You become more conscious of your responsibility to take care of every person in that organization to help them become better.

Focus on securing their legacy. Secure leaders focus on legacy, not securing their bank account, not securing their real estate, not securing their cars. This is the spirit of mentoring. Stay in touch with people. Make them your priority. Give your life away. Distribute yourself to your generation. Become a mentor of mentees who mentor. Live for the success of other people. Make your dream the dreams of other people being great. "It is good for you that I am not present. Because if I am present, you cannot do greater works." May that be your prayer as well.

Chapter 9

Make Room for the Maverick

THE MEETING BEGAN promptly at 10 a.m. as the chairman of the board entered the room. I looked around and surveyed the assembled members, confidently sitting in fifteen high-back, leather chairs around a beautiful mahogany table that filled the room. Their collective wisdom represented decades of experience. The chairman took his seat and motioned to a young man who seemed intimidated by the evidence of age in the many silver heads in the room, confirming his youth and inexperience.

"Good morning, everyone! This is Mr. Femi Odeyo, our new product-development manager who will take us into the future and keep our company on the cutting edge."

To what seemed to be less-than-enthusiastic applause, the manager, dressed in his blue jeans, casual sport coat, and multicolored necktie, rose and gave a slight bow of respect to these corporate giants in this hallowed hall.

"Good morning, gentlemen and ladies! I am thrilled and honored to have the opportunity to join a team of such distinguished colleagues, leading a company that has broken all records in our industry. It is my hope that I will add to the progressive spirit that has driven this company to the heights it has enjoyed for so many years, and I look forward to working with and learning from you."

With a slight smile on his face, the chairman invited the new executive to present his first proposal to the board for its review and consideration. He walked to the front of the boardroom, activated the projector for his Power-Point presentation and began unveiling the new concept and product for the company's next cycle. As the presentation progressed, the audience became quiet and then restless. Grunts and deep breaths escaped the mouths of board members. Obviously, the reaction to the new manager's fresh ideas was shock, awe, disbelief, and suspicion. Eventually you could almost cut the tension in the room with a knife.

He concluded his talk and then opened the floor to questions and comments. After a long hesitation, one hand went up, and as if a dam had broken, members began blurting out their responses and queries.

"This is a complete departure from our traditional product line and may cause confusion in the minds of our long-time customers," said one board member.

"And how do you intend to convince the down-line managers to buy into this new approach?" asked another board member.

"I am deeply concerned that this new idea may change the reputation we have in the marketplace and threaten our long-standing history as a conservative company," said still another member.

"All great leaders at some time have been considered mavericks, rebels, and non-conformists."

Soon it was clear to the chairman that the board's response to the new associate's ideas was as expected. Tapping his fingers on the dark, wooden table to get the attendees' attention, he began: "Ladies and gentlemen, this is exactly why I appointed Mr. Femi Odeyo to this position, to challenge our set ideas and open this company to new horizons. We are here in the room not to protect or worship history but to make history. I support his proposal and hope we all will be willing to open the closed windows of our minds to let in some fresh air that will inspire us all to go places we have never been. Let us give him a hand for leading us to the future."

This story is as old as time and is repeated in every organization, every country, and every generation. It is the principle of the maverick. A maverick is somebody who is always asking the wrong question at the wrong time and introducing something that destroys all tradition. There is at least one in every organization, in every staff meeting. You know who they are.

A maverick can embarrass you. He or she will come to you and say, "Why does the company still put up with this problem? It would be so easy to fix."

"Well, we have been trying to solve that for forty years. We have tried everything. It just cannot be done," you say.

"On the contrary, if we just do that and do this, this, this, and that, it will be solved. Let me try," the maverick says.

In two days the maverick reports that the problem you have not been able to resolve in four decades is now history.

Are you thinking, "I hate that show-off"?

Imagine that you have just hired a recent graduate of one of the finest colleges for an entry-level position in information systems. She came highly recommended and earned a master's degree in computer science with honors. As part of her orientation, you invite her to observe an upper-level management meeting. Instead of sitting quietly, she asks several questions. Finally, she butts in to suggest that your method of tracking shipments is outmoded but that she could correct it easily, if you adopt the new software she created in graduate school.

You immediately dismiss the suggestion and take umbrage at her impudence. You are thinking, "Who is she to question my managerial decisions?"

You blurt out: "Well, we have always done it that way. This is a long-standing practice here at ABC Manufacturing. It's been our policy, and here come you people just out of school with your half-baked, new-fangled ideas and glitzy technology."

Not only is this probably embarrassing to her, but also it is bad for the company. You might have alienated and stifled the one person who could assure the continued success of the company, quadruple profits, and expand operations into global markets. This could be your successor. Admit it. She reminds you a little bit of yourself at that age when you had just come into the company. Right?

Back then, you quickly gained a reputation for being a bit of a maverick, and you still pride yourself on having an independent streak. Now when others come forward with innovative ideas and unconventional tactics, you tend to shut them out and push them out of the company. A maverick will test your capacity to remain civil and polite. We do not want anyone around us smarter than us. We have these kids coming out of college now with a degree in cyberspace and Internet science, and you are just trying to type with one finger. They are in your department, and they make more money than you do and you have been there for fifty years. You are wary of them because they are mavericks.

Who needs those troublemakers? You do because they are the leaders of tomorrow. Failure to make room for mavericks is among the main reasons we do not reproduce leaders. Do not become jealous of mavericks. Embrace them. Do not be afraid of new ways of doing things. Adopt them immediately. That is very important. The maverick is the one who will bring progress to the company. Progress is never born by traditionalists. It is birthed by those who break tradition. If you are going to develop good leaders, you will have to make room for those who make you think.

Instead, we often try to silence them, rein them in, or push them out. In doing so, we stifle creativity, growth, and progress. We run the risk of seeing our own success, our legacy, die with us. Our culture reinforces conformity and discourages self-discovery. All great leaders at some time have been considered mavericks, rebels, and nonconformists. Nonconformity is a requirement of leadership.

Mavericks are the ones who go beyond what others have done and make history. Jesus was a maverick. John the Baptist certainly was a maverick. The Virgin Mary was a maverick. Martin Luther King Jr. was a maverick. Mahatma Gandhi was a maverick. Eleanor Roosevelt was a maverick. Bill Gates is a maverick. Hillary Clinton is a maverick. Barack Obama is a maverick. The list is long, and it is hard to think of any great leader who does not fit the bill.

The Change Agents

The term *maverick* itself comes from the last name of a Texas rancher who did not follow the tradition of branding his cattle, as everybody around him did, which caused trouble and controversy among his neighboring ranchers. The word has come to mean independently minded.

"Maverick" generally describes a person or a personality who interjects new, untested, unconventional ideas into an environment. People like this do not allow the traditions and conventions of an organization or a company to entrap them. Usually a younger person comes in with fresh ideas because he or she is not immersed in the historical traditions of the organization. These mavericks are, therefore, willing to test the boundaries or push the envelope. They are willing to gore some sacred cows to try new ideas. This naturally threatens the status quo.

Mavericks are usually agents of change. Change is healthy for any organization because change is the only component in life that is inevitable. Whether we initiate change or become victims of change, change will win. One benefit of having the spirit of the maverick in your operation is that it can make you an initiator of change, a cultivator of change, and an agent of change rather than a victim of change. A wise manager will not suffocate the maverick, but will encourage the spirit of exploration, experimentation, and innovation without feeling threatened. The wise mentor may even recognize that he was once a maverick himself.

The greatest mentor of all time, Jesus Christ, not only embraced mavericks but also challenged His mentees to think beyond the norm and break traditions. He was not intimidated by questions, but encouraged them. In fact, He was a maverick who challenged the traditional leaders of His day with unsettling questions. He never accepted the norm, but created new norms. He defied tradition and introduced new paradigms that we are still working with two thousand years later. Not only was Jesus a maverick, but He also created and attracted mavericks.

Look at the way Peter challenged Him on occasion. Peter was the one who resisted when Jesus washed the feet of His dining companions. When it was his turn, Peter had a problem with this. Washing someone's feet was something a servant should have been doing. By the time Peter's turn came, he was so uncomfortable with the idea of the Master washing his feet that he decided to say something. Of course he did. He was a maverick. "Master, you do not have to wash my feet," he said.

The Gospel John describes the scene this way.

John 13:3–9 Jesus knew that the Father had put all things under his power, and that he had come from God and was returning to God; so he got up from the meal, took off his outer clothing, and wrapped a towel around his waist. After that, he poured water into a basin and began to wash his disciples' feet, drying them with the towel that was wrapped around him. He came to Simon Peter, who said to him, "Lord, are you going to wash my feet?" Jesus replied, "You do not realize now what I am doing, but later you will understand." "No," said Peter, "you shall never wash my feet." Jesus answered, "Unless I wash you, you have no part with me." "Then, Lord," Simon Peter replied, "not just my feet but my hands and my head as well!"

It is interesting that Christ's student Simon Peter was not only His most-outstanding maverick, but also was in His intimate mentoring program. The ultimate leader Jesus Christ chose twelve men to mentor, but from among those He selected three for a more intimate level of training. From among those three, Simon Peter was arguably the most challenging. Yet Jesus chose him to take responsibility for the future of the organization. He demonstrated that if you want to secure the future, you must give it to the maverick.

Peter had quickly turned around after Jesus corrected him on the foot-washing issue, but the mentee's first instinct was to challenge Him. Even after Jesus chose Peter to carry on and build His church, Peter questioned what Jesus was saying about His departure.

Matthew 16:18–23 "And I tell you that you are Peter, and on this rock I will build my church, and the gates of Hades will not overcome it. I will give you the keys of the kingdom of heaven; whatever you bind on earth will be bound in heaven, and whatever you loose on earth will be loosed in heaven." Then he warned his disciples not to tell anyone that he was the Christ. From that time on Jesus began to explain to his disciples that he must go to Jerusalem and suffer many things at the hands of the elders, chief priests and teachers of the law, and that he must be killed and on the third day be raised to life. **Peter took him aside and began to rebuke him. "Never, Lord!" he said. "This shall never happen to you!"** Jesus turned and said to Peter, "Get behind me, Satan! You are a stumbling block to me; you do not have in mind the things of God, but the things of men."

Peter was different in many ways. He was always coming up with ideas. At the Transfiguration of Jesus, he wanted to build tents honoring Jesus, Moses, and Elijah (see Mark 9:5). Then he was the one who cut off the ear of a servant to one of the soldiers who came to take Jesus, and he alone followed them to where they took Jesus for trial.

> **John 18:10–11** Then Simon Peter, who had a sword, drew it and struck the high priest's servant, cutting off his right ear. (The servant's name was Malchus.) Jesus commanded Peter, "Put your sword away! Shall I not drink the cup the Father has given me?"

Mentoring the Maverick

Each time Peter would challenge Him or act out, Jesus would correct him, even telling him he was full of the devil. Peter was the mentee, Jesus the mentor. Jesus knew Peter was a maverick. Ultimately, He chose the maverick to carry on His leadership.

Make room for the maverick. That should be the first one you mentor. Seat the maverick right next to you in the board meeting. Listen to everything this young innovator has to say. Encourage mavericks to speak their minds. New ideas will spring from them.

You will also have to put up with someone who may be difficult to mold, somewhat of a misfit, impossible to silence, and eager to move ahead. In the final analysis, you might not pick the maverick to succeed you, but take this rebel under your wing, learn from him, and encourage him to use his gifts to help carry out your vision. Your company, agency, or organization will be better for it.

Points to remember:

Embrace and encourage the maverick.

Jesus Christ challenged His mentees to think beyond the norm and break traditions.

Nonconformity is a requirement of leadership.

Chapter 10

Refuse to Be a Seedless Grape

ONE DAY I went to the supermarket to run an errand for my wife. While there, I walked over to the produce section. As I surveyed the many fruits, vegetables, and juices, I noticed signs that said "seedless grapes" and "seedless oranges." At first I thought it was a gimmick because I had never heard of such things. I thought, "Is it possible for there to be fruit without seeds?"

I asked the attendant in the store. "Is the information on these signs correct?" He smiled and said, "This is the new trend." I reached out and picked up a beautiful orange. It looked normal. It smelled normal. I thought to myself, "Is this our future?" and the answer exploded in my mind. This fruit has no future.

Suddenly, I realized the future of everything exists in the seeds of that thing, and where there is no seed, there is no future. I walked away from that supermarket forever changed, fully understanding that the principle of the seedless fruit applies to all life. Every organization, political party, church, corporation, and even family must cultivate, identify, secure, and develop the potential seeds within its context that will guarantee the perpetuation of that entity. That is mentoring. The process of mentoring and the principle of succession protect all organizations from becoming seedless fruit. Seedless fruits only satisfy the present, focusing on immediate gratification at the expense of posterity.

The responsibility of mentoring and the commitment to effective succession must never be an experiment but rather must be intentional. Jesus planted seeds. He did not leave "leadership development" to chance. He had a program. He spent three and a half years training, developing, molding, shaping, and modeling leadership to His twelve students. By the time He left, the ultimate trainer made sure they could preach, teach, pray, heal, cast out demons, and perform miracles. His greatest success was not what He did, but what His students and their students did after He left.

While He was with them, Jesus told this story:

> **Matthew 13:31–32** He told them another parable: "The kingdom of heaven is like a mustard seed, which a man took and planted in his field. Though it is the smallest of all your seeds, yet when it grows, it is the largest of garden plants and becomes a tree, so that the birds of the air come and perch in its branches."

"Mentoring is the seed that we plant for future generations."

Mentoring is the seed that we plant for future generations. Many leaders, however, are like seedless grapes. They do not produce a seed that can readily reproduce more of the same. If you recall the three stages of life I introduced earlier (see chapter 6), a fruit is dependent on the tree. If you leave it on the tree, it will eventually release itself when it is ripe and will fall to the ground. The fruit becomes independent, but that is not the final stage. You might think the goal of an orange tree is to produce fruit, but that is not true. The goal is to produce seeds. When the fruit falls from the tree, the greatest gift that it can give to the world is the seed that it contains. The purpose of a tree is not to produce fruit, but to produce seed. The greatest gift that a fruit carries is not the fruit, but the seed. You can go to the grocery store and buy seedless grapes and seedless oranges. That is fruit with no future. It cannot reproduce itself.

As I outlined in chapter 6, the ultimate goal of life is not independence, but interdependence, the ability to contribute to the ongoing development of the species. Mentoring assures that we do not become like seedless fruit.

As a leader, your greatest contribution to life is not your leadership, but the seed—the leaders that you produced and carried to maturity. You can reproduce your own kind. You can transfer all that you have become into the next generation.

Leaders who fail to mentor are seedless fruit. In order to mentor and bear fruit, you have to banish these tendencies, issues, and emotions:

Entitlement. Leaders who do not mentor desire job security for themselves. To mentor means that you are working yourself out of a job and that you do not see your job as a permanent position of private ownership or entitlement. Many leaders derive their self-worth from the position. Their self-esteem depends on it. They see that job as their security. They are afraid to mentor because they feel they would be undermining their own life.

Fear. Mentoring implies that you intend to leave. Resistance to mentoring comes when leaders believe they have nowhere to go. They fear that unknown dark hole called retirement. They also feel mentoring will undermine their job, their financial security, and their pension. "If I mentor, I'm going to end up losing all of that," they think. Retiring can be very frightening to a leader who has no life to which they can look forward. We must remember that our lives are bigger than our jobs and that our jobs are temporary phases. We must not be afraid to prepare others to take our place.

Resistance. Nothing frightens humans more than change, especially uncontrolled change. When you mentor someone, you are creating the prospect of change that directly affects you. We do not mind changing other people's lives, but we do not want to change our own. We do not mind removing other people from our department, but we do not want to remove ourselves. Mentoring requires that we be willing to change who we are, where we are and what we are. Those are frightening prospects.

Poor self-esteem. If you get your sense of worth or value from your position and title, you would want to retain them as long as you live. Obviously, you will not feel it is in your best interest to prepare someone else to take your job. If we recognize, however, that our own worth comes from our unique gifts and transcends the job we have today, we can free ourselves to mentor others to grow into our position.

Doubt. Many leaders will declare they are mentors and promote the idea that one should mentor and prepare a successor. Underlying their public declarations, however, is a fear that the people in their present circle could never fill their shoes. They lack faith in their own people. They do not mentor anyone because they do not think anyone around them is worthy of taking their place.

Misplaced love. Leaders can fall in love with the people at their job so much that they are afraid to live without them. When you are in an organization twenty to thirty years, the people in it can become like family. Mentoring is about giving up power, giving up authority, transferring influence, and giving up control. Mentoring would suggest giving up "family." We need to remember that all of life is transitional. We should never attach ourselves to anything or anyone to the point that our very sense of individuality and our sense of self-worth depend on those relationships.

Investment. You have invested your whole life in this organization, church, or company, and now you have to mentor someone who might take your investment or even destroy it after you are gone. This is the attitude of a leader who does not understand that the only way to preserve the investment is to mentor a successor. If you have mentored well, your investments will be in good hands.

No Excuses

Most of our reasons for failure to mentor—for being seedless grapes—boil down to lack of confidence in ourselves and in others.

It comes down to fear of the future and lack of faith. Our fears are indicators of poor leadership. This is why Christ has come into our lives. Jesus came to shake us loose from false self-worth or lack of self-worth. If you have been in a leadership position for a significant time, you should know your worth and have the confidence to have produced, developed, refined, and cultivated the people under your influence to become leaders. Leaders develop people who can become successors.

Many people today who have held jobs for decades are losing them because of the global economic crisis. They are disgruntled, depressed, and disillusioned. Many of them are turning to drugs, alcohol, or both to try to numb the pain. Some are giving up completely—committing suicide—all because they lost a job or a title.

What if economic forces wiped out your entire company or industry? You have worked your whole life, but all of your training is for an industry made extinct by the Internet or outsourcing to foreign countries. I believe that is a great opportunity for you to reassess your priorities and do an inventory of yourself: What is my worth? Where are my values grounded?

A clear sense of self-worth enables you to mentor because mentoring initiates the process by which you eventually remove yourself from a position of leadership. That is a frightening process.

Jesus, our example of the ultimate mentor, was not worried about His leadership position. He was secure. Early in His ministry, He put His departure on the agenda. He began talking about leaving.

> **Matthew 16:21** From that time on Jesus began to explain to his disciples that he must go to Jerusalem and suffer many things at the hands of the elders, chief priests and teachers of the law, and that he must be killed and on the third day be raised to life.

> **Mark 8:31** He then began to teach them that the Son of Man must suffer many things and be rejected by the elders, chief priests and teachers of the law, and that he must be killed and after three days rise again.

> **Luke 9:22** And he said, "The Son of Man must suffer many things and be rejected by the elders, chief priests and teachers of the law, and he must be killed and on the third day be raised to life."

Why call a staff meeting in your organization and say, "Look, I'm not going to be with you forever. So I want to train you to do without me."? Plan your departure the day you begin so you will not be a seedless grape.

There Is Life after Mentoring

Among the greatest fears about mentoring that plague the insecure leader are: "If I successfully train my replacement, then what is my future? Do I still have a place? Is there life after mentoring?" The answer is, "Absolutely, yes!"

Mentoring guarantees that your life will never be stagnant and that your success will never imprison you in your position.

Jesus Christ knew that He came to Earth to leave. All throughout His life with the disciples, He kept reminding them, saying things like: "I am leaving. I am going to die. I am going to leave. You know, I will be going soon."

That should be the spirit of a true leader. Because you know that you are transitional, you can focus on people. You are free to focus on mentoring. Your departure is a given. You need not fear retirement.

Jesus had no fear of the future or going into the unknown because He knew the unknown was in the hands of His Father. All true leaders must understand that they do not belong to themselves. They belong to God. He gives them every position of leadership for His season.

Jesus was conscious of this. He often said, "I go to my father. I go to prepare a place for you." He kept talking about a sense of another assignment. True leaders are always conscious that change is inevitable and should be anticipated and expected. They can make preparations because change is certain. True leaders know that no position is a destination, and none is a permanent address, but rather they consider each position a prep course for their next phase of life.

This ultimate leader, Jesus Christ, did not resist change but, in fact, initiated change. It is the very consciousness of guaranteed change that gives birth to the need to mentor. Jesus had no fear of mentoring because He loved change. He actually challenged the disciples many times to do things they were afraid to do. He encouraged innovation. He told Peter to walk on the water. This is innovative encouragement. He told His mentees to feed the five thousand with just a brown-bag lunch. He forced them to "repurpose" fishes and loaves. He challenged their resistance and forced them to change. His leadership proved that He believed in Himself. His favorite words were "I am"—words that represent self-worth, self-concept, and self-esteem. "I am the bread of life. I am the word of life. I am the way. I am the truth. I am the door. I am the resurrection." Everything He said expressed His sense of confidence in Himself.

He also had confidence in the successor He was grooming. A brief review of His relationship in Peter reveals that Jesus had confidence in Peter from the very beginning. Once Peter bragged that he would never forsake his mentor. Jesus told Peter he would be tested on that point but would survive the challenge and come back.

> **Luke 22:31–33** "Simon, Simon, Satan has asked to sift you as wheat. But I have prayed for you, Simon, that your faith may not fail. And when you have turned back, strengthen your brothers." But he replied, "Lord, I am ready to go with you to prison and to death."

Even after Peter had denied Jesus three times (see Luke 22:57–62) while He was on trial, the risen Jesus had confidence. After His death and resurrection, the mentor called a meeting and wanted all of His students to be there. The angel told those who came to the tomb:

> **Mark 16:7** **"But go, tell his disciples and Peter,** 'He is going ahead of you into Galilee. There you will see him, just as he told you.'"

Mentors have to remember that their mentees will fail sometime, but your confidence in them should bring them back, and that is what brought Peter back. The confidence of his mentor drew Peter back into the leadership.

Holding on Too Tightly

Is love for the people at your job keeping you from mentoring? Jesus did not love us so much to the point that He wanted to stay with us. He said, "It is better that I go away so that you can do greater works."

Sometimes you love your staff or your children so much that you hinder their growth by not giving them time to be alone. This is also true in marriage. I think spouses need to be apart for periods to regain themselves. Married people are often with each other so much that they lose touch with themselves. Partners need time apart to build self-confidence and maintain their own identities.

The process of mentoring requires that the mentor and the mentee spend time together. This is because mentoring is not just a matter of instructing and teaching, but more importantly, it also calls for observing. However, the effectiveness of mentoring is tested by the absence of the mentor. In essence, mentors need to give the mentees their space to prove their own progress and development.

Jesus did not love the job to the point that He wanted to remain on earth in His body forever. He knew that this life and this body were temporary. He was not afraid of losing His investment. He turned over everything He had, all His authority and powers, to the disciples—all the work He had done in salvation and redemption. He said, "You go now and take it to the world." Jesus turned over the investment to them. He had mentored them, protecting His investment. His legacy was safe. Jesus told Peter, "I'm teaching you this so you can teach it to others." He transferred the investment so that others could be the beneficiary and could benefit others. He had planted the seed.

The greatest leader of all time expressed this principle of succession thinking in very simple words:

John 17:20 "My prayer is not for them alone. I pray also for those who will believe in me through their message."

He was thinking about the future.

As leaders today, we have to do the same—mentoring to plant the seeds for the future. Everything changes, and no one lives forever. If we do not plant the seeds of leadership, nurture them, and cultivate them until new leaders reach maturity, we cannot reap a legacy of success that outlives us. We need new seeds, new growth.

During the past thirty years, I have had the privilege of building an organization that has become a national and international success with hundreds of full-time and volunteer workers. I was always conscious of the transitional nature of life; therefore, at the earliest stages of our organization's development, I intentionally instituted not just a career-path process but also a mentoring environment. I sought out young, talented, highly motivated individuals who held the prospect of securing the future of my vision. I began immediately to draw them into my circle of influence. Their response to this invitation determined the level of my commitment to mentoring them. I was very conscious that I was growing older every day, and I refused to live under the self-deception that I was indispensable. I wanted to make sure, as all leaders should, that the beautiful, successful, fruitful dream we have cultivated bears seeds. The future is in the seed.

Points to remember:

Lack of confidence is the primary reason for failure to mentor.
Mentoring protects organizations from becoming seedless fruit.

Part 3

The Purpose—Make Your Vision Endure

Chapter 11

Hand Off the Baton

IT'S A RELAY RACE

THE ORGAN PLAYED softly as scores of people filed into the church. From my vantage point, I could see the casket positioned up front as many family members and friends lined up to view the remains of the beloved departed one. The man who died had once been a famous athlete. Most of the mourners were well-known sports heroes. Next to the altar stood a larger-than-life photo of the man they revered, shown in a running pose, depicting his athleticism in the profession of track and field.

Finally, I decided to pay my respects along with the friend I had accompanied to the solemn event. As we joined the dwindling line of viewers, I caught my first glimpse of the lifeless body of this great patron who had won so many gold medals for his country. Suddenly, I was standing face to face with the reality of death as I saw the motionless frame of what was once a human powerhouse.

My eyes soon focused on the instrument in his hand. On closer inspection, I was shocked to see the dead man's hand tightly gripping a silver-colored baton, the kind used in relay races. I was amused at first and then stood there almost transfixed in a daydream as I contemplated an amazing paradox, experiencing a revelation.

Returning to my seat, I lost track of the proceedings as my mind was deep in thought and mystified by what I saw. It was a lesson I will carry to my grave. What was that lesson? The image of that dead hand holding tightly to the rod will always be a reminder that batons were never made to be kept. This picture was one of the greatest leadership lessons I have ever learned. It reminded me that many leaders would rather die gripping the baton of their legacy in their hands than to pass it on to the next generation of leaders.

"The greatest accomplishment of leadership is not attaining it, it is releasing it."

It is important to understand that leadership is a relay, not a sprint or a marathon. Leadership is about passing on knowledge, experiences, wisdom, and achievements to the next generation. Remember, in a relay the whole team wins!

In many endeavors, we have people who are eighty years old who are still trying to be in charge. Talented young lions are waiting to do something great for the organization, but some old lion is blocking them, declaring, "The Lord says, 'The race is not to the swift but to those who endure' (Ecc. 9:11). I'm going to die here."

That is the attitude of a marathon runner. Leadership is more like a relay than a marathon.

What is a relay? A marathon only has one winner. When you run a marathon, a thousand people could start the race. Only one wins. That runner gets all the glory. A relay is different. One runner starts for each team. Each person runs only a leg of the race. The team shares the glory.

Endurance is valued in the marathon. A victory in that event rewards individual performance and persistence. The prize goes to the one who crosses the finish line first after a grueling, long race that pits individuals against each other. In a relay, each runner runs his leg of the race and hands off the baton swiftly and securely before the next runner can start. Only when the last team member crosses the finish line is a victory declared. The team has won.

We see a dramatic variation of this every four years when runners of many nationalities carry the Olympic torch around the world to the next venue for the games. Each runner covers the assigned distance, passing it from one to another, until that last bearer enters the host country's arena during the opening ceremonies and lights the fire that serves as a symbol of the games.

This is a good model for leadership succession. You have to know when you have finished your leg in this company, in this church, in this organization, or in this government. You are not supposed to die holding the baton. You do not have to stay on the marathon course at eighty.

We have learned that in life or business we should press on until the end. That is one idea of leadership that is misguided. It is why people do not mentor. "Be faithful," they say. "Stay till the end." That is not good advice as a leader.

Leadership is about successful transition. You have the baton now, and some people want to take that baton home in their pockets. They write their names on it. "That isn't yours. This is mine." They actually put in their will: "This baton should be in my casket."

Who in your organization has an arm extended, hand open waiting for the baton? Can you think of someone? They are begging you: "Your leg is finished. You have run out of ideas. You have run out of creativity. You have run out of steam. You are living on old experiences, unable and unwilling to accept change. Let me run with the baton for a while." Still, the marathon runner prefers to stay on, even if he has to limp to or collapse at the finish line.

You can ask the people in your company who look as if they have been around for a while, "How long have you been working here?"

"Fifty-two years."

"Right here?"

"Yes."

"Doing the same thing?"

"Oh yes. I'm an expert."

They are proud of that. They are marathoners.

We have people who prefer to stay on and clog up the system. Many of us are guilty of it. I have to keep protecting myself from it. It is so easy to be caught up in it, but leadership is a relay. Can you imagine a relay in which one person just would not pass the baton? Everybody is looking. The next designated runner is thinking, "Where is he? He is supposed to be here, but he passed by still holding the baton."

That runner is like the person who will not mentor anyone, pick a successor, and hand off the enterprise to the next generation.

Jesus Christ is the greatest relay runner of all time. He was thirty-three when He transferred the baton. God wants us to pass it on. This book is about the transfer, learning how to recognize where you are in the race, learning how to appreciate the value of getting rid of the baton, and learning that you do not have to die to celebrate the win.

Choosing the Next Runner

In life, business, government, church, family, or any organization, we can only run the distance of our one limited life and then pass the baton. We must hope the next generation is capable of going the distance to the next handoff, perhaps running faster, or better, or just differently than we did.

The most difficult thing about being a leader is giving up leadership, leaving it to someone else. The greatest act of leadership is not attaining it. It is releasing leadership. I would estimate that ninety percent of all leaders fail in this area. They fail to effectively transfer, give up, and release leadership. They have no idea how to pass the baton and most do not want to.

Most of the leaders you know probably died with the baton in their grasp, and the next generation had to pry it out of their cold, dead hand. That is true in politics and business. It is true in the church, community organizations, and the family.

That is why the relay race is an excellent metaphor for mentorship and succession. In a relay race, the one who starts out is aware that he will not finish. Most leaders of any significant organization or business who have a vision do not start out thinking, "I am not the one who will finish this." This is a hard thing to accept because we pride ourselves on finishing things, and we expect to get the credit. Perhaps it would be a better perspective for the leader not to think so much in terms of finishing the entire course, but to think of running your leg of the race well. The goal is to complete your lap in the eternal stretch of time.

What I like about a relay race is that each runner is already in place, so the approaching runner knows when he should hand off. I think many times in leadership we run past the other runner. That guarantees the loss of the race. Our whole team will lose. Many leaders go beyond their time. They refuse to hand over. They refuse to release to the next leader, and they forget that life is not a mad dash to the finish line. It is a sprint to the next runner or leader. We must not think that we alone should finish the race. We should finish our leg of it and pass to the next generation. Instead, we often drop the baton at the hand-off point.

The relay race underscores two other ideas. The race represents the broader vision. Our responsibility is a portion of that race. The runner who receives the baton has been designated ahead of time. That team member can start running to get up to speed before receiving the baton from his predecessor. The next runner does not start from a standstill.

We could define succession as effectively identifying the next runner and successfully handing off the baton to that leader. If there is no one to carry on, all is lost. If one runner drops the baton, the team can be disqualified. To prevent this, it is the leader's obligation to mentor and prepare the next bearer of the baton—training, grooming, and counseling until that runner is up to speed and can carry on.

Fifteen years ago, I ordained my replacement. I mentored him, laid hands on him in public, and told the church, "That is your pastor. I am gone." He runs the church. That is why I can travel the world preaching and teaching.

When I go home, I can tell them, "Hello, I am back."

Some of them will say, "Oh, we did not know you were out of town." That is good.

True leaders provide opportunities for others to find their gift. Let an associate preach some Sundays. Let someone else chair the meeting or teach the class while you listen. Create opportunities for your understudy to go on stage. Give someone else the solo.

For me, nothing is more exciting in my church than to sit on the front row and let another pastor preach. I take notes. That gives credibility to others. It gives them confidence, and it gives other people confidence in that person.

Transfer the torch. Secure leadership does not see the development and success of followers as a threat. True leaders rejoice when their followers become greater. I like the way John put it.

> **3 John 3–4** It gave me great joy to have some brothers come and tell about your faithfulness to the truth and how you continue to walk in the truth. I have no greater joy than to hear that my children are walking in the truth.

We rejoice when our children can do things for themselves. We keep track of "firsts." When they first sit up, walk, tie their shoes, read a book, or drive the car by themselves, we are delighted. We should rejoice when others do not need us for everything we used to do for them. The transfer of our skills, knowledge, and gifts is proceeding on schedule.

We are supposed to give all our gifts, use them up, before we finish the race. We need to die empty and have nothing left to take to the cemetery. True leaders work hard because they are on a race against death. Your greatest motivation should be death. As you run every day, work every day, your main thought should be, "I have to be empty before I hit the cemetery." You will never be bored. Leaders are people who discover an assignment that is bigger than their lifetime. When their time is up, they can pass their legacy on to the next runner.

Gone Fishing

The first act of true leadership is to identify your replacement and train them. I dare you to do what Jesus did. Jesus was starting His ministry when He was about thirty years old. The first place He went was to the beach. He saw some men fishing. He essentially said, "Take me out with you." He catches fish for them and inspires them. At this first meeting, Peter fell down in the boat. He said, "Get away from me, Lord. I am not worthy to be in your presence."

Here is how the meeting went:

> **Luke 5:1–11** One day as Jesus was standing by the Lake of Gennesaret, with the people crowding around him and listening to the word of God, he saw at the water's edge two boats, left there by the fishermen, who were washing their nets. He got into one of the boats, the one belonging to Simon, and asked him to put out a little from shore. Then he sat down and taught the people from the boat. When he had finished speaking, he said to Simon, "Put out into deep water, and let down the nets for a catch." Simon answered, "Master, we've worked hard all night and haven't caught anything. But because you say so, I will let down the nets." When

they had done so, they caught such a large number of fish that their nets began to break. So they signaled their partners in the other boat to come and help them, and they came and filled both boats so full that they began to sink. When Simon Peter saw this, he fell at Jesus' knees and said, **"Go away from me, Lord; I am a sinful man!"** For he and all his companions were astonished at the catch of fish they had taken, and so were James and John, the sons of Zebedee, Simon's partners. Then Jesus said to Simon, "Don't be afraid; from now on you will catch men." **So they pulled their boats up on shore, left everything and followed him.**

Jesus looked at Peter and probably thought, "That is the one I'm going to mentor. This is the guy." At that first meeting, Jesus basically says, "Peter, get up. Follow me. I will make you somebody."

This is very important. Do not just follow anyone. Follow someone who can make you somebody. Jesus identified His replacement and worked on him for three and a half years. Leaders make leaders.

The purpose for leadership is to make the follower just like you in knowledge, in wisdom, and in skill. Christ said the student should become just like the teacher. The student should not remain something less than but should become equal to the teacher. The student does not stay under the teacher forever.

> **Matthew 10:24–25** "A student is not above his teacher, nor a servant above his master. It is enough for the student to be like his teacher, and the servant like his master."

An effective master creates a masterpiece. An effective teacher creates a teacher. I find it intriguing that Jesus Christ's first act when He began His ministry was to go find potential successors.

The first person He chose to be a potential successor was Peter. This implies that He began from the beginning to mentor His potential successor. His first act was to identify, His second act was to mentor, and His final act was to appoint His successor.

A true leader works himself or herself out of a job. When you gain authority, what do you do with it? You are now a bishop, a chief financial officer, a college president, supreme officer of the fraternity, head of the agency, or commander of the division. You have authority. You are the authority. Use authority to empower others. The higher you go, the more leaders you should create. Pass the baton! That is what Jesus did.

> **Matthew 28:18–19** "All authority in heaven and on earth has been given to me. Therefore [you] go and make disciples of all nations."

He gave them the baton and urged them to do likewise.

Points to remember:

Leadership is more of a relay than a marathon.
The leader must mentor to prepare the next runner to bear the baton.

Chapter 12

Find Better Things to Do, Look Forward to Greater Things

YEARS AGO, WHEN my children were very young, my wife and I took them to the world-famous Disney World in Orlando, Florida, for a vacation. I had just bought my son an ice-cream cone that he held in one hand. In his other hand, he held cotton candy. My daughter had just gotten a hot dog and was about to bite into it when my son began to cry for one. He wanted what she had. My good-natured daughter reached out her hand to give it to him, but he had a problem. Both of his hands were full, and yet he wanted something else.

His dilemma was one that successful leaders often face: How do I get what I want without losing what I have? How do I enjoy the next opportunity and hold on to the present one? Finally, my son turned around and reached out his hands toward me as plea for me to hold the runny ice-cream cone and the sticky cotton candy so he could take hold of what he wanted next—the hot dog.

His boyish doings taught me another great life lesson: You cannot go to the next level in life if you are not willing to "let go" of the present level. This is a fundamental principle of mentoring and succession. You have to move on so that you can move up to your next assignment or phase in life.

Most people in leadership have the attitude that they will stay in their positions forever. They defend and protect their turf. They are aggressive. They watch for threats. They arouse antagonism in others. They look forward to collecting their pension from this job. They are going to stay in this position until they retire or die. That is not leadership. It is insecurity. It is the epitome of selfishness and self-centeredness.

Great leaders look for opportunities to leave because they have bigger, more-exciting things to achieve. They want to explore different aspects of life. They want to expand themselves. For a great leader, every position is temporary. This is why that leader needs to identify a successor. Mentoring becomes the major focus.

"Your vision should be larger than your current role."

We are all "temporary" in the grand scheme of things. If you have been running the company or the country for forty years, you are still temporary. We have all heard people say that someone has been running things for so long that he thinks he will live forever. I assure you, he will not.

Your interest should always be in the future because that is where you will spend the rest of your life. Visionary leaders are ready to move on when the time comes because they always have something bigger and better to do. Your vision should be larger than your current role. Be eager to leave this success behind and go on to greater accomplishments. Continually be thinking, "What else can I do? How much more can I contribute? What new things can I accomplish? I am really looking forward to doing new things."

Even Jesus had plans for what He would do and how He could continue to serve after He died:

> **John 14:3** "And if I go and prepare a place for you, I will come back and take you to be with me that you also may be where I am."

He was already planning a greater role for Himself. What are you planning next?

Leadership succession is two-sided: Not only should you train and mentor your successor, but you also should retrain and mentor yourself for life afterward. It would not be a bad idea for a leader to counsel himself while he is counseling his successors. While you are preparing your successor, prepare yourself for succession. Ask yourself what you will do, not just who will succeed you.

Historically, people focused on one skill, one career, and one trade, and they died in that trade. This was especially true after World War II, when many people worked in factories that turned out the same product for years. Now the global economy and new technology routinely displace people. We cannot count on having a job for decades, and workers have to find new ways to earn a living.

Leaders are in a similar position at the end of a long career. Suddenly, they have to think beyond their position. They must know how to prepare to leave.

Dream New Dreams

As I mentioned earlier, the Bible says that even Jesus is still working. It is important to reiterate that after the ultimate leader and mentor, Jesus Christ, had completed His redemptive act as a sacrificial substitute for all humanity, His last words were not, "I am finished," but "It is finished." These two statements are very different and important. The latter implied that an assignment was completed. The former indicates that a new phase would begin. Jesus Christ completed His earthly assignment, transferred the responsibility to His successors, Peter, James, and John, and then moved on to His next position. The first-century apostle Paul stated in his letter to the Roman church, "Christ Jesus, who died—more than that, who was raised to life—is at the right hand of God and is also interceding for us" (Rom. 8:34). Here, we see that leadership never stops. It simply enters new phases.

Death should not determine when and how you leave your position. Rather, leave because you are moving to the next phase of your life.

Earlier I talked about the importance of vision in leadership because I believe it is vision that comes first. Vision creates the leader. Often, however, as leaders become comfortable with the perquisites of leadership and fulfill their initial vision, they stop dreaming. They stop planning. They have not begun to envision what they will do after retirement from this particular job. They have not created new visions.

One day they will have to retire because they are too feeble mentally and physically to do all the things they used to do. They have not made plans to get out while they still have time to do other things. In these days, when many of us can look forward to longer, healthier lives, that is tragic. It is understandable that leaders will not relish the day they have to retire if they have a vision of sitting on the porch in a rocker, whiling away the time, forgotten by those they once supervised. Some look forward to years of leisure, but many still want to live useful and productive lives.

The desire to retire should never be the motivation for mentoring and succession. Rather the motivation should be the desire to be released from your present limited position in life to find new ways to contribute to the ongoing of humankind. Interestingly, neither the word nor the concept of retirement exists in the Hebrew Scriptures, which seems to indicate that the Creator never intended for us to stop working but to keep changing the nature of our work. Even death itself is considered only a transition, not a termination in the Hebrew text.

While you still have time, why not plan an entirely new career? Create a charity. Move to a new industry or a different kind of ministry. Take up coaching or teaching to share with a new generation what you have learned. Use talents or skills you did not need in your old job, apply your knowledge to new endeavors, train for an entirely new field, or be like the woman who once headed a county prison system, but now describes herself as "a full-time volunteer."

How many times do we hear of people who are seventy or eighty years old completing a college degree? Yet how many times have we heard of athletes who cannot seem to find a new purpose when their career on the field ends before they are forty? It is a matter of perspective.

The Next Horizon

You may think you are too old for something new, but if you retire from an executive job at sixty-five, you could conceivably live twenty-five to thirty-five more years. That is long enough for another career. Studies have even indicated that intellectual and physical activity will prolong life and productivity. The secret to a vibrant life is to keep renewing your life. The danger of renewing your life is that you have to start over again, and human nature resists that.

Life should never be lived out. It should be lived in. We need to keep moving to the next life intended for us. Jesus left because He had work to do in preparing a place for us and interceding on our behalf. He moved on to a new life.

Personally, I have lived three or four lives. What I am doing now, I will not be doing in the future. I do not want to keep doing just the same old things. I am preparing for change.

In 1980, I initiated an organization, and after the first ten years of growth and development, I determined that the time had come to begin mentoring and delegating responsibilities to others. Today many of the individuals I mentored are now responsible for leading, supervising, and managing the entire organization. I also have had the privilege of officially appointing a leader to oversee the entire vision with full authority and accountability to our board. This relinquishing of my positions and responsibilities was the key to my ability to expand our organization from a national to a global influence. This should be the attitude of every leader. Mentoring and succession do not result in losing a position or authority, but rather they make it possible to increase and expand your influence and impact.

Most of the work done in my organization happens while I am away. I estimate that I now spend less than twenty percent of my time with the organization every year, and yet the organization expands, grows, and runs effectively. That is a greater measure of pride for me than if I were there giving orders every day. I am content to have my leadership measured by what happens while I am not there.

If I were to die today, there would be not one hiccup in the organization because my successor is already in place. Now I am training a successor for him. In fact, a group of people is being trained to take over should the need arise. We are looking at the next generation of leaders after that and mentoring them as well.

The Escape Plan

Mentoring is continual work. If you do not mentor to produce a successor, you will never expand beyond what you are doing. If you hold people down, remember you have to stay with them, so you will never move beyond them.

Succession sets you free to achieve greater success. This is why many leaders do not go beyond what they are doing now. They will not produce successors so they can move on to greater success.

I said earlier that finishing well is more important as a measurement of leadership than starting well. You had a great ministry, powerful works, a dynamic megachurch, the largest music and dance ministries in the state, and an awesome radio and television operation, but when you died, a big fight erupted, broke up your church, and ended it all. Did you finish well?

Whether you are a pastor, business leader, or any other kind of professional, you are temporary. The only way to finish well—to know your legacy will continue—is to mentor and prepare for your transition to a new role in this life or a place in the next one. Leadership is not a permanent condition. Will you always be the pastor or the CEO, or will you pursue a bigger, grander vision?

True leaders do not retire. They just go to the next phase. They go from player to coach, and from coach to advisor, from advisor to owner, from owner to...They just keep moving and evolving. You are bigger than your current position. Do not let your position trap you and limit your exposure. Train people to take your place so God can expand your territory. If you are such a great visionary, surely you must see new things, greater challenges in your future. Look toward a new horizon. Get a new vision. Dream something new. Draw up a fresh ten-year-plan. This assignment is done. It is finished. Find something better to do. Look forward to even greater things.

Points to remember:

Visionary leaders move on because they have something bigger to do.
We are all "temporary."

Chapter 13

Know When to Fold 'Em

THE HOUR HAS COME

ONE OF THE fellow trustees of our global leadership organization, Dr. Joshua Turnel Nelson, who passed away some years ago, used to sit on a stool in my kitchen for hours and talk. He was the former superintendent of the Pentecostal Assemblies of the West Indies and from Port of Spain, Trinidad. We would discuss all kinds of dreams, and he would teach me so many things and share his heart with me. I used to keep telling him, "You need to write some of this in books." We spent hours talking like this, and then he was gone. He was not old. We still remember him as energetic, running here and there—teaching us. Now he is free from this earthly state.

Life is that fast. Invest in people. He invested in me. That is why I revere his name and keep his memory alive. He invested in people. His legacy is in us.

Have you started mentoring your successor? You know that you will die.

I discovered something about death. Lately, it has no respect for age. When I was a child, only old people died—or so I thought. You remember those days. Only old people died. Now we know anybody can die at any age, so we must be ready to leave the stage at any hour, confident that someone can carry on in our role.

At the Apollo Theater in Harlem, New York City, New York, when the audience boos an "amateur night" contestant, a tap-dancing, clownish character appears to coax and gently pull the failed performer off the stage. The disappointed amateur quickly accepts this fate and meekly exits stage left. In leadership situations, rarely does someone show up to force you off stage. You get to decide. You will have to summon the judgment and the wisdom to know the hour has come.

"Succession is proudly bowing out, leaving the stage without regrets."

Make succession decisions before your deathbed. It is too late to think about it then. It is too late to select and train the right person. It is too late to communicate your desires, too late to let the next leader settle in, and too late to allow others to get used to the new chief. Select someone while you still have time to mentor, guide, and correct him when he makes mistakes. Do not choose your successor on your deathbed. That is the wrong place. Choose your successor now even before they know you are training them. Let the chosen one observe you and learn from you while you are still in your prime, not when you are too feeble to tell them and show them what they need to know. Bring that person up to speed, make it clear to others that this one has your blessing, and then let God commission your successor. You will also have time to change your mind if your choice is an utter failure.

Leaders must know when it is time to leave a position. You will know the right time to leave if you watch for these indications:

- Leadership is like a party that is getting a little wild. It is better to leave early than to stay too late and have regrets. In most endeavors, leaders do more damage when they stay too long than when they do not stay long enough. Move on if you detect any signs that you are holding up the next generation.

- You might have overstayed your assignment already if that job you once loved is killing you now. When your time is up, the very thing that you gave your life to will destroy you. Your staff will become restless and plot against you. People will drop hints about what you cannot do anymore and suggest that you check out some nice retirement communities they discovered. The board will try to push you out or work around you.

- If you have overstayed, you will feel pressure from the bottom. Your followers will become very agitated. They will complain more, question your ability, and challenge your creditability. They no longer see you as a mentor but as a menace. They begin to despise and resent you as the one preventing them from growing, rather than stimulating and cultivating their growth.

These are signs that you are overstaying your time. The Bible says there is a season for everything, including "a time to give up, a time to keep and a time to throw away" (Eccl. 3:6). This may be your season.

Succession is proudly bowing out, leaving the stage without regrets. Succession is moving out of the spotlight back into the shadows without jealousy. It is not waiting until someone pushes you out of the spotlight or shuts it off while you are still on stage. Succession is pulling another person into the spotlight while you are still leading.

John the Baptist had already told his followers someone greater than him would be coming. One day while he was preaching, he spotted Jesus approaching. The time was right. John pulled Jesus into the spotlight, introducing Him to the crowd.

> **John 1:24–31** Now some Pharisees who had been sent questioned him, "Why then do you baptize if you are not the Christ, nor Elijah, nor the Prophet?" "I baptize with water," John replied, "but **among you stands one you do not know. He is the one who comes after me, the thongs of whose sandals I am not worthy to untie.**" This all happened at Bethany on the other side of the Jordan, where John was baptizing. The next day John saw Jesus coming toward him and said, "Look, the Lamb of God, who takes away the sin of the world! This is the one I meant when I said, 'A man who comes after me has surpassed me because he was before me.' I myself did not know him, but the reason I came baptizing with water was that he might be revealed to Israel."

Likewise, at God's urging, Moses put Joshua out front. Some folks want to die in their positions. God essentially says to us, "No. Be like Moses. He chose Joshua early." As the Scripture describes it:

> **Numbers 27:18–23** So the LORD said to Moses, "Take Joshua son of Nun, a man in whom is the spirit, and lay your hand on him.

Have him stand before Eleazar the priest and the entire assembly and commission him in their presence. Give him some of your authority so the whole Israelite community will obey him. He is to stand before Eleazar the priest, who will obtain decisions for him by inquiring of the Urim before the LORD. At his command he and the entire community of the Israelites will go out, and at his command they will come in." Moses did as the LORD commanded him. He took Joshua and had him stand before Eleazar the priest and the whole assembly. Then he laid his hands on him and commissioned him, as the LORD instructed through Moses.

It Is All Temporary

God may not come to tell you personally that it is time to go, and He may not show you your successor, but a secure leader knows the hour is at hand. In Deuteronomy 31, Moses formally bows out, announcing the end of his leadership and proceeding with the succession plan. By then he is an old man whose abilities are waning. He will not get to the Promised Land.

> **Deuteronomy 31:1–3** Then Moses went out and spoke these words to all Israel: "I am now a hundred and twenty years old and **I am no longer able to lead you.** The LORD has said to me, 'You shall not cross the Jordan.' The LORD your God himself will cross over ahead of you. He will destroy these nations before you, and you will take possession of their land. Joshua also will cross over ahead of you, as the LORD said."

This passage shows Moses was conscious that he could no longer lead, and he announced that fact to the people. Imagine saying that to your department or organization. "I am done here. I am washed up. My time is over. I just cannot do this job anymore." That would take a great deal of self-confidence and courage. Moses stood before the people of Israel, letting them know his time was past and that he had prepared someone to take the lead. In verse 3, Moses transferred his position. He transitioned, appointing a trained successor.

Moses did not wait for his death to force the situation and allow the people to fight over his leadership. He presented the leader to them himself. In effect, he says, "This is the one. Be strong. Joshua, you must go with these people into the land of God." He is telling Joshua in front of the people, "This is my successor. I want you to follow him. He will take you to places I have not yet been. I did my part. He will take you to the next phase."

It is a beautiful succession.

> **Deuteronomy 31:7** Then Moses summoned Joshua and said to him in the presence of all Israel, "Be strong and courageous, for you must go with this people into the land that the LORD swore to their forefathers to give them, and you must divide it among them as their inheritance."

A few verses later, notice that while Moses chooses his successor, God makes it official.

> **Deuteronomy 31:14** The LORD said to Moses, "Now the day of your death is near. Call Joshua and present yourselves at the Tent of Meeting, **where I will commission him**." So Moses and Joshua came and presented themselves at the Tent of Meeting.

For me, this chapter underscores that God expects you to identify the successor first. What we do today is reverse. We say, "I will leave it up to the Lord. Let the Lord choose and let Him take over. It is all in God's hands."

That might sound righteous, but in reality it is a cop-out. It is both unwise and cowardly. Lay hands on someone while you are alive. Make your successor your greatest contribution to the future.

Prevent Overstaying Your Welcome

Plan your departure, prepare your replacement, then shut up and leave! Get out while you are still at the top of your game. Leave before you have had a chance to undo all the good that you accomplished, like a gambler who stays at the poker table long enough to lose everything he had won when the night was young.

Many leaders overstay their welcome and leave bitter memories for things they did late in the game and not the golden memories of the many triumphs they had earlier in life. Think about someone like Richard Nixon, the former United States president who held on too long as the Watergate scandal festered and saw everything he had accomplished tainted by the public disclosures of his role in it.

We have seen many examples of leaders who cling to their offices by preventing or rigging elections and attacking their opponents. All over the world, dictators prey on challengers to maintain control, often long after they should have stepped down. Some would rather see their countries in ruins than hand over power. The same is true in many corporations, churches, and families. A leader's stubborn refusal to yield strangles out new leadership.

Whenever you leave a position on time, or before time, you will never be blamed for any future failure, but if you overstay your time, you are at great risk for being blamed for any future failure. History always seems to recall that you should have allowed another to step in at a certain time. This is why, no matter what happens, we will always admire Nelson Mandela. He left on time. He is a great example of mentorship and succession. He was not afraid to give up all that power he had. He gave it up early, declining to seek reelection in 1999 and announcing that he would shift responsibility increasingly to his choice, Thabo Mbeki.

Great leaders move themselves out of the spotlight, and Mandela is one of the greatest leaders I have met personally. He was elected president unopposed, handed power on a silver platter by the South Africans. No one could oppose him because he had earned the right to be trusted. He was president for one term, and then he made a decision to step aside. Everyone was thinking he was going to be there for twenty years to fix South Africa, but he was not hungry for power. He sought out his replacement. He began to mentor Mr. Mbeki at his first opportunity.

Most of us could not do that. When we get to a position of power, we settle in and begin to make plans for how we are going to stay there and make sure no one can move us out. Mandela could not wait to relinquish power because he did not feel that he needed to pursue authority. He was willing to make himself unnecessary. He knew when to leave the stage.

If you have made the right decision and mentored a successor properly, you can move on and rest assured that the ship is in the right hands and proceeding on course. As we have seen, Jesus was always preparing His team for the time He would leave. From the beginning of His ministry, He talked about His death (see Matt. 17:22–23). Why talk to your nearest team members about your death all the time? Ideally, you are trying to build into them the acceptance of your dispensability and vulnerability. It underscores that you are not bound to the position. You are not equating your value with your position. You accept your own mortality. The secret to succession begins with the leader's acceptance of his mortality. It begins with the consciousness, "I am temporary." That allows confident mentors to find a replacement, develop that person, and plan for departure.

The Last Act

When leaders refuse to make room for others and mentor them, they restrict and retard the capability of others. By leaving, they allow others to come into their own.

Jesus had three and a half years to plan an effective transition. Do you remember when Jesus told His students this?

> **John 14:12** "I tell you the truth, anyone who has faith in me will do what I have been doing. **He will do even greater things than these,** because I am going to the Father."

He was talking about going to the Father. He tied the capabilities of others to His absence.

You may remember that He also said:

> **John 16:7** "But I tell you the truth: It is for your good that I am going away. Unless I go away, the Counselor will not come to you; but if I go, I will send him to you."

In the first case, He was saying in effect, "If I do not go, then your capacity or potential will never be fulfilled." In the second instance, He was saying something different. "It is better if I go away. If I do not go away, then the replacement cannot come." In other words, leaving makes room for the other leader.

Both are relevant to the discussion of succession. Leaving provides the opportunity for other people to reach their full potential and provides an opportunity for someone else to shine.

Many people measure their success by how long they can stay. In reality, that is a contradiction because you know you are not going to stay forever. You will get sick, get into an accident, or die. Life is unpredictable.

Jesus knew this and He knew when His time was almost up. John 12 records that He predicted His death yet another time.

> **John 12:23–25** Jesus replied, "**The hour has come** for the Son of Man to be glorified. I tell you the truth, unless a kernel of wheat falls to the ground and dies, it remains only a single seed. But if it dies, it produces many seeds. The man who loves his life will lose it, while the man who hates his life in this world will keep it for eternal life.

He knew He would have to leave to be glorified. At Gethsemane, Mark says Jesus was certain His time was up.

> **Mark 14:41–42** Returning the third time, he said to them, "Are you still sleeping and resting? Enough! The hour has come. Look, the Son of Man is betrayed into the hands of sinners. Rise! Let us go! Here comes my betrayer!"

Jesus knew it was time to meet destiny and turn over His command. He told His followers so. Jesus was healthy and whole when He left the position. We too must recognize when the hour has come. Timing is everything. Leave the party early if you can. Say your good-byes and get out while your reputation and your dignity are intact. Leave with pleasant memories and not regrets.

Points to remember:

It is better to leave early than to stay too late.
Know when the hour has come.

Part 4

The Plan—What Are You Looking for in Your Successor?

Chapter 14

The Wrong Choice

You HAVE A fabulous staff. They are all well-trained, efficient, and productive. Many of them have been in your service for many years and have the experience it takes to lead the enterprise. They have wonderful ideas on how to make it grow and the abilities to execute them. You have heard that some of them are getting impatient for the opportunity to lead. A few of them may even be praying for your departure or scheming for your removal. A handful of people on the board have already created a system to get rid of you. Rumors are circulating madly.

How do you choose one to mentor and take over the company, department, church, or school when you leave?

Who is there for you to give all your powers, all your accomplishments?

If you have read this far in the book, you probably are at least beginning to accept that you have an obligation to find your successor, mentor that individual, and get ready for new challenges. By now you might even be looking forward to it. Still, you may be wondering how to make such a big decision—one that caps off all your accomplishments so far and establishes your legacy for all time.

No pressure. Right?

Let me try to help. First, we will deal with the kind of person you should *not* choose. If you were expecting advice first on what kind of people to consider, study the following list. I think it is far more important to know what kind of people to avoid. By process of elimination, you can zero in on the good candidates.

Through my years of reading about and observing the transition of leadership in real-life situations, I have come up with six principles for disqualifying a potential successor. Do not choose one who:

"Choose the one who loves you and not your vision."

Loves your vision. This is shocking to most people because we normally think the person who captures our vision and loves our vision is the kind of person who should succeed us in the organization. I have found this is not always the case. If you are a success, you expect people to be attracted to your vision, but that does not qualify them to be successors. You do want to mentor those who are willing to carry out your vision, but those who focus merely on the vision and not on you may not carry on your legacy in the way you would want. They may see the vision through different eyes. The final product may not at all be what you had in mind. Their methods of achieving it may not be what you desire. They may try to reach the goal without exercising the values you emphasized, or want the vision so badly that they push you out prematurely, or get rid of the staff you protected, or disenfranchise the heirs you love.

People will be attracted to what you are doing. They will express their admiration and encourage you, telling you how wonderful your work is. They will even be willing to help you do it. They may be sincere. They want to serve you and believe you have "a great vision from God." Or, "You are a genius." Or, "I just love your company. You have a great marketing plan." That is the wrong person to choose because whoever loves only your vision could try to take it over or cause a split in the organization. Be careful of those who express excessive interest in your vision; they may have ulterior motives. They love your vision, but are not necessarily committed to helping *you* carry it out. Choose those who respect the vision but respect you more.

Loves and admires your gift. Of course your gift attracts people, and many of them associate with you for the right reasons. They enjoy hearing you speak or watching you succeed. They want to learn from you and help you. That does not mean you should automatically entrust everyone who loves your gift with the future and rush to teach them everything you know, lay your hands on them, and give them your blessing to follow in your footsteps. Some people say, "I just love the way you write. You are such a wonderful writer. I just admire you." Many of them are sincere, but others come around you to get what you have.

While many people will have a commitment to or appreciation of you as a person, others may not care much for you or your personal needs or success. Your gift, however, benefits them in some way. Being around you gives this type credibility, allowing them to advance their personal ambition. They want to move ahead by using their association with you. They want your name and your influence. They are with you but not for you. These few are dangerous people.

I think this is what Jesus meant when the people came to Him and asked for a miracle. They loved His gift. But His answer was short. He said that only a "wicked and adulterous generation" seek out miracles (see Matt. 12:38–39). He identified their motives. They were not interested in Him, but rather in what He could do.

After Jesus multiplied the fish and bread, the crowds had followed Him. They came after Him because of His gift.

> **John 6:26–27** Jesus answered, "I tell you the truth, you are looking for me, not because you saw miraculous signs but because you ate the loaves and had your fill. Do not work for food that spoils, but for food that endures to eternal life, which the Son of Man will give you. On him God the Father has placed his seal of approval."

Some people come to you because of your gift, not because of you. Do not trust everybody who applauds you. Do not be so quick to delegate authority to people who seem to celebrate you because they might be celebrating only what you do for them and how they benefit from being with you. Some people's relationship with you is for their benefit, not yours. Jesus knew that some people followed Him only because He had fed them on fish and bread. They were attracted to Him because of the miracles He had done. The people who love your gift may be with you because of what you can do for them, because you can make them look good or feel good. The people who love only your gift may want that gift or the benefits derived from it for themselves. Choose those who are sincere in their admiration of your gift, but appreciate you for who you are.

Wants to emulate you. Many people may imitate you just out of true admiration. You may be the only positive role model in their lives. Your mentoring is working in them. Others who copy everything you do may be trying to compete with you and possess what you possess. Beware of prospective mentees who seem to want to *be* you and to have everything you have—the title, position, and influence. They might even turn up wearing the outfit you wore last week. They drive the car you drive. They emulate your lifestyle too much. They are always asking where you bought something and how much it cost. "Man, I want me one of those!" Maybe you have people like this around you now. They are not trustworthy. In extreme cases, they might try to depose you, embezzle from you, steal possessions, or run off with your spouse. They want the bling, not the business. They are not candidates to succeed you. Choose those who imitate the right things they see in you for the right reasons.

Wants your power. Choose those who are confident in their own anointing and who do not covet your power. One guy in the New Testament became so excited when he saw the apostles exercising power that he offered them money to have the same gift, but Peter rebuked him.

> **Acts 8:18–24** When Simon saw that the Spirit was given at the laying on of the apostles' hands, he offered them money and said, **"Give me also this ability** so that everyone on whom I lay my hands may receive the Holy Spirit." Peter answered: "May your money perish with you, because you thought you could buy the gift of God with money! You have no part or share in this ministry, because your heart is not right before God. Repent of this wickedness and pray to the Lord. Perhaps he will forgive you for having such a thought in your heart. For I see that you are full of bitterness and captive to sin." Then Simon answered, "Pray to the Lord for me so that nothing you have said may happen to me."

Some people may approach you nicely and say, "I want your anointing." That is the wrong person to choose. Your anointing is for you. They should have and realize their own anointing. That is not something you bestow. Be wary of those who just love being around power and who just want the power that comes with your position. Do not choose a successor who is too fixated on watching you control things and use your influence. Avoid the ones who only like to flirt with your power, asking, "May I make the announcements for you? May I present the report? Let me represent you at the meeting." They can be dangerous if they only want to take on your power, not your sacrifice.

The person who merely loves your power would not necessarily use it to carry on your vision or build on your success. He or she has other agendas. Mentor the ones who are confident in their anointing and are willing to observe and learn how you use your power to benefit others.

Wants your position of authority. Authority is different than power. Authority is permission. Power is ability. Authority is position. Power is control. You can have power but not authority. You can have authority without power. As a leader, you might have it within your power to control or influence most of the people in an organization, but if you are not the sitting president, you do not have the *authority* to direct the organization to take action.

Watch those people who desire the authority you have. They want you to promote them so they can have your blessing to exercise control over others. They want the gavel that goes with the office. They may even try to convince you that what they want is good for you. A genuine desire to serve a leader and the desire to use a leader are two very different things. One says, "I want to serve you; I want to be your number two man"—but does not necessarily mean it. Another comes with the right attitude: "I just want to make you look good. I can do whatever you wish. Let me know what you need me to do." The latter is someone to keep an eye on for succession. One who covets your authority will not submit to your authority while you are still in charge and may try to undermine you.

You want someone who submits as Jesus submitted to John's authority to baptize.

Matthew 3:13–15 Then Jesus came from Galilee to the Jordan to be baptized by John. But John tried to deter him, saying, "I need to be baptized by you, and do you come to me?" Jesus replied,

"Let it be so now; it is proper for us to do this to fulfill all righteousness." Then John consented.

John implies when he talks to Jesus, "You are greater than I am," but Jesus told him that was not true, recognizing John as the authorized forerunner of the Messiah. He seems to say, "I do not have the authority, so I have to submit to the one who is introducing me." When we desire another's authority, we should not get it. When we desire to serve the leader who has authority, we attract authority.

Believes he or she is wiser than you are. You want people who are not trapped by the past to take the organization forward. No one knows everything, and no one will ever know everything one needs to know. We need to identify people who are perpetual learners, who are willing to change, be changed, and bring change, even to discard their own sacred knowledge when it is inadequate or irrelevant.

Some say they will help you and serve you, but they are always criticizing you, questioning your methods. They are telling you they know a better way to do it. They are actually trying to diminish your confidence. Such a person may say, "Show me how to do that. I really want to learn it." You say, "Okay, meet me on Wednesday at three o'clock and I will give you your first lesson." When she shows up, she keeps interrupting you to tell you what she thinks you should be doing and explaining to you what you really mean. "I think we should be doing it this way," she says because she thinks you do not know what you are doing. These are signs of someone who will undo everything you accomplished as soon as you are out of the way.

Do not choose experts either. This is especially important in these times. The word *expert* is very frightening to me because traditionally it defines a person who is so well versed in a subject that he or she no longer feels the need to learn anything else. That is a dangerous person. The bottom line is that you cannot teach someone who thinks he is already smarter than you are, and you cannot trust him to be the caretaker of your vision. Such a person is already thinking, "If you were not here, I would be where you are. I should be in charge. They should have picked me. I know how to run this place better than she does."

Expertise is particularly treacherous. I constantly fight against becoming an expert because I do not ever want to be so impressed with myself that I stop considering myself a student. This is why I discourage choosing "know-it-alls" as potential successors.

A case in point is the global crisis that rendered economists ineffective. This is why they have been so silent. They were experts, but experts in a system that did not work anymore. The crisis cancelled out many of the books they wrote and the theories they cherished. So what is expertise? Expertise is a frozen knowledge that could melt away with new experiences. Never choose an "expert" as a successor. Choose a student of life who understands that what he knows is not all there is to know. Mentor one who is willing to learn new things.

Narrowing the Options

Right now you probably have people in your organization who are jockeying for position, trying to get rid of others to eliminate the competition for succession and conniving to narrow the field. Jesus had to put up with people like that too.

Jesus had twelve men around Him, but of the twelve, He identified three to work with personally—Peter, James, and John. Of those three, Jesus identified one that He really trusted—Peter. Even though He pulled James and John into His inner circle, He was concerned because they had some defects. For example, James and John wanted power. They also thought they were wiser than Jesus. They essentially told Christ, "Look, there are some people down the street who are not operating the way we are operating. Let me give you some advice, Jesus. Call down fire and burn them up." They wanted to destroy people who did not welcome Jesus. James and John loved His power.

> **Luke 9:49–56** "Master," said John, "we saw a man driving out demons in your name and we tried to stop him, because he is not one of us." "Do not stop him," Jesus said, "for whoever is not against you is for you." As the time approached for him to be taken up to heaven, Jesus resolutely set out for Jerusalem. And he sent messengers on ahead, who went into a Samaritan village to get things ready for him; but the people there did not welcome him, because he was heading for Jerusalem. When the disciples

James and John saw this, they asked, "Lord, do you want us to call fire down from heaven to destroy them?" But Jesus turned and rebuked them, and they went to another village.

James and John were not qualified to succeed Jesus because they wanted power. They admired Jesus' power and authority, and they wanted to tell Him how to use it. They thought they were wiser than their leader.

> **Mark 10:35–37** Then James and John, the sons of Zebedee, came to him. "Teacher," they said, "we want you to do for us whatever we ask." "What do you want me to do for you?" he asked. They replied, "Let one of us sit at your right and the other at your left in your glory."

He told them they did not have what it takes to drink from His cup, and He did not choose them to succeed Him.

Now to review:

The Don'ts

Never choose one who:

- Loves your vision.
- Loves and admires your gift.
- Wants to emulate you.
- Wants your power.
- Wants your position of authority.
- Believes he or she is wiser than you are.

Chapter 15

Establishing the Qualifications

TAKE A FEW minutes to consider who around you exhibits the kind of attitudes and behaviors I just described. Cross them off your list. You may think that eliminates all the people you were considering. Look around your department, your company, your ministry. Who is left? Consider that quiet person over there in the corner who has been with you for a while, has never moved up to any significant position, has never been pushy, never asked for anything, but just loves what he or she is doing and loves being around you. Keep an eye on that one as a potential successor.

Choose the one who:

Loves you and not your vision. The one who loves you will carry on your vision and protect your legacy. Jesus and Moses by process of elimination chose the ones who loved them.

> **John 21:17** The third time he said to him, "Simon son of John, do you love me?" Peter was hurt because Jesus asked him the third time, "Do you love me?" He said, "Lord, you know all things; you know that I love you." Jesus said, "Feed my sheep."

> **Numbers 27:15–18** Moses said to the LORD, "May the LORD, the God of the spirits of all mankind, appoint a man over this commu-

nity to go out and come in before them, one who will lead them out and bring them in, so the LORD's people will not be like sheep without a shepherd." So the LORD said to Moses, "Take Joshua son of Nun, a man in whom is the spirit, and lay your hand on him."

Search out individuals whom you have discerned have a deep love for you. Whether it is in politics, business, religion, or a family, you have to identify the person who loves you. It may be one, two, or three people, but identify those who genuinely love you. You can tell who they are. Do not give the baton to the person you love, give it to the person who loves you. The person you love might not love you. The person who loves you is the one to entrust with your future.

"The person who loves you more than your power, your authority, and your gifts is the right choice."

Loves you and not your gift. The ones who love you more than your gift should not be so hard to spot. People like this are with you in the bad times as well as the good. You mentored them, and they often tell you how much it meant to them and what they learned from you. They hang around because they like you, not because you are famous or rich. Even when your gift has not paid off or has evaporated, they are there. They were there before you were a household name, and they are still there now that most people have forgotten who you were and what you accomplished. Many people once enjoyed your hospitality because you were a good cook and generous host when you could afford to be. Then when you were out of work and had nothing to share, only the few who truly loved you invited you to their homes or took you out to lunch. They still provide for you. When you can no longer pay them a salary, they volunteer to do some of the work for nothing. You used to give them rides when they were young and had no car, now when your eyes are failing and you can no longer drive, they chauffer you wherever you need to go. When you can no longer take care of them or do anything for them, they minister to you. They will have the kind of loyalty Ruth demonstrated toward her mother-in-law when the good times were over and she insisted the younger widow go back to her people.

Ruth 1:16–18 But Ruth replied, "Don't urge me to leave you or
to turn back from you. Where you go I will go, and where you
stay I will stay. Your people will be my people and your God my
God. Where you die I will die, and there I will be buried. May the
LORD deal with me, be it ever so severely, if anything but death
separates you and me." When Naomi realized that Ruth was determined to go with her, she stopped urging her.

Protects what you have. This person will protect you personally, your family, your staff, and your property. He does not covet what you have and will
fend off those who do. He will protect you at his own expense. Do you have
people like that around you? The protector will not join in criticism against
you and will protect and defend you against attacks or pettiness. You want
to give the power to someone who defends you as Joshua tried to defend
Moses (see Num. 11:27–28) and as Peter rushed to defend Jesus (see John
18:10–11). Neither wanted what the mentor had. They wanted to protect
the mentor.

Loves you more than your power. Reward those around you who are
particularly loyal. They are the ones who will not divulge sensitive information about your business or office. They will not tolerate gossip about you
or threats to your good name. They are as protective of you as they would
be of their own child. They are not yes-men or -women either. They will
tell you what you need to hear, not what they think you want to hear. Their
love is for you as a person. If you are a rich person who bestows lavish
gifts on your friends, you will have many friends. If you are an elected official who has been in a position to distribute favors, many people will want
to associate with you. Just watch what happens if you lose the money or
the power. Who loves you now? Humans naturally gravitate to power. We
love being around a powerful person. We want to know powerful people
because we like to be in the environment of power. Power is intoxicating.
Some of the people around you may worship your power. They are impressed by it. They love the way you influence people. They like to tell
everybody they know you. Up to a point, that is good, but what happens
when your power diminishes? What happens when you cannot or are not
willing to use your power to help them? Who is still left in the room an
hour after the election results come in showing that you—after many terms

in office—have lost by a landslide? Who will be with you a month or a year later? Those who love you for who you are—not what you were or could do—will still be there, like those who stood by the convicted, disgraced, and tortured Jesus as He hung on the cross (see John 19:25). God usually provides someone. This person will work to get you back in office, help you rebuild your power base, or just be there to hold your hand and listen to your sorrows. While you are still in the limelight, it is important to identify those who have this kind of love for you. You want to mentor them and see them succeed you.

Is willing to die for you. Not too many people will qualify here, but this is important. When I say die, it could be literally, but it also could mean people who are willing to allow their own ambitions to die. They are willing to set aside their own ambitions, their own interests, and their own preferences for you. They are willing to give up privileges, a birthright, for your sake. You have to ask, "Would they die for me? Would they defend me when everybody else is on the attack?" Peter literally was willing to die for his Master (see Luke 22:33). You want to give the company, the ministry, or the government to the one who is willing to die for you—not for the vision, for you. Love for you and yours will keep your successor in the path you envisioned for achieving your vision and preserving your legacy beyond your lifetime.

Would take a risk for your benefit. The one who loves you will be willing to risk his reputation, his security or job for your sake. If your company were failing, the one who loves you would invest her life savings to help you save it. If someone unfairly accused you of a crime, those loyal to you would risk their good names to testify on your behalf. The one who loves you will sacrifice his own comfort, time, or even money to be with you and to help you achieve your goal, as Peter did by standing by during the capture, trial, and conviction of Jesus. Though Martin Luther King Jr.'s untimely death left him with no clear successor, during his life he was surrounded by a number of aides who risked their lives for him and with him, men like John Lewis, Andy Young, and Ralph Abernathy who modeled nonviolence in the face of violence and went to jail many times. The Bible offers Joseph as one example of a willing risk taker. Out of his love for God and because an angel told him to, Joseph defied custom and gambled on marrying a woman who was carrying a baby that was not his.

Matthew 1:18–20 This is how the birth of Jesus Christ came
about: His mother Mary was pledged to be married to Joseph,
but before they came together, she was found to be with child
through the Holy Spirit. Because Joseph her husband was a righteous man and did not want to expose her to public disgrace, he
had in mind to divorce her quietly. But after he had considered
this, an angel of the Lord appeared to him in a dream and said,
"Joseph son of David, do not be afraid to take Mary home as your
wife, because what is conceived in her is from the Holy Spirit."

He took the angel's word on faith and, risking scandal and ostracism himself,
accepted the mission to see that the Messiah came into the world safely and
that the boy Jesus was reared under the protection of his household. The Bible suggests that Joseph did not even question the angel.

Matthew 1:24–25 When Joseph woke up, **he did what the angel
of the Lord had commanded him** and took Mary home as his
wife. But he had no union with her until she gave birth to a son.
And he gave him the name Jesus.

You want to see that kind of dedication and sacrifice in your successor. God
chose Joseph to be the custodian of His legacy for a while. For your successor, choose the one who would set aside his own needs and take a risk
on your behalf, the one who accepts a risk in the short term for the greater
good.

When Jesus was ready to depart the world, He chose Peter to carry on the
work because he had that spirit. Jesus saw him as a man who would die for
Him, not merely as someone who liked the rabbi's preaching style and His
great ministerial vision. If Peter merely had wanted to carry out the vision
in place of Jesus, he could have scattered with the others when the soldiers
came and emerged later when danger had passed to do the work in exile, not
knowing if Jesus had lived or died. The vision from Jesus might have sur-
vived in some form. Peter could even have claimed credit for it with Jesus
out of the way.

However, Peter loved Jesus the man and mentor, not just the Master's
words, goals, or gift for making miracles happen. Peter had trusted Him

enough to risk drowning. Peter was loyal when armed guards surrounded his teacher and was brave enough to attack the servant in a vain attempt to protect Jesus—both at great risk to himself. He could have been killed on the spot. Peter loved his teacher enough to stay within sight of Him in the enemy's camp as a trial proceeded. He could have been jailed, tried, and condemned as well. Jesus saw in Peter someone who loved Him when He was powerless to save Himself. Peter loved Jesus, not just His message, or His miracles, or His vision.

Test the Love

Are there people who are still with you when the whole city attacks you? In my own country, when I was beginning this work, I used to be a daily offering on the altar of criticism. I have people with me today who were with me through it all, and I trust them with my life.

It is often tough, however, to identify who loves you because you might not know why some people are around you. You will have to put them to the test. It could be a small thing, such as whether they are willing to reach into their own pockets to serve you. As the chairman and founder of Bahamas Faith Ministries International, I take note of which of our many trustees come to my island without any promise of getting any compensation and how many pay for their own plane tickets and hotel bills. If they only come because they are speaking or because they are being paid, then I question their love for me.

The way you know people love you is to let their association with you cost them something. Jesus told the disciples that if they wanted to follow Him, they would have to deny their mothers, fathers, children, farms, or fishing corporations (see Matt. 8:21–22). He was stripping them of all ulterior motives. Are people with you because they love you or because of what they can get from you? Let it cost something to associate with you, and you will see.

It Is All about You

Please notice that these principles all focus on *you*. This is a completely new paradigm for succession. The one who is qualified may not be the one who is talented, who is educated, who is famous, who can speak well, who has personality and charisma, or the one who has influence over the crowd. It is the one who loves you. The person who loves you more than your power, your authority, your gifts, or all the great things about your personality is the right choice.

Look again at one of the biblical examples. Take the case of Moses and Joshua. After the Israelites had their fill of manna and began to complain about the blessing they received in the desert, God told Moses to gather seventy elders so God could put Moses' spirit on them. They began to prophesy, but the spirit or the anointing also began to flow onto some people who were not in the meeting. They were at home, in the tents. They too began to prophesy. Joshua, the young aide to Moses, was in the camp at the time and ran to tell Moses these people were taking his job. He had competition. Joshua wanted Moses to put an end to it. He did not, but Moses understood the young man's protectiveness and frustration.

> **Numbers 11:26–29** However, two men, whose names were Eldad and Medad, had remained in the camp. They were listed among the elders, but did not go out to the Tent. Yet the Spirit also rested on them, and they prophesied in the camp. A young man ran and told Moses, "Eldad and Medad are prophesying in the camp." Joshua son of Nun, who had been Moses' aide since youth, spoke up and said, "Moses, my lord, stop them!" But Moses replied, **"Are you jealous for my sake?** I wish that all the LORD's people were prophets and that the LORD would put his Spirit on them!"

"Are you jealous for me?" Moses said to Joshua, meaning, "Then you can be my successor." The one who is jealous for your sake and the one who wants to protect you are the ones to keep an eye on. That is the man or woman who is going to take the company. Even Moses' sister, Miriam, did not want to protect him. She wanted his job.

He did not give it to Miriam. You remember her attitude. Some of you have that same attitude: "Who does he think he is? God can speak to me too." Moses' brother, Aaron, did not want to protect him either. He and Miriam were preparing a coup until God put a stop to it.

> **Numbers 12:1–2** Miriam and Aaron began to talk against Moses because of his Cushite wife, for he had married a Cushite. "Has the LORD spoken only through Moses?" they asked. "Hasn't he also spoken through us?" And the LORD heard this.

God says in effect, "Miriam, I am going to kill you because of your attitude." He gave her leprosy (see Num. 12:4–10).

Moses chose Joshua because he did not ask for the job. True leaders never ask for the job. Destiny and devotion choose them.

"If You Love Me..."

To protect the people you love, choose a successor who loves you. That is the one who will protect the family, staff, or country that you leave behind. If you are president, whoever takes over will love the country the way you loved it. I find these examples in Peter and Joshua. The young Joshua hated the things that Moses hated and loved the things that Moses loved. Peter loved Jesus so much he was willing to risk his life.

Whoever loves you will:

Love the ones you love. If I love you and you are my friend, I would take care of your wife, your kids, your business, and your legacy if you died. Whoever loves you will love the people you love. Can you trust your spouse to someone after you die? Could you say, "Take care of her. See that she is provided for and has the things she needs." Your successor should be someone who would do that. The one you could trust to do that is the person you want to succeed you. The one who brings security to your children is the right choice. You are confident about what is going to happen to your own family when you die if the person who succeeds you loves you. That person does not merely want your organization, your vision, your money, or your building, but rather desires to see you prosper and to see your legacy live on.

Love what you love. If your successor loves you, he or she will love what you built. The person you chose will honor what you worked for throughout your life. Their values are your values. The successor will maintain it and take it to new levels.

Protect what you love. The right successor will preserve what you built after you die. He will protect it and make sure nothing happens to it because he respected and loved you. The love he has for you motivates him to keep your legacy alive and thriving. The one who loves you will defend the enterprise to which you devoted your life. He will watch over it and help it grow in tribute to you.

Value what you love. The one who loves you will value your vision and the legacy you have built. He will value your personality. The successor who loves you will keep alive the things that make you valuable. He will keep your memory alive and never say, "Take his picture down." Instead he will remind everyone, "This man put fifty years of sweat and blood into this, and we will honor his memory." That person will love your name and protect it. A successor will preserve the mentor's success because she loves the mentor, and she wants to honor what the leader she loves has achieved.

Jesus knew that love was the key to preserving a legacy. If you love me, you will love the people I love. If I love you, I will take care of your husband. If I love you, I will take care of your son. They become mine. I have seen horrific examples of unsuccessful succession in the church after a pastor's death. These experiences would make you stop believing in God—situations in which a pastor who built a powerful, thriving ministry with his spouse for forty years died, and in one week the board fired the pastor's wife and children out of the ministry—the whole family—and put them out of the parsonage. I ask, "How could you have done this? This man and his family built this ministry from nothing." The board says, "Yeah, but it's our time now."

These were his deacons, board members, and elders, the inner circle, but they did not love him. That pastor, not the board, failed because if he had chosen one who loved him to mentor and had transferred the vision, that person would have protected his legacy and his family.

For Jesus, the church was His wife. Peter loved what Jesus loved so much he was willing to die for it. The church of Jesus Christ was like a beautiful woman, referred to in Revelation as Christ's bride (see Rev. 19:7, 21:2, 21:9,

22:17). Peter loved his master so much he preserved His wife. If I die to-day, what would happen to my wife? Will your successors defend your wife or dump her? Will they put your husband off the board and kick him out of his office? If you mentor people effectively, they will protect you later.

If you like power and you train the people around you to value power more than other things, they may come after your power. If you are in ministry or business just for money, you are training the folks around you that money is valuable. That is where their values will be, so they will be after the money. However, if they sense that you love, respect, and want to invest in them, in people, they will protect you out of gratitude.

Mentoring guarantees succession. One of the most successful transfers of power was Moses to Joshua. Normally when we see a transition of power, a war begins. Board meetings become violent, wrestling matches break out, and people start jockeying for position, lining up and laying claim to different pieces of the organization.

No war accompanied the transfer of power from Moses to Joshua because as an aide to his leader since his youth, Joshua wanted nothing but to protect Moses. You want to mentor people who do not want your position, but who want to protect your position.

Those who love you will be there to protect you as Joshua was for Moses. When Joshua urged Moses to stop others from prophesying, he seemed to be thinking, "I don't want them to take my boss's job. I have to protect him." I believe this is the moment that Moses decided, "This kid gets the company because he doesn't want it. He wants to protect me." When people talk about your boss or your pastor, what do you say to them? When people gossip about your leader, what do you say? Do you protect your leader?

"Don't you talk to my president like that! Stop. You don't talk about my leader like that."

"You should never say that about my pastor. How dare you!"

Do you defend your boss, or do you join in and criticize? If you join in, you will never be a successor.

A true successor becomes a protector. Peter and John valued Jesus so much they carried on the miracles, the work, and the teachings. When the Romans jailed them and tried to stop them from preaching and healing, they refused to quit.

Acts 4:18–20 Then they called them in again and commanded them not to speak or teach at all in the name of Jesus. But Peter and John replied, "Judge for yourselves whether it is right in God's sight to obey you rather than God. For we cannot help speaking about what we have seen and heard."

Which one of your children should inherit the family business? Go back to the list. Choose the one who loves YOU. Which person in your department should you take on to mentor and train to take your place? Use the list. Who is the best candidate to become the next pastor or chief executive in your place? Use the list.

Now, to review the qualifications:

The Do's:

Choose one who:

- Loves you, not your vision.
- Loves you, not your gift.
- Protects what you have.
- Loves you more than your power.
- Would die for you.
- Would take a risk for your benefit.

Chapter 16

What's Love Got to Do with It?

WHOEVER LOVES YOU will make sure your work does not die. At the Last Supper, Jesus broke bread and said, "Do this in remembrance of me." He gave this act to protect and preserve His legacy.

Out of love, Christians through time have continued this ritual act as He asked. "If you all love me, you will do what I say." We often do what people say because they command it or because we are afraid. We may fear that someone will fire us. Jesus said, "If you love me, you will do what I say." We are to show obedience, submission, and cooperation because of love, not because of fear.

John 14:15 "If you love me, you will obey what I command."

You might be thinking, "All that love talk sounds fine for churches or families, Pastor Myles, but I work in a Fortune 500 company. Who can expect to find 'love' in this cutthroat corporate world?"

That is exactly why I wrote this book, because all of our organizations today—businesses, churches, governments, and other types—do not understand and practice sound mentoring programs and succession planning. They have a void that could be filled by love.

Just because you work in a major corporation does not mean colleagues should not act out of love for one another. If the CEOs in our corporations loved the workers and they respected one another, we probably would not see the corruption and destruction we do today in business. We would not read daily about the abuse of privileges, the destruction of people's livelihoods, and the corruption of the system. Love is the missing element. In its place, competition and spite often reign.

We see corporate terrorism with people conspiring to destroy their colleagues. They are willing to sacrifice their morals and their values on the altar of opportunity to achieve their private ambitions. We need a new corporate and political culture in our society. The culture that existed in the twentieth century cannot serve the twenty-first century.

Look at where we are today in business, civic life, and other spheres. A few greedy CEOs are to blame for igniting global economic crisis. It is impossible for greed to exist if love is present. We must restore love to the equation.

"When respect, care, and love are missing from the work environment, it is difficult to plan for effective succession."

I hope this book can provide motivation and incentive for leaders to revisit the atmosphere that exists in our companies, in our departments, in our organizations, and even in our churches. Yes, churches have a shortage of love too. In other words, this love deficiency is not a corporate problem or a political problem. It is a human problem that we need to examine. If you are a CEO of a company or head of a political party, maybe you need to be the first one to reinject love into the system. The components that encourage high productivity are love and respect for one another.

Surveys have indicated that the number one complaint employees have about their companies does not concern money. The primary complaint is lack of respect and caring. In other words, the very thing we do not give our employees is what they want the most. People want love and respect more than they want monetary compensation.

Productivity is a by-product of love. In our organization in the Bahamas, we have workers who have been with us a very long time, and we have extremely low turnover. Why? Because our corporate culture is one of love and respect. We encourage people to work because we love the company, we love the leadership, we love the employees, and we care for one another. Our focus on love has produced faithful employees.

Rooted in Love

When respect, care, and love are missing from the work environment, it is difficult to plan for effective succession. Remember the first mandate of this book: The first act of a leader is to identify his successor and mentor that person. I want to challenge every senior executive reading this book to stop letting the company's present needs be your first priority. Let your company's future be your first priority. Preserve it by identifying a successor. Review your staff. Look at your executive team. Talk to the board about this issue because you want to leave the company in good hands.

Today's CEO might have to review his executive team to determine who has the highest respect for him. We may call it respect instead of love in that context because the one who respects you the most and who believes in you the most is a good prospect to mentor for succession. No CEO should abandon his post and recommend that the board endorse a successor who has no respect for him.

It should not be so difficult to find love in our organizations because chances are that an organization began out of love—love for a mission, an idea, a product, or a constituency. Every great political party, for instance, began out of love. The problem is that politics takes over. What really motivated the founding of the ancient nation of Israel? It was not politics. It was Moses' love for a people. Think about Nelson Mandela. What really started him on his journey? It was not politics. It was love for a people. What really ignited the civil rights movement in the United States? It was not politics. It was love for freedom and love for people.

How does any entrepreneurial project begin? With love. An entrepreneur is someone who loves an idea so much that he or she is willing to sacrifice financial security for it. Love always gives birth to a new enterprise, but along the way the love becomes raped by politics and greed.

We have to go back in time. Where is the love in our community? Where is the love that started our organization? Where is the love that gave birth to our political party? Where is the love that germinated the power and the ministry of this church? Go back to the love.

Do you remember the greatest complaint Jesus had in the last book of the Bible about the church? "Yet I hold this against you: You have forsaken your first love" (Rev. 2:4). He did not say return to your power or your building or your equipment. He said return to your first love. He says in effect, "I know your works. I know your power. I know your faith, but you are missing the thing that started you." He called it your "first love." In context, the Scripture reads:

> **Revelation 2:2–5** "I know your deeds, your hard work and your perseverance. I know that you cannot tolerate wicked men, that you have tested those who claim to be apostles but are not, and have found them false. You have persevered and have endured hardships for my name, and have not grown weary. Yet I hold this against you: **You have forsaken your first love.** Remember the height from which you have fallen! Repent and do the things you did at first. If you do not repent, I will come to you and remove your lampstand from its place."

He says, "I know your deeds." In other words, "You are doing a great job as a company. I know your work. I know your perseverance." Corporations use these words all the time. He says that I know "you cannot tolerate wicked men." That means you have integrity. I know "you have tested those who claim to be apostles but are not." In other words, "You ruled out all of those who are not committed to the company. You have persevered and have endured hardship." I hear Jesus saying, "You have made it twenty or thirty years in the company, but you forgot your *first love*. You forgot what started this company."

The next verse says, "Remember the height from which you have fallen." Applying that today, I would say, "Change the way you think and do the things you did at first. Go back and fall in love with your company."

Without love, you cannot mentor. You cannot mentor in an environment of cutthroat competition. You cannot mentor in an environment of antagonism. You cannot mentor in an environment of distrust, hatred, and deception, and yet we need to mentor. Without mentoring, we are perpetuating self-destruction, organizational destruction, and national paralysis. We need to go back to our first love so we can restore the environment of care and respect in our institutions.

We need love to mentor. We need love to be motivated to plan for succession—love for those we leave behind and love for the generations to come.

Points to remember:

Chances are that our organizations began out of love.
We must restore love to the equation.

Chapter 17

Who Loves You?

PETER'S EXAMPLE

RUNNING HIS HAND over what was left of his receding, thin silver hair, Jack stood by the window looking outside at the vast cityscape, with towering business centers shaping the skyline of the metropolis. His mind drifted back and forth between where and when he had started his company and what it has become today, a multimillion dollar empire employing thousands of workers both at home and abroad. This is the most important night of his professional and business life. This was the night he would determine who among his five sons would succeed him. To whom would he hand over the helm of this ship that consumed his life? Which son would he trust with his entire life's work, investment, and pride? To whom would he give his entire past and the promise of the future?

His face knotted up as he walked back to his desk, pondering at the hour of decision that would affect the lives of his spouse, his family, and thousands of people who depend on this company for their livelihood. It also would affect the children who look to them for their future and the millions of customers who had placed their trust in his company's products. The decision weighed heavy.

Staring down at the yellow pad on which he had scribbled for the tenth time the names of each of his sons, he knew it was time to choose. The eldest son was an intellectual and had graduated from the top Ivy League university in the nation. He was smart and had a great personality. The second son was an excellent manager who had helped to build the five production plants the company had in foreign countries. The third son stayed close to Jack and wanted to make sure he always had what he needed. He was not the intellectual his eldest brother was, not a manager as his older brother was, but he understood the passion of his father.

Jack remembered offering the third son a top position with great influence and power in the head office, but he declined, saying he would prefer to serve his father as an assistant so that he could better understand his heart. Jack recalled how this son always was the only one available to come to his house and take his car to be cleaned, pick up his laundry anytime he needed, and always make sure his mom was secure. Jack also recalled that when his company was attacked by the media, this son called a press conference to defend his father while the others opted to go on vacation to avoid the negative exposure.

> *"He was willing to protect and defend the Lord at his own expense."*

The final two sons were young and still in college. They were working summer jobs at one of the company's factories but were not ready to assume great responsibility. Jack knew that his desire was for all of his sons to be involved in the future of his company and had already included them in his projections for the company's development, expansion and future progress. He knew that they would have to choose eventually whether they would carry on the family's business legacy, but he also knew that it was his responsibility as their father, mentor and leader, to make the provisions.

Jack leaned back in his large, leather-covered chair, closed his eyes, and meditated a moment. He thought, "Do I need someone with the intelligence to run the company or the management expertise to grow my resources, or do I need someone who loves me enough to protect and preserve all I have loved all these years?" This question was the most important one on his mind. Suddenly, leaning forward, Jack took his pen and underlined the name of his third son. The decision was made. He chose the son whom he felt loved him. The criterion for succession in Jack's mind came down to love. Afterward, Jack wrote a memo calling a meeting with his family, knowing that his decision was not in keeping with the traditional or industry standard for succession planning, but he felt a deep sense of peace, joy, and confidence. He then turned his yellow pad over and began to design an intensive mentoring program for his son David.

The fact that you are reading this book is proof that you are a visionary leader in some capacity, and therefore you will have to face the same challenge Jack faced: How do I choose a successor and what criterion should I use?

I had to make that decision some years ago and traveled the same path Jack did. Our conglomerate of companies under the umbrella of Bahamas Faith Ministries International is more than thirty years old now, and I founded the organization with a vision that I knew would exceed my initial leadership position, territory, constituency, and lifetime. I worked diligently to build the vision, and today it is a global brand. Then a day came when I began to feel that urge to expand the vision to the next phase. To do so, I needed to release the position that held me fast. I knew I could not go where I needed to go if I held on to where I was. I had appointed a team to work closely with me, and they were all talented, gifted, passionate, dedicated, and submitted to the vision. I began to mentor them in leadership as we grew the organization together. They all seemed perfect as potential candidates to succeed me. I began looking around me for the person to whom I could transfer the trust of the thousands of people who looked to me for leadership, along with the physical and monetary assets the company had accumulated. I knew that choice would be critical. I had heard horror stories of hostile or manipulative takeovers, and I wanted no part of that experience. I had read accounts of leaders who spend their entire life building an organization only to have it destroyed by others who devalued the original vision and the visionary.

One member of my founding team was my college friend Richard with whom I shared my life's vision and passion for the world back in 1974. He not only encouraged me at that time, but also returned to my hometown after we finished our post-graduate studies, and he left his job with the Bahamas government to come join me in carrying out my vision. He also married my wife's sister, and thus we became "brothers" in two ways.

During the first ten years we spent developing the organization, he served in every capacity that I asked of him and submitted his gifts, talents, ambition, and personal future to the vision I had shared. I knew he not only loved my vision, but also loved me personally. Therefore, it was not difficult for me to identify him as the successor to the leadership position. We love each other on two levels, as colleagues and as family. I trust him with everything that I carry in my spirit and in my heart because his love is *for me*. He has loved everything that I have done and everything we continue to do in the organization. I have no hesitation in entrusting everything I have built into his hands. I know he will protect it, preserve it, and further develop it. It is his. He loves it as much as I love it.

Furthermore, I chose him because he was with me through my years of doubt, when the community misunderstood me and misunderstood what we wanted to accomplish. He stayed with me when I was publically criticized, maligned, and attacked in the media. I chose him because he never competed with me, nor expressed a spirit of jealousy or distrust. I chose him because he was willing to stand with me when everyone stood against me. He defended me in private and in public. I chose him because he was never interested in taking my position, my influence, my success, or my achievements. I chose him because all he wanted was for me to be successful.

I chose him because he was the personification of one who loves *me*, not merely my vision, my gift, or my power. When times called for it, he has been willing to protect and defend me at his own expense, and I trust that he would be willing to die for me or take a risk for my benefit. I have seen him sacrifice for and invest in our organization. He has often set aside his own ambitions, priorities, needs, or cares for my sake.

In my experience, he never coveted my gift or lusted for what I have. He never coveted or usurped my authority or criticized me in way that implied he was wiser than I was. He never attempted to take credit that was due me, never attempted to run off with any of my responsibilities, including the people. He was the obvious choice for me to mentor to become my successor. I have watched him grow into a powerful and outstanding leader. This is the joy of effective mentorship. At this stage, what I do in the organization is to provide long-term, visionary guidance and international networking. He provides the leadership on a daily basis.

Why Choose Peter?

As I mentioned previously, when leaders consider the prospect of succession for their organizations, ministries, and family businesses, it is a common temptation to establish criteria that are limited to talent, education, skills, experience, and academic achievements. That may seem reasonable. However, as I also stated before, in many cases this approach has resulted in great conflict, disappointment, and even organizational failure. After many years of observation, interaction, and personal research, I have concluded that these criteria do not take into account the best and most-effective prerequisite for successful succession.

My careful study of historical cases of successful succession—the Hebrew deliverer, Moses, and his aide Joshua; the prophet Elijah and his protégé Elisha; the great king of Israel David and his son Solomon; and ultimately Jesus Christ and His student Simon Peter—indicates that the most important prerequisite is love. Ask the ultimate question: Does this potential successor love *me*? When Christ had to decide who could carry on His ministry, Peter stood out above the others, a rock in times of uncertainty and hardship. Why Peter? The reasons might not be obvious to us. You will recall that he was a maverick.

At their first meeting, even he thought himself unfit among those Jesus had chosen.

> **Luke 5:8** When Simon Peter saw this, he fell at Jesus' knees and said, "Go away from me, Lord; I am a sinful man!"

From time to time, he pestered Jesus with questions.

> **John 21:21** When Peter saw him, he asked, "Lord, what about him?"

Initially, he refused to have his feet washed.

> **John 13:8** "No," said Peter, "you shall never wash my feet." Jesus answered, "Unless I wash you, you have no part with me."

Peter challenged Jesus on why He had to die, disputing the necessity of it.

> **Matthew 16:22** Peter took him aside and began to rebuke him. "Never, Lord!" he said. "This shall never happen to you!"

Peter was hotheaded. Remember, he was the one who cut off the servant's ear.

> **John 18:10–11** Then Simon Peter, who had a sword, drew it and struck the high priest's servant, cutting off his right ear. (The servant's name was Malchus.) Jesus commanded Peter, "Put your sword away! Shall I not drink the cup the Father has given me?"

Peter, as you know, even denied he knew Jesus in His hour of need—and not once, but three times.

> **Luke 22:54–62** Then seizing him, they led him away and took him into the house of the high priest. Peter followed at a distance. But when they had kindled a fire in the middle of the courtyard and had sat down together, Peter sat down with them. A servant girl saw him seated there in the firelight. She looked closely at him and said, "This man was with him." But he denied it. **"Woman, I don't know him,"** he said. A little later someone else saw him and said, "You also are one of them." **"Man, I am not!"** Peter replied. About an hour later another asserted, "Certainly this fellow was with him, for he is a Galilean." Peter replied, **"Man, I don't know what you're talking about!"** Just as he was speaking, the rooster crowed. The Lord turned and looked straight at Peter. Then Peter remembered the word the Lord had spoken to him: **"Before the rooster crows today, you will disown me three times."** And he went outside and wept bitterly.

Peter feels he has let Jesus down and weeps in shame.

All these things that seem to show Peter's failings are true, but look again. Try to see Peter through the eyes of Jesus. Take a fresh look at how Peter's denial of Jesus reveals his steadfast love and loyalty to his mentor. Most of you probably learned to see his denial as a failure or betrayal. It is a story parents and teachers tell small children. "Peter denied Christ three times!" They warn young people sternly never to disown the Lord. Congregations recite this passage without fail every Easter, and they hear it as an indictment of weakness and shame. They vow not to be like Peter. They have learned and believed all their lives, as I did, that Peter did a bad thing by denying Jesus, but nobody ever emphasizes *his love*.

Love in Denial

Take another look. Peter had followed the soldiers and risked hanging around to be near Jesus. He even lingered when it was clear his cover was blown. The real cowards had scattered as soon as the soldiers showed up to grab Jesus. Peter stayed within sight of Jesus so he could monitor what His accusers were doing to Him. The Scripture reveals that he was so close that Jesus could see him as the ordeal unfolded.

If Peter had not denied being who he was, a friend and student of this radical, doomed rebel on trial, the guards could have thrown Peter out of the courtyard, or worse. Peter proved on that night, as he had many times before, that he loved Jesus. That is why Christ left him in charge of His global vision of establishing the Kingdom of Heaven on earth, appointing him at the final meeting with the disciples, postresurrection.

> **John 21:15–17** When they had finished eating, Jesus said to Simon
> Peter, "Simon son of John, do you truly love me more than
> these?" "Yes, Lord," he said, "you know that I love you." Jesus
> said, "Feed my lambs." Again Jesus said, "Simon son of John, do
> you truly love me?" He answered, "Yes, Lord, you know that I
> love you." Jesus said, "Take care of my sheep." The third time he
> said to him, "Simon son of John, do you love me?" Peter was hurt
> because Jesus asked him the third time, "Do you love me?" He
> said, "Lord, you know all things; you know that I love you." Jesus
> said, "Feed my sheep."

Joshua had risen to Moses' defense when he thought others were copying him and stealing his thunder, as we learned in Numbers 11:26–30. Note Moses' response to Joshua: "Are you jealous *for my sake?*" (v. 29). Joshua was jealous "for" Moses, not "of" Moses. Joshua desired to protect Moses' position and influence.

Just as Joshua defended Moses, Peter had jumped at the chance to protect Jesus, even resorting to a violent act when he cut off the servant's ear. Peter took risks. He was willing to protect and defend Jesus at his own expense. He was willing to hang around in enemy territory where he might be recognized and taken into custody along with his rebel teacher. Peter must have been willing to die for his teacher because his actions could have cost him his life.

I have been taught all my life that when Peter denied Jesus it was wrong. That is how most of us have learned to see this episode in Jesus' life, but we can look at the context: Jesus was in the Garden of Gethsemane, praying at the heaviest moment of His life. He was about to take on His ultimate assignment. Jesus knows this is His last moment, and He feels the weight of it. He tells the disciples in so many words, "You guys stay awake because something is going to happen tonight. Something is coming down." He is struggling with His assignment.

The soldiers show up with Judas. Most of His disciples run. Eleven had been there with Him, and they were supposed to be His best friends. Yet in the midst of all those soldiers with their daggers, swords, spears, and shields, only one—Peter—pulled out his sword and was ready to take them on. Where is John whom Jesus loves so much? Where is James who is so powerfully attached to Him? Where is Bartholomew? Where is Jonas? Where are all the others? Where is their loyalty? Why have they abandoned their great teacher now? Only one was willing to die for Jesus. Only one would have taken on an entire guard, and Christ allowed him to swing the sword to cut the ear off one of the attackers.

Christ could have stopped Peter before he wounded Malchus, but I see this as a test. Jesus allowed it to happen to see who loved Him best. Only after Peter struck did Jesus tell His defender to put away the weapon, and He healed Malchus on the spot.

Envision the time from this Gethsemane moment to the last meeting where Peter is named as the successor (John 21:15–17 as we read earlier in this chapter) as a period of transition. It began when Peter pulled that sword out. With that act, in essence, Peter is saying, "Before you guys take my boss, you have to take me." This is the highest qualification for succession. Peter was willing to die, willing to sacrifice.

In effect, Peter gave his life for Jesus before Jesus gave His life for Peter. Jesus allowed him to do it. Jesus had the power to stop the assault, but He let it run its course. He was testing. "I have eleven guys here with me. Let's see who will make a move to protect me."

The only one who did was Peter. Jesus already knew it would be Peter, and Jesus had the power to stop Peter's attack, but He wanted to prove something. When Jesus told Peter to put away the sword, He was saying, "Okay. You qualify. You love me. You are the one."

Jesus demonstrated His power by undoing the damage Peter did. Afterward, as Luke told it, Jesus fixed the servant's ear as if to say, "Thank you very much, Peter, but we'll just pick this ear up here and put it back on, now that you have made your point and passed my test."

> **Luke 22:51** But Jesus answered, "No more of this!" And he touched the man's ear and healed him.

If Jesus could do that, surely He had the power to prevent the act.

Later, when Peter denied Jesus, it did nothing to diminish his role as successor. He had proven his love. Since Christ had predicted the denial, Jesus probably was glad it happened. Jesus essentially told him in advance, "Make sure you deny me. By the way, you know, when you do, the rooster will give me the signal." In other words, Jesus implies, "You have to deny me. It is necessary. If you do not deny me, the building of my church will not happen."

To Be Near the Master

When Jesus surrendered to the soldiers, they put Him in chains, tied Him up, and took Him away for a late-night trial. Matthew's account of these events underscores Peter's courage and determination.

> **Matthew 26:56–58** "But this has all taken place that the writings

of the prophets might be fulfilled." **Then all the disciples deserted him and fled.** Those who had arrested Jesus took him to Caiaphas, the high priest, where the teachers of the law and the elders had assembled. But Peter followed him at a distance, right up to the courtyard of the high priest. He entered and sat down with the guards **to see the outcome.**

If someone we love is accused of a crime, or is a victim of one, we want to be in the courtroom for the trial "to see the outcome." If our loved one is on trial, we want to be sure the authorities treat him or her fairly. Peter wanted to know Jesus' fate.

Peter remained as close as he could, alone in a hostile environment. John 18:15 says that another, unnamed disciple had followed with Peter and was able to go to the inner courtyard with Jesus because the high priest knew that disciple. Later, this colleague arranged for Peter to get in too.

> **John 18:16** But Peter had to wait outside at the door. The other disciple, who was known to the high priest, came back, spoke to the girl on duty there and brought Peter in.

Waiting among strangers, perhaps Peter was thinking, "I do not care what happens to me. I am going to stay near my boss. I cannot be with Him, but I am going to follow Him even though it is dangerous."

Have your associates stayed with you when the whole country criticized you? Have people denounced your church as a cult? Did your team stay with you when the media spread lies about you? Who came to the courtroom every day when you were prosecuted or sued? Who went on record defending you? Did you have staff members who said, "I am still here. I am standing behind him. I know him better than that. I still believe him, and I am sticking with him"? Who took a risk for you? Alternatively, did everyone run away?

As a leader, you might face times when you will be disgraced or misunderstood. That is when many followers will forsake you. Even the young people you have mentored will make themselves scarce, or worse, join your competitor's camp. When you have cleared your name and have regained your fame and fortune, some of these former associates will want to creep back into the fold. You might forgive them and even accept them back on your terms, but they do not deserve to be successors.

Peter loved Jesus so much that he thinks, "I need to supply moral support. I need to be there." Do you have aides who love you like that? Peter knew that if he was caught, he could be killed. Yet, the story shows, he stayed within sight of Jesus. I believe when Christ looked around in that courtroom and saw Peter in that corner He thought: "I have found a successor. He is the only one here. All the other guys who talked so big are gone."

The denial was love. Peter wanted to stay so badly that he lied out of love. He says, "I am not one of them." He said it because he wanted to stay. As Christians tell the story now, they really have wronged Peter, making it seem as though he did an evil thing. I would say that the others, the ones who hid, did the evil thing. They wanted to protect their own hides, not protect their leader.

Generations have accepted the belief that Peter failed, when in fact this one believer was the most qualified to succeed Jesus because of this loving act. Churches teach that Peter was trying to distance himself from Jesus, but if he were, he would not have risked waiting to be let in. That could have been another chance for him to run. Instead, he drew closer to the proceedings. It would have been illogical for him to insist on staying after someone identified him. His actions say, "I don't care what you all say, or who you say I am, I am staying to be near my teacher. I want to know what you are doing to Him. I want Jesus to know I am here for Him."

It would seem that after placing himself in danger of being arrested by the temple guards by assaulting one with the sword, Peter's motivation for following Jesus was greater than his fear of losing his own life. It is my conviction that the motivation that forced him to deny Jesus in order to stay close to the trial was his deep love for his Master.

When he denied Him, he was saying, "I don't know the man, but let me stay with Him." To the logical mind, this is a contradiction. It says, "Because I do not know Him, I will stay close to Him. I want to see what you all are doing to this man." The others were the ones who denied Jesus. They were not even close enough to say they did not know Him. The fact that Peter had to say it is proof that he loved Jesus and wanted to stay near Him.

After Peter's third denial that he was associated with his Master, Jesus Christ, realizing that his motivation to remain with Jesus conflicted with his conscience because he had to fabricate a justification for staying close to his Master, he wept in deep remorse and personal regret. I do not believe that Peter wept because he desired to stay close. I believe he wept because of the justification he used to stay close to his Master.

The Risk Taker

This was not out of character for Peter. He was always the one stepping up. He was the one who told Jesus he would never leave Him.

> **Luke 22:33** But he replied, "Lord, I am ready to go with you to prison and to death."

Those are very strong words, and the only disciple who ever said them was Peter. John had wanted to sit on His right, James on His left. They wanted to be as great as Jesus was, but Peter wanted to protect his leader's greatness. Peter told Jesus he was prepared to die for Him, and Jesus knew Peter was the next leader.

Peter had shown great faith on a different occasion. As some of the disciples were out on the sea in a boat, Christ came across the water toward them. After they spotted Jesus, only Peter was brave enough to step out in faith to join Him. All the others were afraid to walk on water. Only Peter asked, in effect, "Master, is that You? Can I come?" As soon as Jesus told him to come, Peter started walking. As the Bible describes it:

> **Matthew 14:26–29** When the disciples saw him walking on the lake, they were terrified. "It's a ghost," they said, and cried out in fear. But Jesus immediately said to them: "Take courage! It is I. Don't be afraid." "Lord, if it's you," Peter replied, "tell me to come to you on the water." "Come," he said. Then Peter got down out of the boat, walked on the water and came toward Jesus.

Only when he let fear take hold did he begin to sink, but Jesus caught him and got him back to the boat. Notice though that Peter's first instinct had been to believe and obey Jesus. He seems to think, "Well, if the Master says I can walk on water, then I can. I am just going to step out on the sea." He was always the one thinking, "I am going to believe my Master. I am going to stay with my Master." What an amazing man he must have been!

Who Am I?

Peter also had been first to recognize and identify this strange, young rabbi as the Messiah. You may recall this story:

> **Luke 9:18–20** Once when Jesus was praying in private and his disciples were with him, he asked them, "Who do the crowds say I am?" They replied, "Some say John the Baptist; others say Elijah; and still others, that one of the prophets of long ago has come back to life." "But what about you?" he asked. "Who do you say I am?" Peter answered, "The Christ of God."

Matthew also gives this account:

> **Matthew 16:15–16** "But what about you?" he asked. "Who do you say I am?" Simon Peter answered, "You are the Christ, the Son of the living God."

Peter recognized Jesus' greatness. Peter knew He was the Messiah. Peter saw Him for who He really was.

Check the Criteria

When Jesus was ready to announce a succession plan, He surely remembered all of these things. He called the whole board together for a final meeting. He is resurrected by this time and is about to identify His successor.

He has His associates gather, and He has to announce a decision. He is about to decide who is going to be in charge of an organization that would eventually serve two billion believers at one time. It would be a global company with a global product—salvation—and Jesus would essentially direct the sales and distribution team to, "Go to all the world and take my product." He was about to turn over billions and billions and billions of people, souls, and resources to one top leader. He is about to turn over a defined earthly assignment to a flesh-and-blood human. That is a big decision. Who is the one?

First, look at *how* Jesus chose. Does He ask Simon Peter, "Are you famous? Are you intelligent? Do you have good personality? Are you competent? Do you have skills? What expertise do you bring? Do you have experience? Do you love my vision? Do you want my power? Do you value my mission?" Does He inquire about Peter's academic achievements, his references, or his style of management? Does Jesus ask Peter how well he gets along with the other associates? Does Jesus even ask how many converts Peter has brought into the fold or how many miracles he has performed?

Jesus is about to transfer the greatest organization in history. Is His criteria: "Are you highly educated? Do you have the academic credentials? Are you an effective, strategic planner? Do you have what it takes to be a chief executive officer?"

No! Jesus asks, "Do you love me?"

That is it. That is the test. Jesus asks this three times (again, see John 21:15–17), and Peter must be thinking, "How can Jesus even ask such a question? I proved myself a long time ago. I stayed near the courtroom when I could have gone to prison myself. I am the one who could have gotten my head cut off by slicing off that man's ear. Even before that, I was the one who could have drowned trying to walk on water. He knows I love Him."

Peter loved Jesus more than the others did. He had passed the test. He was in charge. Jesus turned over the keys to him.

Did Peter have flaws? Of course. Was he brash? Sure. Impulsive? Yes. Hard to control? Certainly. Yet Jesus saw the quality He needed in this particular servant: love.

The criteria used by Jesus for choosing His student Peter to take over His global vision was not Peter's intellect, his personality, his experience, his contacts, his management ability, his wisdom, or his achievements. Although all of these are very valuable and helpful for all leaders, Jesus used the simple criterion, "Do you love me?" This criterion challenges all the theories used in the leadership training and development industry and sets a new standard for mentoring a successor.

Perhaps leaders today should study the wisdom of this great leader and apply His principles for longevity of vision and His criterion for choosing a successor.

The Takeover

The instruction Jesus gave to the chosen successor to oversee the ongoing work of His global vision—"Feed my sheep"—was also important. In the days Jesus lived on earth, many other "rabbis," or master teachers who were founders of schools of thought and institutes of learning, were also active. Their students were called simply disciples. Therefore, it is essential to know that Jesus was the founder of the amazing school that taught a vision of global expansion of the influence of the heavenly kingdom of God on earth. In other words, His vision was the colonization of earth by the Kingdom of Heaven. This was a massive vision and required the training of humankind to understand and implement this vision in succeeding generations.

Jesus in John 21:15–17 uses the metaphor of "sheep" to describe His entire school of students—disciples. Drawing on an image often invoked in the Scriptures, Jesus saw Himself as the "shepherd," or teaching guide of His school. He had built this school to become well-respected and influential in the community and nation. Thousands followed His school from city to city, and many joined His institute. Now He is about to leave and decides to turn over His entire organization—the human resources, reputation, credit, and goodwill to the one He had chosen, Peter. That must have been a defining moment for Jesus, Peter, and all the other students. The transfer that day was the greatest lesson in mentoring and succession in history. It was God transferring a heavenly vision to an earthly man. Peter passed the test and exhibited the qualification for succession: love.

Peter loved the church because that is what Jesus loved, and Jesus knew this was the person to protect it.

Matthew 16:18 "And I tell you that you are Peter, and on this rock I will build my church, and the gates of Hades will not overcome it."

When it comes time for you to choose a successor, do you know if any one of your associates could pass the test? Do you know if any of them loves you? Are they jiving, playing games to get a position, and jockeying for power? As a leader, you know the schemes. You recognize commitment. You know who is serious about working with you. You know whether your staff members are working for money or for love. Which of your staff members would you leave in charge? Who loves you?

Do you know what motivates the people around you? I know which people around me are motivated by love. They check on things in my life that only someone who loves me will check. When I am coming home from a long trip, they will cook something for me and bring it to the house. They say, "This is for pastor. I know he is tired, and no one has had time to cook." That is love. To think that far ahead is love.

Look for people like that. Choose such people for your leadership team. Do not get experts. Get lovers. You want people around you who will protect you and love you. You want people who will love and protect what you love. When it comes time for succession, you will not have to ask, "Do you love me?" You will have seen love in action.

Points to remember:

Peter proved his love for Jesus many times, even to the point of risking his own life.

Peter loved what Jesus loved.

Love is the most important credential for a successor.

Chapter 18

All in the Family

FEELING THE LOVE

MY MOTHER CALLED me at work one day some years ago and asked, "Can you come right now?"

"Mom, I am working," I replied. "I cannot do that."

She insisted, so I left work and went to see her.

When my mom wanted to talk, she would beckon me to her bed. She said, "Sit here." As I did, she continued, "Son, you know I do not know how long I am going to live. I do not know what is going to happen. Your daddy and I are talking about the future and about what is going to happen with your younger sister. I have some money here, some savings."

I found out some things I never knew. She had savings under the mattress.

"I know you are not the oldest one," she said. "But I want you to know that Dad and I want to turn our estate over to you. We are going to give you all of our books, all of our bank account numbers. We want you to take care of everything."

I began to protest, saying, "But I have three brothers, seven sisters. I am sure my oldest brother expects certain things."

I am the middle child in a family of eleven children. Usually, by law, the oldest son would take such a role.

She said, "Son, just keep quiet."

I said, "Mom, why me?"

She put her hand on my head and simply said, "Son, because you are my boy. I know you love me."

In a week, my mother was dead. Her reasoning in choosing me was not who was qualified by law to inherit this role, but who was qualified by love.

From that moment on, I took care of my father. Until this day my father does not work. I told him. "For the rest of your life, do whatever you want." I took care of my youngest sister, who was still at home then. My mother told me to take care of them. I think it was a transfer of leadership, a rite of succession.

"Inheritance of leadership is not automatic."

All my brothers and sisters know how I feel about them. If they need something done, they just call me. They all look toward me. If they want something to happen, they call. It is unspoken, but I think it is because I never wanted anything for myself and never asked for anything. I am the one who always wanted to make sure everyone else was all right. That always has been my position and my view. Every family seems to have a person like that, someone who holds everything together. It is the one qualified by love.

Now, in addition to being their brother, I pastor all of my siblings in my ministry in the Bahamas. I think my coming into this leadership position in the family is similar to what happened to Peter on the day of Pentecost. Everybody knew something strange had happened, but when it was time for someone to speak up, they all looked at Peter, the one the Master had left in charge. He stepped into the role and began preaching.

Acts 2:12–14 Amazed and perplexed, they asked one another, "What does this mean?" Some, however, made fun of them and said, "They have had too much wine." Then Peter stood up with the Eleven, raised his voice and addressed the crowd...

He went on to preach about how the One who was crucified had come as the son of God and about His plan for salvation. The Bible says about three thousand people became baptized believers that day. By speaking up, Peter had stepped into the leadership for which Christ prepared him.

Thicker Than Blood

If you own a family business, you might assume that your son or daughter is the natural heir and is ready to step forward to carry on your enterprise. However, just because someone is in your family does not mean that he or she is the natural successor. Do not assume that the person who succeeds you in whatever you do has to be a family member. You might prefer that it be, but it does not have to be. Whether it is a company you have established or some project that you have built, you might want your family to inherit it, but it does not mean that your children will protect it.

Even in a family, you can see the destruction of your dream. I have heard many stories about families who have built successful businesses, but whose children did not have the passion of the father or mother for the business and who would sell it for almost nothing. They would destroy the family business because they have no interest in what their parents built.

Blood does not qualify people to succeed you. It does not give someone the same interests, skills, drive, or determination that you had. Having your DNA does not make them a leader. Kinship does not guarantee shared vision. More importantly, it does not guarantee that someone will love you enough to protect your legacy.

Which one of your children loves you? Families are strange. You love your family members because you are obligated to do so, not because you chose them. Maybe you started out cutting grass and eventually built a landscaping company that is now worth millions. One of your children might be willing to give up a career to keep what you built from dying, but your children stopped cutting grass a long time ago. You were able to send them to the finest schools, and they went on to become professionals. Now you are getting too old to run the firm on a day-to-day basis. One child says, "Daddy, I am a doctor, but I do not want to see what you started die. I am going to stop practicing medicine and take charge of the company." That child loves you enough to carry on your legacy at the expense of his career.

Another child says, "Well, that's my daddy's business. I respect that, but it is not what I want to do with my life. If it dies when he dies, that's his problem. I'm a dentist; I have to take care of my dental career." He is not willing to sacrifice that for your dream, and that too should be understandable. That child has his own area of gifting and must pursue his own purpose.

To choose him as a successor and insist that he carry on your legacy would be a disaster.

Many family businesses die because we as founders assume our children will carry it on. You work for years building the company that has provided their livelihood, give it to your son, and within five years he is bankrupt because he did not love what you love. He could not appreciate the cost you paid to build that company. He did not value you.

I have seen parents who accumulated millions of dollars in real estate or finance and gave it to a son who lost everything in ten years. He did not qualify as the one who will love, protect, and defend what the parents built. Choose the one who would protect and defend you at his own risk.

That one who loves you and will protect your legacy might not be a relative. A leader might think, "Well, if I built this massive legacy, then it should be inherited by my family."

Inheritance of leadership is not automatic. Your children have their unique gifts and must pursue their own purpose. They might contribute to the future of your enterprise, but you might have to look elsewhere for a successor.

God is bigger than your private family. Let your children do what God created them to do.

Squandering the Vision

Some of the most miserable people on earth are those forced into the family business, and some of the worst failures are those of dynasties left to a family heir. I am not looking for my family to inherit the organization I build. That might happen, but it might not. I searched for the person who loves me for who I am. He will love those things that I love when I am gone.

Succession should be determined not by relationship, but by love. This remains true in families today. Children in very rich families can destroy the family's fortune because they do not respect the price their parents paid to build it. Wealthy organizations who entrust themselves to those who are not relatives but who care about the family's legacy and work hard to protect that name fare far better.

Many times the family members are more interested in the money accu-

mulated than they are in the source or product of the visionary's passion. I
think Paris Hilton is a good example of that. Her great-grandfather Conrad
Hilton Sr. built a global hospitality company. Her father and grandfather
continued in a similar fashion. She wanted to go play games and buy clothes.

Succession Is Not by Entitlement

Many organizations founded by an individual tend to suffer from the "entitlement syndrome," a condition in which blood relatives to that individual
feel the organization is obligated to choose them as natural successors. This
concept does not come out of any biblical truths or sound business model.
Today I know of many ministries and companies founded by individuals who
forced family members into the same line of work or profession. In many
cases, these heirs destroyed the organization. In other cases, they were only
there because their families expected it of them, not because they wanted to
be there. As a result, they were under great stress, working under duress, not
doing well, and not fulfilling their own purpose.

When we look at biblical examples, we see that Peter was not kin to Jesus.
Whenever God calls you to do anything, it is not a guarantee that He will
call your offspring to do the same thing. It is not an assurance that your family will be a dynasty. Leadership is not a dynasty of kinship. God's dynasty is
based on conditions or hearts, not genetics.

When we look at biblical examples, we see that Peter was not kin to Jesus.
Yet he was the chosen successor. Jesus chose the one who loved Him, not
the ones related to Him. We believe that Jesus had half brothers and sisters,
but He did not choose any of them as the successor for the leadership of His
organization.

Joshua was not a relative of Moses. He could have chosen a relative. Moses
had a sister, Miriam, and a brother, Aaron, but he gave his whole organization to Joshua, not siblings. Miriam was jealous and Aaron could not be
trusted, but Joshua loved him. Joshua was the one who loved him. Joshua
defended Moses, stayed with him, and went to the mountain with him.

> **Exodus 24:12–13** The LORD said to Moses, "Come up to me on
> the mountain and stay here, and I will give you the tablets of

stone, with the law and commands I have written for their instruction." Then Moses set out with Joshua his aide, and Moses went
up on the mountain of God.

Miriam seems to have gotten jealous when her brother started hanging out
with this young fellow Joshua. That is when she started talking about Moses'
wife and about hearing from God directly (see Num. 12:1–2 as I discussed
in chapter 15).

She implies that Moses was spending too much time with this teenager.
"You do not spend time with your big sister. Who brought you up?"

Some people feel you are obligated to pick them because they have been
with you a long time. Succession is not by seniority either. It is by love. You
might have people who have been with you for twenty years. Yet you have
made no promises that any of them could take over when you are gone. Now
some of them are angry with you over that. Then here comes someone who
has just been with you for three years, and you spend hours pouring your life
into that person. The ones who have been with you longer feel jealous and
angry. They even attack the new person or talk about you and your relationship behind your back.

In every case that we read in the Bible, we see a trend in which the one
who loved the leader is the one who succeeded, as in the cases of Jesus
and Peter, then Paul and Timothy. They were not relatives. The Bible does
mention certain instances where succession went to a relative. David and
Solomon, for instance, were father and son. More often though, biblical successors were not kin.

When it comes time to choose a successor, pray and observe everyone
around you in your organization. Study the staff, look closely at each family
member, and try to discern who qualifies. If you decide your enterprise
should go to one of your children, it should be the one who loves you. The
goal in family life is to cultivate an environment in which people can express
and communicate their love for one another. However, I know of no principle that states succession must be a result of genetic coding or dynastic
relationship. Therefore, no child in any family should feel an obligation to
follow in the profession of the parent. It is very important to allow people to
discover and pursue God's purpose in their own lives.

Even children who have the same parents may have completely different

purposes. We would love to see our children work in the environment that
we built, but they do not need to work in the same position we had. If you
build a family company and you have four children, each might have very
distinctive gifts that can be useful in different ways. All of them could have
gifts suitable for purposes very different from yours. Yet all of these children
could be useful in the same company.

Even if they do not inherit your position, they could participate through
their gifts in that company that you built—if that is their purpose. One is an
artist who could be useful in designing new products or working in adver-
tising. The other is a financial genius who could reorganize the accounting
systems or lead the company into new investment strategies. Perhaps none is
a master of marketing as you were, but together they could cover that function or hire someone to do it if you were gone.

Different Kinds of Gifts

We need to learn not to make our offspring feel obligated to follow in our
footsteps. In the church, I have seen people who believe that their children
are supposed to inherit the ministry automatically, and some children try it.
That does not mean they are succeeding at it.

I do not encourage my children to follow me into the ministry. That
would contradict my own teaching. I cannot preach all over the world,
telling people they should develop their own gifts and pursue their purpose,
then come home and force my children to follow in my footsteps. They are
busy with their own purposes.

People ask me, "You have a son and a daughter. Which one is going into
the ministry?"

Probably neither one. I told my children that I did not want them to feel
obligated to take this ministry. It is not mine. I am just God's hired hand.

"Find your own call to your own generation," I say. "You find your purpose. You pursue it. I will train, teach, and give you everything that I have.
I want you to dream bigger than I dreamed. I want you to learn everything
about God for yourself. The beat goes on." I have no plans for them to take
this ministry. It is not mine to give. We cannot call people to the ministry.
God does.

My son, Chairo, or Myles Jr., and daughter, Charisa, have accepted completely different calls for their lives. They certainly seem to have purposes other than mine. My son is studying business administration, and my daughter is studying psychology and social work. I must not force them to be me.

The ministry that I built during thirty years is not their inheritance. The ministry is not a monarchy. My investment in building this ministry does not guarantee my children's future. Their purpose may be bigger than this ministry, and I want them to find their spot, their unique place, and then flourish.

When my son was having difficulty finding a job in his field after college, I started a family business that is in keeping with his gifts and interests so he could use them running his own thing. I told my daughter that if she wishes, when she finishes her education in the United States, she can work in the family business with my son and they can inherit it. That might not be her desire or her calling.

I do not want to force either of them into the ministry. I cannot trap them in this ministry. I do not even consider ministry my whole life. It is but an aspect of my life. It is not my permanent assignment. I am on my way to something else, taking the advice I provide in chapter 12. It is important to set children free so they do not feel obligated or entitled to follow in the footsteps of a successful family member. They must know their own calling.

What God Has for You

I see a good example of this in the words of Jesus near the very end of the Gospel of John. The risen Jesus was about to leave the earth. Just after Jesus grilled Peter on whether he loved his mentor and after Jesus gave Peter the flock, we find something very interesting. It has to do with expectation and succession. The Scripture says Peter turned and saw another disciple following them as they talked.

> **John 21:20–22** Peter turned and saw that the disciple whom Jesus loved was following them. (This was the one who had leaned back against Jesus at the supper and had said, "Lord, who is going to betray you?") When Peter saw him, he asked, "Lord, what about

him?" Jesus answered, "If I want him to remain alive until I return, what is that to you? You must follow me."

"What about him?" To me, those words imply that Peter wanted Jesus to
choose John to join him as a leader. Jesus turns it back on him, saying in effect: "What does that have to do with you? What I have for John is none of
your business. I already gave you your assignment."

We can also note that while Jesus gave Peter the ministry, the Master had
already made John His successor in taking care of His family.

> **John 19:26–27** When Jesus saw his mother there, and the disciple
> whom he loved standing nearby, he said to his mother, "Dear
> woman, here is your son," and to the disciple, "Here is your
> mother." From that time on, this disciple took her into his home.

These actions support the idea that each of us has our own assignment. Jesus
would tell us, "Son, you do not need to be like your daddy, and daughter,
you do not need to be like your mother. No, what I have for them may not
be anything like what you do."

What God intends for our children is not what we might wish. It is strictly
between God and them.

> **1 Corinthians 12: 4–7** There are different kinds of gifts, but the
> same Spirit. There are different kinds of service, but the same
> Lord. There are different kinds of working, but the same God
> works all of them in all men. Now to each one the manifestation
> of the Spirit is given for the common good.

Points to remember:

Kinship does not qualify people to succeed you.
Your children must pursue their own purposes.
If you decide a relative should succeed you, choose the one who loves you.

Part 5

The Practice—Making Succession Work

Chapter 19

Leadership Is "Caught"

I WAS SPEAKING at a conference. When I arrived at the airport, my host had sent a driver to pick me up. During the ride, I asked the driver, "What do you do?"

He said, "I don't have a job. I am a businessman. I was the area director of a fried-chicken chain."

This obviously sounded like a six-figure job, so I asked, "What are you doing picking me up?"

He just said, "I am your chauffeur for the next three days."

I was impressed that an executive wanted to drive me. He was smart. I think I know why he wanted to do this, and I would find out soon that I was right. He had seen my television programs. I could see one of my books on the seat of the car. It was a well-thumbed, messed-up copy.

I was very busy on this trip, and we did not talk much as he drove me from place to place during the next three days. When it was over, I said, "I want to pray for you before I leave." So we prayed. I asked him about his family, and he told me about his wife.

He drove me to the airport and said, "Would you mentor me?"

I looked at him. I liked his spirit. He just wanted to serve. I said, "I will mentor you, but it will cost you."

He said, "Whatever it takes. I will follow you to the Bahamas. I will spend time with you. I will just be with you."

I mentored him. Today he has his own firm training entrepreneurs and leaders, and he speaks at my conferences.

Some of the people I mentor are in other countries. At times, I tell them to meet me at some destination and accompany me for the rest of the trip. I mentor as we travel. They get to see how I handle problems, decisions, stress, misunderstandings, or counseling. They are in my environment. That is how you learn. That is what I mean when I say leadership is "caught" not taught.

"The mentee learns through interaction with the mentor."

I have another associate whom I am very proud of mentoring. Everything I told him to do, he did. He did not question my instructions, even when he did not understand them. He invested money in his own development. When I said, "I want you to come with me to Africa," he said he would have to borrow money to do it, and he did.

He bought a ticket and came with me to Africa. I did not buy a ticket for him because he was pursuing me for mentorship, but I wanted him to go with me to experience the vastness of my audience. When I saw him invest, I was happy to give him a microphone to speak before a huge crowd while we were on the trip because he had demonstrated his willingness to learn. He had made a sacrifice to do that.

When people ask me to mentor them, I tell them to write a letter to me and pray about it because what they are requesting will require hard work. Not for me, but for them. I am going to give them plenty to do. "Wait till you get my mentoring package," I say. "You will be sorry that you asked me to mentor you. Read these four books this week and give me a report."

"Oh my! What did I get myself into?" they ask.

"And by the way," I add. "I also want you to pray an hour a day about these twenty things."

Our formal mentoring program at Bahamas Faith Ministries International draws applicants from all over the world. What I ask of those in the program is nothing compared to what Jesus asked of His protégés.

Jesus told His disciples to leave their families. "If you want to come with me, you have to forsake something. Are you sure you want to come with me?"

Matthew 8:21–23 Another disciple said to him, "Lord, first let me go and bury my father." But Jesus told him, "Follow me, and let the dead bury their own dead." Then he got into the boat and his disciples followed him.

To be a good mentee, you have to be present. At every opportunity, the mentee should be with the mentor. The mentee learns through interaction with the mentor and through the environments, experiences, and opportunities the mentor provides. This kind of association transforms the thinking of the protégé. Mentoring has more to do with association than with mere instruction. Being with a mentor is more important than receiving instruction from a mentor. When you associate, you can transform your life.

Mentoring is a two-way street. The mentor agrees to mentor, and the "mentee" must submit to be mentored. To learn, you must submit to the teacher, and the teacher has to accept responsibility for transferring knowledge.

"Follow Me"

From a historical perspective, a disciple was a student who lived with the teacher, similar to the way many Olympic athletes today might leave their families or even their countries to train with an outstanding coach. For much of history, anyone who wanted to learn an art, a craft, or a trade would have to apprentice—that is, to leave home at a young age to go live, observe, and work with a master in that field. Similarly, preteens or young adults intending to become rabbis, priests, monks, or nuns left their parents to live and study with their instructors.

When Jesus began His own ministry, His disciples or students left their homes and lived with Him for three and a half years. They traveled with Him. They ate with Him. They slept near Him. Most of what they learned was from observation and interaction. Just as the lion's cubs learn by observing, they learned by watching Him deal with issues. This is why they were so successful as successors.

Only through association can transformation take place. You cannot mentor a person if they do not associate with you. It is important to note also that the disciples did not just gather around Jesus. He chose them, and they agreed to follow. Others could observe, but He said, in essence, "If you are going to be my trainees, then you have to be with me." He told them they would have to leave their families in order to serve Him. "If you are you associated with me, you have to be with me."

> **Luke 9:57–62** As they were walking along the road, a man said to him, "I will follow you wherever you go." Jesus replied, "Foxes have holes and birds of the air have nests, but the Son of Man has no place to lay his head." He said to another man, "Follow me." But the man replied, "Lord, first let me go and bury my father." Jesus said to him, **"Let the dead bury their own dead, but you go and proclaim the kingdom of God."** Still another said, "I will follow you, Lord; but first let me go back and say goodbye to my family." Jesus replied, **"No one who puts his hand to the plow and looks back is fit for service in the kingdom of God."**

> **John 12:26** **"Whoever serves me must follow me;** and where I am, my servant also will be. My Father will honor the one who serves me."

Often you have to leave the places and the people who are familiar to you so that you can learn and grow. You have to step out of your comfort zone. In the mentoring relationship, you have to enter the environment of the mentor.

Points to remember:

To be a good mentee, you have to be present.
Leadership is "caught" more than it is taught.

Chapter 20

Mentorship Is by Agreement

I STOOD ON the receiving line, surrounded by the elite of our society: the governor, diplomats, politicians, wealthy business owners, bankers, judges, and a mass of other socialites gathered at a beautiful, private venue. We were all waiting to meet and shake hands with a man the world had come to love, respect, and admire—Nelson Mandela.

I remember the historic moment during that evening that I had the privilege of meeting this global icon, the first president of the new South Africa. He had just been freed from the prison on Robben Island a few days earlier, and his first official trip was to my small nation of islands, the Bahamas. His decision to travel there was a result of his relationship with our first prime minister, Sir Lynden Pindling, who had been a university colleague of Mr. Mandela's in England. Pindling was the world leader who presented the case of Mr. Mandela's imprisonment to the United Nations to demand his freedom from the apartheid-driven government prison on Robben Island.

As for me, as a man who grew up in an environment of racism and oppression in this former British colony, I understood the nature of prejudice, and I had always admired the sacrifice, commitment, and dedication of this freedom fighter. I had embraced him as a distant source of inspiration. To me, he was a mentor. At least, that is what I thought.

Finally, my time came to shake those hands that had become so hardened and calloused after twenty-five years of cracking the hard rock of Robben Island with a hand ax during his incarceration. The prime minister of the Bahamas at that time, Mr. Hubert Ingraham, introduced me to this towering figure who was bigger than life to me. I reached out my hands and felt myself melting under the warm radiance of a smile I will never forget. My eyes filled with tears as I felt my hands touch history. I surrendered to the emotions of the moment and hugged him.

"Thank you, sir, thank you," I heard myself mutter.

He simply held me close to his heart and said, "Thank you, son."

Here I was in the shadow of my long-distance "mentor" and touching a legend who would change the world's view of human dignity.

"The two parties in a mentoring relationship must reach an agreement and have an explicit understanding at the outset."

Those of us on the receiving line were guests for a private dinner held in his honor, and I sat a few seats away from President Mandela. During the meal, I watched him closely and observed everything he said and did. The way he was kind in spirit, gentle in all responses, and without guile, hatred, and bitterness reduced me to childlike wonderment. Many questioned him about his feelings toward his oppressors and about the impact his experience had had on his life. His response was consistently one of forgiveness and reconciliation. I saw love in its pure form and made a decision that I would always try to emulate this monumental example of leadership.

As the evening drifted on, I listened as a student, basking in the depth of knowledge and experience leaking from the lips of this rare human specimen. I began to acknowledge that even though I had held up Mr. Mandela as a personal mentor for years, I did not know him. I had to accept the fact that he was not my mentor, but rather a source of inspiration and motivation to me.

That night I was able to observe him directly and to see how he listened intently to others, waited with thoughtful meditation before he calmly answered questions about his painful past. I noticed how he used his hands to gesture and how he wore the unique shirt that has become a trademark. I was for the first time understanding what true mentoring is, even while accepting that this was not the nature of our relationship. I was interacting with true character.

I realized that true mentoring involves more than distant observation of a character or person. Mentoring is more than reading the writings of an author, even though that might inspire and motivate you to act on the ideas. Mentoring is more than learning about the accomplishments and achievements of another person or admiring their dedication to a cause or vision. Those things might ignite your own passion and encourage you to dream and believe in your vision, but they are not examples of mentoring.

I came to understand that true mentoring is the intentional submission of one person to the personal influence, counsel, instruction, correction, observation, understudy, and intimate exposure of another person's life, environment, lifestyle, actions, and behavior. That includes their processing of ideas and management of a variety of circumstances in life. Submission to mentoring requires expectation and accountability on both sides. This submission is with a verbal or official understanding and agreement that the relationship is for the purpose of mentorship. In essence, mentoring requires mutual agreement between both parties.

I had to accept the fact that President Mandela was an inspirational character, a role model, a motivational icon, and an example of sacrifice and commitment to a cause, but not my official mentor. We had no agreement or mutual consent as a teacher and a student. You could say my relationship with President Mandela was "distance learning."

I have since traveled to South Africa almost every year to facilitate leadership training seminars and conferences and have encountered him only one other time, but Mr. Mandela will forever be an inspiration and motivation to me.

Misunderstanding the Relationship

If mentoring is to be effective and successful, then the two parties in a mentoring relationship must reach an agreement and have an explicit understanding at the outset. As in marriage, the relationship will work better if the two understand each other's expectations.

"You have been my mentor for years," people tell me.

"How is that possible?" I normally ask. "I do not know you."

"Oh, I have read your books," they say. "I watch your television programs."

I tell them, "Then I may have inspired or motivated you, but I would not say I am your mentor."

That is not mentoring in its true sense. As I said earlier, this is distance education, not mentoring. You can become a disciple of leaders through their resources, materials, or programs, but that is different from mentoring. True mentorship involves face-to-face, direct, and interactive communication.

I think we witnessed a misunderstanding about the mentoring agreement during the 2008 presidential campaign in the United States. The media frequently characterized the American pastor Jeremiah Wright as a "mentor" of Barack Obama, who was then a senator and candidate for the Democratic presidential nomination. It is clear, however, that no agreement on mentorship had ever existed between them.

When Obama arrived at Wright's church years earlier, it was not as a mentee seeking direction. He went there as an adult looking for a place to fulfill his spiritual needs and his desire to help the community, not to be mentored by the Reverend Wright. Young Obama had heard that the church lived out its Christian values through the kind of community projects that he wanted to do as well.

The frequent use of the term "mentor" in the context of their relationship was unfair. As far as we know, the Reverend Wright never said, "I am going to train you and mentor you. You are going to do what I say. Follow me." No. The fact that Obama attended the church does not mean the pastor was his mentor. Obama did not say to the minister, "I'm here to learn from you. I submit to your authority and teaching. I want you to mentor me." Neither did the relationship evolve into one of mentorship. They never had an agreement.

This is an essential point, as millions of individuals commit themselves to many churches, mosques, temples, clubs, and other civic or religious organizations. They, or others observing them, could make the mistake of regarding their relationship with the leader in that environment as an official mentorship relationship. They are not necessarily that. If you attend a church, the pastor is not automatically your mentor. He is your pastor and spiritual instructor. His words and example might inspire you, but the two of you have no personal agreement for true mentoring.

As I noted earlier, mentorship is an intentional, conscious agreement between two individuals. It is intimate. It is explicit. To determine whether a mentorship exists, examine the specifics of the relationship. Was Barack Obama at Pastor Wright's side? Did Obama carry the minister's Bible for him or spend days at his house? Did Obama travel with his pastor? No. Then no mentoring agreement was in place.

Even people in a relationship may assume that a tacit mentorship agreement exists, but you cannot assume that someone is your mentor or mentee. The mentor must agree consciously and explicitly to mentor. At times, we assume or presume that we are training someone, or that someone is training us, when that is not the case. Many times people want you to train them, help them, or develop them, but no communication has taken place between the two parties. That is like expecting a marriage to take place when the parties have had no first date, no courtship, no engagement, and no license issued. Mentorship has to be an agreement. You want me to mentor you, and I decide to do it.

Again, mentorship requires commitment, dedication, submission, responsibility, and, most important, accountability. One reason an agreement is so important is that the relationship will require the mentor to assign tasks, offer correction, or dispense discipline. The parties must agree beforehand that the mentee will carry out tasks and accept the mentor's discipline.

Agreeing to Agree

One of the greatest examples of a mentoring agreement is the relationship between the greatest leader in history, Jesus Christ, and His mentees. Let us take a brief look at His official relationship-agreement process. At thirty years old, this Jewish teacher or rabbi, Jesus, was clear on what He wanted to achieve. He knew His vision and mission, and He was dedicated to fulfilling them. You may recall His initial encounter with three of the men who would become His first mentees. These men were business owners. They operated a fishing business in a little town on the northern coast of the Sea of Galilee, the large lake that empties into the Jordan River, flowing all the way to the

Dead Sea in the south. Peter and his brother Andrew, along with James and John and their father Zebedee, were partners who worked these waters for most of their lives.

The account of their first meeting with Jesus tells us the encounter took place at the shores of the lake one morning. They had fished all night, but were unsuccessful in securing a catch. One could assume they were depressed, frustrated, and discouraged. After all, fishing was their livelihood and full-time profession. It was in this circumstance that the Jewish villager Jesus approached them. After solving their business and economic problem, He intentionally invited them into a mentoring relationship. Let us read this account:

> **Luke 5:4–11** When he had finished speaking, he said to Simon, "Put out into deep water, and let down the nets for a catch." Simon answered, "Master, we've worked hard all night and haven't caught anything. But because you say so, I will let down the nets." When they had done so, they caught such a large number of fish that their nets began to break. So they signaled their partners in the other boat to come and help them, and they came and filled both boats so full that they began to sink. When Simon Peter saw this, he fell at Jesus' knees and said, "Go away from me, Lord; I am a sinful man!" For he and all his companions were astonished at the catch of fish they had taken, and so were James and John, the sons of Zebedee, Simon's partners. Then Jesus said to Simon, "Don't be afraid; from now on you will catch men." So they pulled their boats up on shore, **left everything and followed him.**

The New Testament gospel record of the former tax collector and accountant Matthew, who was also an official mentee of Christ, also gives an account:

> **Matthew 4:18–22** As Jesus was walking beside the Sea of Galilee, he saw two brothers, Simon called Peter and his brother Andrew. They were casting a net into the lake, for they were fishermen. "Come, follow me," Jesus said, "and I will make you fishers of men." At once they left their nets and followed him. Going on

from there, he saw two other brothers, James son of Zebedee and his brother John. They were in a boat with their father Zebedee, preparing their nets. Jesus called them, and **immediately they left the boat and their father and followed him.**

It is important to note that Jesus did not allow them just to wander after Him. He invited them specifically, and He established the expectation and accountability factors of the mentorship relationship: "Come, follow me," Jesus said, "and I will make you fishers of men." Did they intentionally agree and accept the invitation?

The gospel writers confirm that they did.

> **Luke 5:11** So they pulled their boats up on shore, left everything and followed him.

> **Matthew 4:21–22** Jesus called them, and immediately they left the boat and their father and followed him.

Here it is clear that He invited and they accepted. After that they followed Him daily, observed, listened, watched, and accepted His correction for more than three years. Their relationship required an agreement of mutual commitment, dedication, submission, and accountability. Theirs was a true mentoring relationship. It was all in the agreement.

The Right Motives

The mentor must be careful to choose wisely for the right person to mentor. As I travel around the world speaking at leadership conferences and corporate training seminars, many people approach me and express how much influence one of my lectures, books, or broadcasts has had on them. Such comments always humble me, and I find them to be a source of personal encouragement and satisfaction. However, many people also come to me and say they want me to mentor them. I usually respond by asking them questions to understand the motives for their request. I observe them for a little while and listen carefully to their responses.

I find that many of them are genuinely interested in receiving help and want to learn. If I feel they could be considered as a potential candidate for my mentoring program, I ask them to write to receive my mentorship introduction packet. It includes a number of introductory items, along with a questionnaire and application to ascertain their deep motivation and understanding of the demands of mentoring.

However, occasionally I also encounter those who do not really want to be mentored or taught by me, but rather they want to *be* me. In essence, they want what I have more than they want to learn how I got it. They are driven more by personal ambition than by a personal desire to submit, learn, and grow through a process. These are the kinds of characters that believe you can wave a wand and make them an instant you. They do not have the right attitude.

As a public figure who has achieved a measure of success, I will always attract interesting characters. Many people have approached me and said they wanted to serve me as an assistant or volunteer to learn from me. Sometimes I allow them to work around me so I can observe their attitude and the content of their heart.

After a while their true motives are exposed. Some really want to serve me, but others want to use me. I discover their real motive was to use their association with me to boost their status, expand their personal network, or to use the age-old advantage of name-dropping by being able to say or claim they know me. These are not potential mentees. These are parasites to avoid. I have experienced these shady spirits so frequently during the years that I am now able to discern them very early and not give them access to my personal space or valuable time. I learned that not everyone who wants to "help" is a helper.

I have identified some qualities that these characters exhibit that are red flags to watch for if you are the mentor. These attitudes will cancel any individual as a candidate for mentorship:

- They are interested in your work and vision more than in you.
- They are aggressive in the presence of your associates.
- They introduce themselves to your colleagues and circle of influence instead of letting you do so.
- They frequently speak of one day having the same power, influence, or authority you have earned.

- They attempt to give you unsought advice.
- They suggest or believe they know more than you do about your own work and vision.
- They possess a spirit of jealousy over what you have accomplished, and they often suggest they could do the same.
- They question what you do, rather than ask questions to learn how you did it.
- They try to keep other people away from you so they can have you to themselves.
- They tend to compete with you rather than submit to you.

The Mentoring Agreement

Assuming you have found the right candidate to mentor, what would the agreement say? I suggest that it incorporate these concepts for the mentor and the mentee:

The Mentor:

The following affirmations should become every mentor's commitment and goal for entering a mentoring relationship.

I agree to mentor. As a mentor, you must be willing to consider and accept the commitment, cost, and dedication required to mentor. You must be faithful to your decision to mentor.

I understand that leadership is "caught" more than taught. As a mentor, you must acknowledge that successful mentoring demands an interactive relationship with your mentee, providing opportunities to observe, listen, ask questions, understudy, and learn in your environment.

I will see potential in each person I mentor. As a mentor, you must see the hidden treasure within the mentee and be motivated by what he could become and not judge him on what he is now.

I will tolerate mistakes. As a mentor, you must be willing to make room for the learning process of the mentee, being ever mindful that you are also a product of many failures and mistakes, which were all a part of the development process.

I will demonstrate patience. As a mentor, you must cultivate a high tolerance level for the developmental process of the mentee and enlarge your capacity to handle the missteps of your student.

I will make time to spend with the mentee. As a mentor, you must be willing to invest your time in and share physical space with the mentee, as well as to accept that mentoring will demand time and effort from you.

I will provide opportunities to learn. As a mentor, you must be willing to create or invite the mentee to share your platform and exposure in different environments and situations for the purpose of personal development and training.

I will be honest with correction and generous with praise. As a mentor, you must be willing to confront the mentee on issues when necessary and not miss any opportunity to convert negative situations into teaching moments. You must also encourage and motivate the mentee with affirmations and also praise your protégé when appropriate.

I will provide recognition. As a mentor, you must be willing to recognize the value of the mentee and share that value with others in your sphere of influence.

I will focus on managing things and developing people. As a mentor, you must be willing always to place the human factor above material or mechanical things. Human development will be your principle motivation.

I understand that transformation comes only through association. As a mentor, you must accept responsibility for transferring your knowledge, wisdom, resources, relationships, and opportunities to your mentee through a close relationship with you.

I will view people as opportunities, not interruptions. As a mentor, you must be willing to allow the mentee to enter your personal space when appropriate and always make yourself accessible. The mentee should never feel that he or she is a burden or interference in your life.

I will have a long-term perspective. As a mentor, you must always be aware that the purpose and goal of mentoring is the future. Maintaining a comprehensive view of the bigger picture is mandatory.

The Mentee:

A mentee entering a mentoring agreement should be prepared to make the following affirmations:

I will initiate pursuit of the mentor. As a mentee, you must be willing to activate your own personal interest in finding a mentor and not wait for the mentor to pursue you.

I will submit to the mentor. As a mentee, you must be willing to submit to the mentee and cooperate with the mentee's instructions, advice, corrections, and training processes.

I will accept that the mentor is acting in my best interest. As a mentee, you must be willing to accept that the mentor intends—through actions, instructions, rebuke, or corrections—to benefit your developmental process and not to restrict or harm your progress.

I am willing to accept the mentor's counsel. As a mentee, you must be willing to receive the advice of the mentor because you trust his or her wisdom and commitment to your success.

I will never abuse the privileges offered by a mentor. As a mentee, you must be cautious never to forget that having a mentor is a privilege and not a right and that any advantage, opportunity, access, or privileges the mentor gives must be protected and respected. At no time should you use any relationship with someone introduced to you by your mentor for your personal gain or interest, being mindful that the relationship is the property of the mentor and may have taken years to cultivate. Mentoring is a privilege for which you must always be grateful.

I will harness the power of questions. As a mentee, you must understand that the mentor is like a buried treasure chest and that the surest way to get to the treasure is to dig it up. Questions are the shovels of life used to unearth hidden wisdom and knowledge. At every opportunity, ask questions of your mentor. Remember that questions automatically create a classroom and the teaching moments that will always benefit the one who asks the questions.

I will invest personal resources in pursuit of the mentor. As a mentee, you must be willing to invest your time, finances, and resources in your own development—understanding that mentoring is costly and will only have value to the degree that you are willing to invest in it.

I will never compete with the mentor. As a mentee, you must understand that the mentor already has accomplished much of the success in life you are pursuing and had to do this during many years of struggle, personal sacrifice, and failures. You can never achieve in your time with the mentor what it took him or her a lifetime to achieve. Remember, the purpose of being mentored is to equip you to live your life, not trying to adopt or compete with the life of the mentor.

I will never take the mentor's advice or criticism personally. As a mentee, you must be willing to receive correction or counsel as teaching tools and never consider the mentor's correction as a personal attack on your character, but rather embrace it as an expression of care and concern. Remember, the mentor has nothing to gain from mentoring you, except the satisfaction that you will be the success for which he or she can share credit.

I will never be jealous of the mentor's success. As a mentee, you must always be aware that what drew you to the mentor was that leader's success, achievement of major goals, or overcoming of great challenges with character and resilience. Your purpose in pursuing that mentor was to learn from those accomplishments. What they have achieved was the result of a lifetime of work, sacrifice, and faithfulness. You must never be jealous of history already lived. You must focus on making your own history.

I will be honest in the relationship with the mentor. As a mentee, you realize that the mentor's time and effort are precious commodities that must never be abused, devalued, or misused. The greatest act of respect and appreciation for a mentor is demonstrated through an honest and open relationship. Mentors cannot mentor a dishonest mentee.

The following chapter will speak more to those who seek mentors and expand the roles and responsibilities of the mentee, but these points should give you an idea of what is expected.

The mentor and mentee might not recite these affirmations verbatim or put them in writing, but they offer guidelines to keep in mind when contemplating a mentoring relationship. Mentoring agreements can be officially stated or unstated. That is why I have written this book. The leaders and parents of the twenty-first century must move away from haphazard, confusing, and "guess work" training, understanding their obligation and responsibility to provide effective leadership for the next generation to carry on their vision. They must establish official mentoring relationships and do it intentionally.

Points to remember:

Mentorship requires an explicit understanding between two parties.
Mentoring demands commitment, dedication, submission, responsibility,
    and accountability.
Being mentored is a privilege.

Chapter 21

The Mentor Chooses/The Mentee Pursues

MENTORING IS ALWAYS the prerogative of the mentor. The mentor determines if mentoring will take place. If you are reading this book because you are in need of mentoring, understand that there are two sides to the mentoring coin.

The first side is mentorship initiated by a leader who is in search of a potential candidate for succession. Intrinsically, all true leaders know they are transitional and therefore must focus not only on managing the present, but also on securing the future of their organization. It is imperative that they mentor future leaders, and thus they must initiate the process by *choosing to mentor*. Many people might seek out a specific leader to be their mentor, but as a priority and responsibility the leader must choose a mentee and initiate the relationship. He might mentor many individuals in an organization before narrowing the selection to choose a successor.

In this case, the mentor selects an individual or individuals by his prerogative and invites them to submit to his tutelage, training, and discipline. This is what the great leader Jesus Christ did when He initiated the selection of His twelve disciples. Many people were following Jesus before He intentionally made His choice of the twelve.

Luke 6:12–16 One of those days Jesus went out to a mountainside to pray, and spent the night praying to God. When morning came, **he called his disciples to him and chose twelve of them**, whom he also designated apostles: Simon (whom he named Peter), his brother Andrew, James, John, Philip, Bartholomew, Matthew, Thomas, James son of Alphaeus, Simon who was called the Zealot, Judas son of James, and Judas Iscariot, who became a traitor.

John 15:16 "**You did not choose me, but I chose you** and appointed you to go and bear fruit—fruit that will last."

Mark 3:13–15 (NKJV) And He went up on the mountain and called to Him **those He Himself wanted**. And they came to Him. Then He appointed twelve, that they might be with Him and that He might send them out to preach, and to have power to heal sicknesses and to cast out demons.

It is important to note that out of all those who joined His group, Jesus intentionally and deliberately chose individuals *"He himself wanted"* to be with Him. These statements are pregnant with the spirit of the mentor and indicate a desire for training and development by the mentor for future succession.

In this context, the mentor selects the mentee. The mentor invests time, energy, and often money in the mentee. However, as the relationship proceeds, the mentee must experience a transfer of responsibility and begin to pursue the mentor, realizing that the relationship is for the mentee's benefit. This dynamic is evidenced by Jesus, who after calling some men to follow Him challenges them to sacrifice everything for the relationship with Him in order to benefit from the training. For example:

Matthew 16:24–25 Then Jesus said to his disciples, "If anyone would come after me, he must deny himself and take up his cross and follow me. For whoever wants to save his life will lose it, but whoever loses his life for me will find it."

The leader may choose an individual or individuals to establish the relationship for mentoring, but the chosen one must also choose or pursue the mentor to whom he or she will submit in order for the process to be successful.

The second side of mentoring is that the mentee pursues the mentor. Those who desire to be mentored must seek out individuals to whom they will submit for this purpose. If you genuinely want and are willing to submit to a mentor for the process, first you will have to find a prospective mentor and persuade that person to mentor you. Then you will have to continue to pursue the mentor if you wish to benefit from the relationship.

> *"First you will have to find a prospective mentor and persuade that person to mentor you."*

The very nature of leadership, which ultimately is the fulfillment of a vision of the future that exceeds the life span of the leader, makes mentoring a successor a priority and an imperative. A true leader knows he or she is obligated to mentor and must prepare a successor, but the selection of a specific person is his or her prerogative, and it may not be you. Mentors by definition are successful people whose time may be limited. Many people may be pursuing the same mentor, and all or most of them may be worthy of the mentor's attention. Only a few will stand out enough to get it. The key is to make yourself genuinely available to serve the mentor, whether he chooses you or not. Your goal is to learn and benefit from the mentor's knowledge, wisdom, and experience.

As a leader, I am willing to mentor individuals who seriously pursue me seeking help and who willingly submit to me for training. Mentees pursue. Mentors choose or accept mentees. However, mentors are usually more inclined to take on mentees who display an earnest desire to be mentored and who demonstrate sincere effort.

Sometimes the prospective mentee's motivation for pursuit of a mentor is negative or questionable. The approach could be motivated by selfish ambition, a desire to associate with power and position, or to use the relationship to advance a mentee's personal goals. The discerning mentor will reject this attitude and the spirit of manipulation.

Not Ready to Commit

Mentors will never mentor an unwilling, uncommitted, *unsubmitted* mentee. One of the most graphic examples of this principle is the succession account of the great biblical prophet Elijah and the mentoring of his successor, Elisha.

The first action taken in the story of Elijah and his relationship with Elisha was the indication of Elijah of his willingness to mentor Elisha.

> **1 Kings 19:15–21** The LORD said to him, "Go back the way you came, and go to the Desert of Damascus. When you get there, anoint Hazael king over Aram. Also, anoint Jehu son of Nimshi king over Israel, and anoint Elisha son of Shaphat from Abel Meholah to succeed you as prophet. Jehu will put to death any who escape the sword of Hazael, and Elisha will put to death any who escape the sword of Jehu. Yet I reserve seven thousand in Israel—all whose knees have not bowed down to Baal and all whose mouths have not kissed him." So Elijah went from there and found Elisha son of Shaphat. He was plowing with twelve yoke of oxen, and he himself was driving the twelfth pair. Elijah **went up to him and threw his cloak around him.** Elisha then left his oxen and ran after Elijah. "Let me kiss my father and mother good-by," he said, "and then I will come with you." **"Go back,"** **Elijah replied. "What have I done to you?"** So Elisha left him and went back. He took his yoke of oxen and slaughtered them. He burned the plowing equipment to cook the meat and gave it to the people, and they ate. Then he set out to follow Elijah and became his attendant.

This account of mentorship and succession offers lessons for the twenty-first-century leader that may save many organizations from ruin. Let us look a little closer at this powerful story.

First, Elijah, the senior in the relationship, came intentionally to seek Elisha for mentorship training, as he was directed (see 1 Kings 19:16).

Then Elijah chooses Elisha for mentoring: "Elijah went up to him and threw his cloak around him" (1 Kings 19:19). This act signified the mentor was choosing the mentee or bestowing on him the mantle of authority. However, the *choosing* was not *pursuing*. It was an invitation for the mentee to pursue. Elisha did not respond with commitment at first, even though the cloak signaled that he was chosen as a mentee and potential successor. So Elijah did not pursue Elisha, but went on his way. Elisha's parents were his priority. He returned home and continued to be with his family for a while. In essence, Elijah and Elisha did not yet have a mutual mentor/mentee agreement. Elisha wanted to put other things first. "Elisha then left his oxen and ran after Elijah. 'Let me kiss my father and mother good-by,' he said, 'and then I will come with you'" (1 Kings 19:20). Here, we see a lack of commitment to enter the agreement and make the necessary sacrifice to be mentored.

Elijah recognizes that Elisha is not ready. "'Go back,' Elijah replied. 'What have I done to you?' So Elisha left him and went back" (1 Kings 19:20–21). We see that Elijah rejected Elisha to test him for commitment, dedication, and interest. Elijah could have insisted or run after Elisha. Eventually, Elisha did something that is symbolic of what all true mentees have to do. "He took his yoke of oxen and slaughtered them. He burned the plowing equipment to cook the meat and gave it to the people, and they ate. Then he set out to follow Elijah and became his attendant" (1 Kings 19:21).

We see by these acts the ultimate sacrifice, commitment, and dedication to the mentor, which are the foundation of the mutual agreement necessary for mentoring to take place. This is the fulfillment of the second side of mentorship: the mentee pursuing the mentor. We see Elijah finally accepting Elisha when he demonstrated his commitment by his sacrifice.

Letting Go of the Old

Elisha came back with the right attitude. He burned his plow, sold his farm, and barbecued the ox. He showed up at Elijah's door with nothing. By his submission, he implied, "I am ready to be mentored by you. Whatever you want me to do, I'm ready."

Elijah, in effect, says, "Now you can come with me, and if you stay with me, you will get the power. You will get the ministry. You will get the company because now it is clear you are ready to serve me." Notice that

Elisha came as an "attendant." This word means bond servant—one who was marked to be with his master forever.

Elijah accepted him. Elisha's burning of the oxen and the selling of the farm were the keys to his being qualified for becoming the successor. As long as he had the farm and oxen, he was not completely committed or dedicated. Elisha would know that he would always have something on which to fall back in case things did not work out with Elijah. Wherever there is an alternative or option, there can never be full commitment and dedication to the first objective. This is why, in my experience, marriages with prenuptial agreements hardly ever work out. The agreement is "an escape clause," dividing the spoils should the marriage end. Commitment and dedication is not possible where an option for escape exists.

Until he surrendered everything, Elisha always would have had a fallback position. He could run back home. When Elijah saw that Elisha had given up his comforts, his assurances, and his security, he essentially said, "Now I will mentor you." Elisha had shown he was ready to invest in the relationship. He had left his comfort zone. If you are going to follow a mentor, you cannot give excuses. As the mentee, you must be willing to submit, commit, and even sacrifice.

Transfer of Power: True Succession

The most important part of this story of Elijah and Elisha is the mutual agreement and deep love Elisha developed for his mentor. Read his declaration of loyalty and love for Elijah:

> **2 Kings 2:1–15** When the LORD was about to take Elijah up to heaven in a whirlwind, Elijah and Elisha were on their way from Gilgal. Elijah said to Elisha, "Stay here; the LORD has sent me to Bethel." But Elisha said, "As surely as the LORD lives and as you live, I will not leave you." So they went down to Bethel. The company of the prophets at Bethel came out to Elisha and asked, "Do you know that the LORD is going to take your master from you today?" "Yes, I know," Elisha replied, "but do not speak of it." Then Elijah said to him, "Stay here, Elisha; the LORD has sent me to

Jericho." And he replied, "As surely as the LORD lives and as you live, I will not leave you." So they went to Jericho. The company of the prophets at Jericho went up to Elisha and asked him, "Do you know that the LORD is going to take your master from you today?" "Yes, I know," he replied, "but do not speak of it." Then Elijah said to him, "Stay here; the LORD has sent me to the Jordan." And he replied, "As surely as the LORD lives and as you live, I will not leave you." So the two of them walked on. Fifty men of the company of the prophets went and stood at a distance, facing the place where Elijah and Elisha had stopped at the Jordan. Elijah took his cloak, rolled it up and struck the water with it. The water divided to the right and to the left, and the two of them crossed over on dry ground. When they had crossed, Elijah said to Elisha, "Tell me, what can I do for you before I am taken from you?" "Let me inherit a double portion of your spirit," Elisha replied. "You have asked a difficult thing," Elijah said, "yet if you see me when I am taken from you, it will be yours—otherwise not." As they were walking along and talking together, suddenly a chariot of fire and horses of fire appeared and separated the two of them, and Elijah went up to heaven in a whirlwind. Elisha saw this and cried out, "My father! My father! The chariots and horsemen of Israel!" And Elisha saw him no more. Then he took hold of his own clothes and tore them apart. He picked up the cloak that had fallen from Elijah and went back and stood on the bank of the Jordan. Then he took the cloak that had fallen from him and struck the water with it. "Where now is the LORD, the God of Elijah?" he asked. When he struck the water, it divided to the right and to the left, and he crossed over. The company of the prophets from Jericho, who were watching, said, "The spirit of Elijah is resting on Elisha." And they went to meet him and bowed to the ground before him."

What a beautiful story of effective mentorship and succession. Elijah was the consummate mentor, and Elisha the excellent mentee. Notice that Elisha not only received the mantel of Elijah, but he also received his influence and his school of prophets. Note too that Elisha pursued Elijah right to the end and became his successor. Elisha told Elijah, "As surely as the LORD lives and as you live, I will not leave you."

Before the mentoring relationship can even begin, you must identify a mentor worth pursuing. So there are two perspectives of mentorship, one is that of the mentor who chooses the mentee intentionally for the purpose of training and preparing that person for potential succession. The other is that of a mentee who, desiring to be mentored, identifies a mentor and indicates the willingness to submit and serve the mentor. This is in order to benefit from the mentor's wisdom, knowledge, experience, and molding. In both cases, the mentee must pursue the mentor if mentoring is to be successful.

The mentor *chooses but does not pursue* the mentee. Anyone who could be considered a potent mentor would probably be busy and consumed by his or her priorities and passion. Thus, the ideal candidate would not be waiting casually for someone to come forward and ask to be mentored, nor would this outstanding leader be preoccupied with looking for someone to mentor. In fact, a person worthy of being a mentor already would have many people seeking his or her attention and wisdom. The challenge is that one leader can mentor only a few people effectively.

The mentor ultimately chooses the mentee, but only after the mentee has pursued a relationship and demonstrated the willingness to be mentored. Essentially, whether the mentor chooses the mentee or the mentee chooses the leader as mentor, the initiative and onus still would be on the mentee.

How to Choose a Mentor

Choosing someone to whom you can submit your entire life, plans, goals, ambitions, dreams, visions, and destiny is a very serious decision. Choosing someone to help form your priorities, values, moral convictions, and future life's work is critical. You must make the decision with great care. What are some of the qualities you might look for in a potential mentor, and where could you find such a person? Here are a few points I wish to submit for your consideration. A mentor should be one who has:

- Lived long enough to have a character that has been tested over time by both his supporters and enemies and is worthy of trust.

- Overcome major obstacles, oppositions, challenges, discouragements, and points of failure in the pursuit of achieving a vision or a cause in the interest of humanity.
- Demonstrated wisdom, knowledge, and understanding of the comprehensive nature of life that makes the mentor's counsel trustworthy.
- Exhibited a longevity and faithfulness to a cause, a vision, or a call with consistency.
- Made major personal sacrifices and demonstrated willingness to bear the cost of a dream and a passion, as well as to help others succeed or achieve their goals.
- Managed failure and success effectively and displayed a spirit of humility and candor.
- Shown willingness to protect his or her integrity and character without compromise.

Getting someone like this to mentor you is not difficult, as I have experienced that every genuine leader or truly successful person wants, desires, and feels obligated to mentor others as a way of giving back. The only requirements or demands would be that the mentee must be serious, committed, and dedicated to being mentored. Leaders do not want to waste their time. Therefore, asking a leader or someone from whom you desire to learn if he or she will mentor you is the first step. However, just as Elijah did, the prospective mentor will test your interest and commitment.

Ready and Willing

If you want someone to consider mentoring you, you must adopt the right frame of mind and demonstrate the right attitude. You must be:

- Willing to serve the mentor and not your personal ambition.
- Willing to sacrifice your personal interests to serve the mentor's interests.
- Willing to submit totally to the mentor's instructions, counsel, advice, rebuke, and correction.
- Willing to stay in the background until invited.
- Circumspect about the mentor's weaknesses and not intent on taking ad-

vantage of them or using them as leverage for exploitation or blackmail.

- Vigilant and aware of all that surrounds your mentor and able to learn his/her habits, desires, preferences, interests, and priorities.
- Respectful of the mentor's relationships or friendships and not intent on taking advantage of them for personal gain.
- Willing to study the process and principles of your mentor, not just his or her results.
- On guard against cultivating a spirit that is jealous of your mentor, understanding that you can never learn from someone if you are jealous of them.
- Open to learning how not to lean on your mentor.

Remember, to be mentored is a privilege and not a right. Be eternally grateful and express it often. Gratitude will always attract help.

The Perfect Mentee

Again we can look at Joshua and Moses as one of the greatest, most-perfect examples of mentoring and succession. A careful review of their relationship as mentor and mentee provides us with an excellent case study for choosing a mentee and submitting to a mentor. Let us read some of their story and extract the unique principles of mentoring and succession demonstrated in their relationship:

> **Exodus 24:13–14** Then Moses set out with Joshua his aide, and Moses went up on the mountain of God. He said to the elders, "Wait here for us until we come back to you."

> **Numbers 11:28–29** Joshua son of Nun, who had been Moses' aide since youth, spoke up and said, "Moses, my lord, stop them!" But Moses replied, "Are you jealous for my sake?"

> **Numbers 27:18–23** So the LORD said to Moses, "Take Joshua son of Nun, a man in whom is the spirit, and lay your hand on him. Have him stand before Eleazar the priest and the entire assembly

and commission him in their presence. Give him some of your authority so the whole Israelite community will obey him. He is to stand before Eleazar the priest, who will obtain decisions for him by inquiring of the Urim before the LORD. At his command he and the entire community of the Israelites will go out, and at his command they will come in." Moses did as the LORD commanded him. He took Joshua and had him stand before Eleazar the priest and the whole assembly. Then he laid his hands on him and commissioned him, as the LORD instructed through Moses.

Deuteronomy 1:37–39 Because of you the LORD became angry with me also and said, "You shall not enter it, either. But your assistant, Joshua son of Nun, will enter it. Encourage him, because he will lead Israel to inherit it."

Deuteronomy 3:27–29 "Go up to the top of Pisgah and look west and north and south and east. Look at the land with your own eyes, since you are not going to cross this Jordan. But commission Joshua, and encourage and strengthen him, for he will lead this people across and will cause them to inherit the land that you will see." So we stayed in the valley near Beth Peor.

These accounts contain all the important principles of mentoring and succession. If you study the relationship of Joshua and Moses, first you will notice:

The mentee must submit to the mentor and possess a spirit of student and servant.

As Numbers 11:28 reads, Joshua "had been Moses' aide since youth." Mentorship had begun. Notice that the mentee *aided* the mentor first. In other words, mentoring begins with serving the mentor. If you want to learn from someone, you have to submit to him or her. To learn from someone, you have to be willing to serve. Thus, mentorship really begins with willingness to serve.

The mentee must be teachable and must not be competitive with his mentor.

The second thing we find about Joshua is that the Scriptures do not call him a servant of God. They always call him an aide of Moses (see Exod.

24:13, Exod. 33:11, and Num. 11:28). That is important because you cannot be mentored when you compete with your mentor. If you want someone to mentor you, you cannot attempt to be equal to your mentor. Joshua just wanted to be a servant of Moses. He had the correct attitude.

The mentee must be present but not too pushy and aggressive with the mentor.

Joshua stayed with Moses all the time. Yet Scriptures cite little that he said, so we can infer that he did not talk much. He is quiet, but he is present. That fascinates me and intrigues me. Joshua was always with Moses because the prophet was his mentor. Joshua followed where Moses went, but he did not assert himself.

The mentee will have access to the environment of the mentor but must never abuse it.

Joshua had this kind of access. Scripture says the young man headed up the mountain with his leader (see Exod. 24:13). Joshua accompanied Moses to the Tent of Meeting. This was a special tent that Moses had set up and where he met with God. They would have intimate conversations there, and the only person who went into that tent with Moses was Joshua. A mentor can get you into places. The Bible says Moses left the Tent of Meeting, and Joshua stayed (see Exodus 33:11). Perhaps he was just basking in the greatness of God. A mentor can get you into the presence of greatness, and you can actually stay there because the great one will start to talk to you. Even then, the mentee must tread lightly, being careful not to abuse the relationship.

The mentee must learn in silence when allowed into the privileged places of his mentor.

No one knows what, if anything, God said to Joshua during those moments in the Tent of Meeting or if Joshua said anything. Maybe Joshua's experience there was to prepare him for future leadership. Joshua experienced God in a way that no other person did because he was brought into God's presence by his mentor. A mentor can open doors for you that no one else can open. Shared influence and connections are important elements of mentorship and succession.

The mentee must never compete with, nor be jealous of his mentor.

When Joshua perceived a threat to his mentor, he expressed jealousy. It was jealousy, not *of* Moses but *for* Moses, which are very different things.

The mentee must not usurp the position of his mentor, but must protect and defend it.

We see Joshua expressing an interesting "menteeship" spirit. Joshua wanted Moses to stop the new "prophets" because the loyal aide saw them as competing with his mentor. This is the kind of person you want to mentor. Joshua wanted to protect Moses from competitors, not compete with Moses. It impressed Moses that this young man wanted to protect his position, not take it. Moses realized that Joshua had an interest, not only in serving him, but also in defending him. Joshua was not looking out for himself. He was protecting Moses' turf.

The mentee must never abuse the privileges of his mentor.

Finally, Joshua did not usurp Moses' authority. He was in the presence of the God of Moses but never tried to claim Moses' relationship with God for himself. The Scripture shows that not only did Joshua know his place, but he also wanted to protect the greatness or authority of his leader. He wanted to make sure others did not encroach on the prophet's powers.

As we see in the example of Moses and Joshua, mentorship presumes a "lesser" and a "greater" in a relationship. Mentoring implies that the lesser is learning from the greater through interaction, interpersonal contact, observation, and experiences. Mentors provide access to their lives, decision-making processes, bank of wisdom, and environment. The mentee has access to the mentor's relationships and resources. Resources can be people, material, and secrets the mentor might have. So mentoring is a very personal—and in some cases a very private—relationship. This separates it from ordinary interpersonal relationships.

Set Up for Success

One of most important processes of mentoring is not just learning from the experience of the mentor, but also learning from the situations the mentor will allow you to experience. The mentor is like a gymnastics coach.

One afternoon I was watching a documentary about gymnastics that showed how these amazing professional athletes train to become world-class competitors. I watched the coach fasten the safety straps to a young girl. After positioning her on the mat, the coach threw her into the air as if she were a bird while he stood right below her. Every time she touched down, he caught her by the waist and threw her again. He never left his post. I saw the initial fear in the girl's eyes, but as the exercise progressed, I noticed the fear turning into a smile of confidence.

The documentary moved on to the next day and there they were again, but this time the straps were off and the coach was still catching her. Finally, the fifth day came, and the coach was on the sidelines with a smile of confidence on his face. He watched his student pace the floor like a pro and with style, grace, and passion, complete her routine without a single mistake and land with a sense of maturity that amazed even the toughest judges on the bench. He had successfully mentored a future leader in gymnastics who eventually went on to compete in the world games.

Many times a mentor may seem to have set you up to experience a measure of failure, but he is really setting you up for success and is standing by just in case you falter. Good mentors will provide opportunities for you to participate in a situation that could teach you a lesson or allow you to use your gifts to prevail. The mentor knows that a mistake or temporary failure is a necessary step toward learning and qualifying for future success as a leader.

The Job of the Mentee

In order to get the most out of the mentoring process, you must understand certain principles.

The Mentee:

Must submit to the mentor. It is impossible to learn from someone if you do not submit to that person. It is like a class that does not accept the teacher's authority. Submission does not mean that you give up your independence, uniqueness, rights, or will. It does not mean that the mentor is smarter than you or more talented. It means the mentor knows something that you want to learn. Be submissive to advice and instruction. I sometimes encounter people who ask me to mentor them but who then refuse my advice or instruction. Right away that cancels our agreement. I cannot help someone who does not submit. Submission in this instance means that you understand and value the contributions that the mentor can make to your life. You are willing to surrender your time and your ability to learn and receive from that mentor. Submission is the first act for the mentee.

Must accept that the mentor is acting in the best interest of the mentee. You *have* to believe that whatever the mentor recommends, instructs, or advises is in your best interest. Your mentor's instructions may not seem to make sense at the time, and they might take you out of your comfort zone. The mentor's counsel might seem strange to you or put you in unfamiliar surroundings. You must trust the judgment and carry out the instructions (within reason) of your mentor. Good mentors will never set you up for destruction. They will set you up for development, if you let them.

Mentors see your future far beyond what you see, so you need to trust their vision. Many times they will tell you do *not* do this or that, or to do something. They are preparing you for something they see for you ten years down the road.

Must be willing to accept the mentor's counsel. Do not ignore their instructions. We often claim that we submit to our mentors, and we still do not accept what they say. If you want to benefit from the mentor, you must take the advice offered. If you claim I am your mentor and you do not take my counsel, I will release you immediately. Do not waste my time, please. If you submit yourself to the teaching and guidance of a mentor, the assumption is that you believe the person has something you need. To get the benefit, you have to accept the counsel offered. When someone rejects advice, mentors often refuse to continue the relationship, ending the mentorship opportunity. To continue is a waste of everybody's time. The mentee must trust the mentor's judgment. You cannot lead people who do not trust you, and you cannot learn from someone you do not trust. Remember, a good mentor does not want anything from you. The mentor did not pursue you. If the mentor gives you advice, he means it for your own good.

Must never abuse the privileges offered by a mentor. A mentor will give you access to such things as her private contacts, environment, or home. Mentors will give you access to the things they are reading, maybe their friendships and other relationships, or even their venues, markets, and audiences. The mentee must be very cautious not to abuse any of those privileges.

If the mentor gives you her private number, you cannot give it to people to prove you know someone powerful or famous. This is abuse. To have that number is a privilege. Alternatively, if the mentor introduces you to one of her contacts, you cannot go behind her back to try to work out a deal for yourself with that contact. That is an abuse of the relationship and an embarrassment to the mentor. It might have taken the mentor forty years to make that connection, and she can give it to you willingly in forty seconds, but do not abuse it.

I expose my mentees to my television programs, let them meet my publishers, or give them the microphone to speak to ten thousand people for a few minutes. I do that because I want to build their confidence and help them, but if the mentee secretly asks the host to invite them alone to speak next time, the mentee is abusing the privilege. People have told others I am their friend when they only met me once at a church somewhere and shook my hand. Do not abuse such opportunities offered by your mentor. You can say, "Yes, I have met that person. I shook his hand some time ago," but do not say that person is your friend when it is not true. I may give you access to the head of a country because you happen to be with me. That does not mean that you are his friend. I am his friend, and you should not disrespect him or me by calling him next week for a casual chat. He does not know you, and that would be an abuse of the privilege the mentor offered. If you have a mentor, you will get access to that person's life. Do not abuse it. Respect, honor, protect, and safeguard the privileges given you by the mentor.

Must initiate or pursue learning from the mentor. Once you have a mentor, the pursuit continues. You have to pursue what you want to learn from the mentor. If you claim you want me to be your mentor, for instance, then you have to prove it by your hunger, passion, and willingness to submit to my authority. The learner must not sit around and wait for the mentor to teach her or to develop her. Anyone worth having as a mentor will be fully engaged in work and other obligations. The one who wants to learn must pursue the mentor by cultivating the spirit of initiative.

You may feel as if the mentor is ignoring you at times, but remember mentors are busy. Just follow the mentor around and watch. Tell the mentor, "I want to see how you handle pressure, people, and stress." The mentor will not come to you to teach you five points on how to handle stress. You have to watch to see how they deal with pressures. Mentoring is more by observation than by instructions, so pursue the mentor. That is what Elisha did.

In the end, he went to Elijah. That was what the disciples of Jesus did. They forsook their fishing businesses and followed Jesus wherever He went. They ate with Him and went to little villages with Him. The very word *disciple* means perpetual student, from the Latin and Greek for "learner" or "one who learns." This implies that it is a continuous thing. Although it has come to be associated with the twelve associates closest to Jesus during His ministry on earth, it is not a religious word. It is someone who keeps learning. The instructor will teach only those who are hungry for education. The one who wants to learn should pursue the teacher.

Should harness the power of questions. As an emerging leader, you must ask questions of the mentor, accessing one of the greatest mechanisms of mentorship. The protégé pursues the mind, the methods, the mechanisms, and the mission of the mentor by initiating questions. Ask questions of the mentor. Nothing is more powerful as a tool for learning than asking questions. Mentors always know more than they tell you. Mentors can always do more than they show you. They can always take you places you have never been, but you have to initiate the journey via questions. A mentor is like a reservoir, full of knowledge and information, experience and wisdom—all wonderful, powerful substances—and you need to pull it out of them. A question is like putting a hole in a dam. The more questions you ask, the more holes you poke. If you ask enough questions, a torrent of wisdom will gush forth.

Good students do not talk much. They ask questions. When a mentee is in the presence of a mentor, he or she must speak little and let the mentor talk. This is usually by the mechanism of questioning. When I studied the process Jesus used to teach the disciples, I was shocked to discover that most of His lessons resulted from a question someone asked. The gospels are full of examples like these:

> **Luke 17:20** Once, **having been asked** by the Pharisees when the kingdom of God would come, Jesus replied, "The kingdom of God does not come with your careful observation..."

> **Mark 13:4** "**Tell us, when will these things happen?** And what will be the sign that they are all about to be fulfilled?"

Jesus shared His wisdom with those who asked for it. To draw out information from the mentor, you have to ask for it. I always tell my students wherever I am around the world that when you are in the presence of a wise or great person, ask questions and be silent. Whenever I meet anyone with much more experience and wisdom and with great accomplishments and success, I start asking questions. Questions automatically give you the ability to be the student. Mentees must ask questions. He who speaks, learns only what he knows; he who listens, learns what the other knows. Through listening, you become wiser. In this way, mentees initiate their own learning.

Sometimes you may be so determined to impress the mentor that you talk too much. If you are always talking, the mentor can become very irritated. If you want answers, do not tell the mentor what great things you do and how powerful you are, how anointed you are, what a good manager you are. How can you learn if you are talking?

Invests personal resources in pursuit of the mentor. Some mentees expect the mentor to pay for their development. Frequently people ask, "Will you mentor me?" and I reply, "Okay, fine, let us agree that I will mentor you. As part of my mentoring program, I offer the elite privilege of allowing you to travel with me to experience my environment." I find it very strange when someone responds, "Great! Can you send me a ticket?" Who is supposed to be pursuing whom? If you want to learn from me, you must be willing to invest your time, money, and resources in pursuit of that knowledge.

We need to understand the power of pursuit. If you want to learn from me, then invest your time, your money, and your resources in pursuit of me. You will have to invest in your own life. I have books, CDs, DVDs, and seminars. If you are my mentee, I expect you to buy all of those books because you need to know my mind, my heart. Forty years of my experiences are in those books. When you buy the mentor's book, you are not just buying the book. You are buying the person.

On occasion, a mentee has asked me a question, and I have refused to answer it because I have answered that question in a book I wrote. I tell them to read the book. Invest that twenty dollars to find the answer for yourself. As your mentor, I do not want your money, but I want you to invest in your own development. Always remember this: the job of a teacher is not to give answers but to stimulate the students to go find the answers themselves. Nothing is yours until you understand it.

Must never compete with the mentor. The mentee must be very aware that he is not in the relationship to compete, but to learn. First, this deals with motive. A mentee is one who wants to learn, who wants to become like the mentor in many different aspects, who would like to benefit from the mentor's knowledge, experience, and wisdom. You cannot easily learn from someone when you are attempting to compete with him.

You will find that mentors will resist the spirit of competition from a mentee because it reveals a spirit of pride or arrogance. It also reveals a spirit of distrust.

Must never take the mentor's advice or criticism personally. If the mentor says things in a moment of anger or corrects you, it is to prevent harm from coming to you or to teach you a lesson. When Elijah told Elisha, "Go back...What have I done to you?" (1 Kings 19:20), it must have sounded harsh, but it was necessary. When Jesus told Peter that he was full of the devil, the words must have stung (see Matt. 16:23). Whatever the circumstances, when the mentor speaks in the heat of the moment, the person on the receiving end must be cautious not to take the words personally.

The mentor might say, "Son, why are you dressed like that at this location? Go home and change into your suit." Do not take that personally. He is trying to protect you because he knows that people at this event will be dressed in a certain way, and they will judge you or even refuse to admit you if you are not attired in a similar fashion. The invitation said "black tie," and you are in tennis whites—nice clothes, but not the right ones.

A mentor might say, "Do not come in here right now. Please wait outside." Do not take it personally. Perhaps it is a matter of protocol. Only people of a certain rank or members of a fraternal group are allowed in today. Maybe he is discussing a confidential personnel matter.

He might say, "You can't come to this reception with me. The president or prime minister will be there, and security is tight. You don't have clearance. Just wait in the lobby." At times, the mentor may not be able to or may not be inclined to give an explanation. Do not take that personally. He knows things you do not know.

A mentor will give you instructions that might make you feel uncomfortable. He may say things that hurt your feelings. Just trust that this too is for your benefit. "I will figure it out later. It hurts right now, but it is for my own good." After Jesus told Peter that he was full of the devil, the disciple still showed up at the next meeting. He did not take it personally. In a moment of anger, a mentor will say things that sting. Jesus Christ was angry because Peter had said, "You will not die" (see Matt. 16:21–22). Peter was attacking the vision. Jesus was correcting Peter, and He did not say it nicely.

Anger is part of the mentoring process because the mentor sees you in your future and attacks the danger that threatens you. It is not personal. It is love. The leader wants to teach you a lesson. When a mentor speaks in the heat of the moment, you have to handle it. Be mature, suck in your stomach, come back and say, "Thank you." Later on you will say, "Wow! Now I see why she did that." Do not despise the anger of your mentor. It too is for your good.

Must never be jealous of the mentor's success. Often a young, emerging leader sees the life of the mentor and assumes or presumes that he could achieve instantly what the mentor has spent years of effort—a lifetime of work—building up. In some cases, the mentor has experienced mistakes, failures, loss, disgrace, depression, or bankruptcy and come back out again to overcome them before achieving what he or she has. The most important question a mentee should ask a mentor is not, "How can I have what you have?" That is the wrong question. Rather ask, "What did it cost you to achieve that? What is the price you paid to achieve that?" The student needs to learn the process and the experiences necessary to achieve the goal.

The mentee must be very cautious not to cultivate jealousy regarding the mentor's observed achievement. If you sought out a mentor, it is because that person is successful. You cannot learn from someone if you are jealous of her. Often emerging leaders see the life that the mentor has and desire it. Mentees have a temptation to want instantly what the mentor gained over time.

The CEO has a jet, a luxury car, a beach house, and more money than you ever dreamed of having, but you do not know what it cost him—fifty years of tough living. Do you covet the aircraft? Why not ask him what it cost to get that private jet? The answer is liable to be: "Oh, twenty years of criticism, five years of depression, two years of ostracism, and ten years of bankruptcy. Then I finally got back on my feet and spent another ten years building my business to the point that I could afford all this. Now I travel three hundred days out of the year and hardly ever see my gorgeous wife and my darling children. I haven't had a home-cooked meal or slept in my own bed in weeks." Never mind. It is not worth the price. Never be jealous of anyone, especially your mentor.

Must follow instructions even if it demands personal sacrifice. Many times a mentor will give the mentee an assignment, an instruction, or a project that may require a sacrifice of time, resources, energy, or relationships. The mentee must trust the mentor to the point of obedience. That is a frightening word, but you have to obey the mentor because he knows more than you do. He has been where you plan to go and has done what you intend to do. If the mentor gives you instructions, just obey them. This is hard for some of you to do because your pride is so tall that God cannot even get above it. Mentees also have to believe in the mentor's belief in them. It is scary to do something for the first time. The mentor may give you an opportunity that you never experienced before, but the fact that he gave it to you is evidence that he believes in you, even when you do not. That is the mentor's way of developing your belief in yourself.

If you want to be mentored, you have to sacrifice. Now, be careful because some people who say they want to mentor you actually want you to buy them things—rings and clothing, for instance. They are not mentors. They are fleece artists. Good mentors make you spend money on yourself, not on them. Be careful about the person who professes to mentor you but wants you to make them rich. That is not a mentor. If so-called mentors take from you, they are not mentors. If they demand that you enhance their lifestyle or that you do anything against God's Word, the Bible, it is not mentoring. It is abuse.

Must be honest in the relationship with the mentor. No pretense, misrepresentation, or lack of integrity should enter the mentoring relationship. The mentor cannot afford to have the precious time he devotes to the relationship misused or devalued. The two parties must demonstrate mutual respect, integrity, and honesty. Do not try to be something before the mentor that you are not. The mentor will dismantle you. Do not lie to a mentor. The mentor will eject you. Be open, transparent. Do not try to misrepresent yourself to impress the mentor. You must have integrity.

Tell the mentor your vulnerabilities, your weaknesses, and your struggles. Be honest about what you do not know. This person can help you. If you are perfect, why do you need a mentor? The mentor can handle your secrets. The mentor knows how to manage your frailty. Mentors can help fix the cracks in your character. Mentors do not use your private information for personal gain. They are there to improve you, so be honest with them.

The mentor cannot afford to have the precious time he or she spends on you abused. Perhaps I have been preparing you for a certain position, and I find out later that you are not available or disqualified because of something else going on in your life or in your past. Both of us have wasted time. If I spent five months mentoring you, and I find out that what you are doing in secret has cancelled everything I did, you have abused my time. Mentoring demands honesty.

The Continuing-Education Program

Submitting to a mentor is a smart decision. It is not demeaning. It does not make you less. It makes you more. Mentorship is critical. The mentor is not in it for gain. The mentor is in it to help you gain. Cherish the privilege and never abuse it. If you do not choose to benefit from the privileges extended by the mentor, the mentor never loses. The mentor knows what he knows, is who he or she is. If you choose not to benefit, you will never become all you could be because you did not complete the mentoring process.

The mentee is more indebted to the mentor than the mentor is to the mentee. Yet each has a role to play and responsibilities in the relationship. Mentors respect mentees. They do not ignore your value. They know that you are important. In fact, a mentor will respect you just because you decided to enter the mentoring relationship.

You never outgrow mentors. You must always be under somebody. The day you think that you do not need a mentor, you are a threat to humanity. I submit to my mentors quickly. Whenever I am in the presence of anyone who has great wisdom, I am a professional questioner. When I first met Nelson Mandela, I met history. I do not have those moments often in my life. I did not want to spend my limited time with him telling him who I was, where I am from, and what I was doing. As far as I was concerned, I had just met a father and I was a child.

I started asking questions because I had to learn a lot in a short time. I do not have to take time to talk about me because I already know about me. My questions gave me the power to draw on his wisdom and learn from him. I was his student, however briefly, and I submitted to his instruction.

Some people who sign up for my mentoring program are seventy-five years old. They are still learning, and they realize that I have something they need. Age is not an issue in mentoring. Peter was older than Jesus. The mentor already has achieved a level of success and effectiveness regardless of age. Mentors reap rewards for fulfilling their purpose, not for their years. The mentee is the one who needs the development, the cultivation.

Do not abuse, misuse, ignore, or devalue the privileges extended by the mentor and squander opportunities to learn. Respect, cherish, and value the relationship. You will be the beneficiary.

Points to remember:

The mentor chooses, but the mentee pursues.
The mentee must submit to the mentor's guidance, ask questions, and cherish the relationship.

Chapter 22

Take the Credit and Rejoice in Your Mentee's Success

THE PEOPLE YOU brought along are taking over. Your successor is ready. Learn to say, "I trained her—now look how far she has come," "I was his mentor. Isn't he great?" or "I taught them. I am so proud of their accomplishments." Then sit back and let them take the enterprise to a higher plane than you were able to do in your allotted time.

When somebody you mentored is doing well, tell people, "That is my boy!" That individual's success is your success. That is your mentee, your protégé.

God felt the same way about His prototype, as noted several times in the gospels. He let people know that was His Son.

Matthew 3:17 And a voice from heaven said, "This is my Son, whom I love; with him I am well pleased."

God took the credit. Are you ready to take the credit for mentoring the emerging leaders around you? If you have succeeded in producing successful leaders and chosen your successor, letting go is hard, but you can do it if you realize the successor is the measure of your success.

Good leaders claim the credit for their successor's success and rejoice in the success of others. If you have done your job as a leader, your successor or successors will go on to have many successes. You can take comfort in and take credit for much of their success. A leader glories in the successes of others. True leaders need not be afraid of their followers' gifts and success. They have no reason to be jealous or resentful. After all, they nurtured those gifts and helped produce the leaders we see today.

Leadership is measured by the success of your successor. That is how you test yourself. Look at the leaders you produced.

This Is a Test

Mentors want the world to discover their protégés and provide them with opportunities to show their true capabilities. Mentors even set up opportunities for people to test their gifts. You see examples in which Moses gave Joshua assignments. He told Joshua to go fight a war, and he rejoiced in his victory.

> **Exodus 17:9** Moses said to Joshua, "Choose some of our men and go out to fight the Amalekites. Tomorrow I will stand on top of the hill with the staff of God in my hands."

In a similar fashion, Jesus provided opportunities for His students to test their abilities, and He was very excited when the disciples succeeded. A true leader does what Jesus did. He sent His followers out to try some things and was pleased when they reported on what they achieved.

> **Mark 6:7** Calling the Twelve to him, he sent them out two by two and gave them authority over evil spirits.

Jesus had modeled the behaviors and the type of ministry He expected of them. Then the Teacher let them loose to practice. He did not just lecture or preach and expect them to go out on their own with no trial period. He showed them and then gave them field experience.

We can recall that Jesus even said He expected those who had faith in Him not only to do what He had been doing, but also to do "greater things than these" when He left (see John 14:11–13).

Secure leaders deliberately choose people who have the potential to be better than they are. Do not be afraid of people who are stronger than you. Do not be afraid of your weaknesses. Always hire people who are smarter than you because they make you look good. Apply this principle to your personal life. Marry someone who is smarter than you are. Your spouse will make you look good. If your children surpass your success, it is to your credit.

"A leader glories in the successes of others."

Secure leaders provide opportunity for others to find and fulfill their God-given purpose and reach their greatest potential. If I stand to speak before ten thousand people and someone I mentor is with me, I invite her to speak for five minutes or so. She might say, "You are crazy! I can't speak in front of all these people." But I insist that the crowd is waiting for her. "How are you going to learn to speak to thousands of people if you never do it? Use my credibility and practice it now." This is an opportunity to colead. I let her feel everything I feel—the anxiety, the butterflies, the sense of how to relate to a crowd. This leader in training can experience that whole environment. Those five minutes can be worth more than ten weeks' classroom study because instead of hearing me lecture about it, the individual experiences it.

Mentorship programs must be more than instruction. They should be experiential. Mentoring differs from teaching or instruction, as I said previously, because teaching may give you information, but it does not model the lesson. Mentoring is modeling in order to train by experiential relationships. Mentoring has more to do with relationships than it does instruction.

Room for All

There is room at the top for everyone. A mentor believes his mentee should be better than he is. A mentor works on making others better. Moses was not upset when Joshua told him people were trying to prophesy as he did. Moses wished for all of them to prophesy—the whole camp. This is my leadership philosophy, that the original leadership model was based on the fundamental principle that we should not focus on building an organization with a leader but rather on building an organization of leaders. It is my desire as president of our organization and chief executive officer of our international company that all discover, develop, cultivate, and manifest the full potential of their leadership gifts.

This same idea excited Moses. He basically said, "I wish all of them were prophesying. Everybody is in charge. I wish everybody were doing what I am doing. What a job!"

That means Moses did not think he needed followers to be a leader. Moses probably measured his leadership by the fact that he was becoming unnecessary. He would not need to prophesy if others could hear God for themselves. That is how Moses thought. He ended his admonition to Joshua saying he wished the Lord would put His spirit on the others the way He had put it on Moses.

The average leader does not think that way. Ordinary leaders wish that no one will come along who has what they have so they can always be in charge. They forget that a true leader works himself out of a job. They do not understand that a true leader desires to become unnecessary.

Tell a young person who pursues you that you are going to make them a mentoring project. "Before I leave or die, I am going to teach you everything I know." When that individual becomes successful, he or she will tell everybody that you were responsible. Take the credit.

Go, Be Better

At a conference recently, I introduced Jerome Edmondson, a young man I had mentored. He had left his home and spent a whole year with me. He and his wife invested a great deal of money in this mentoring experience. Jerome has traveled with me to Africa, Europe, and South Africa, as well as all over the United States and the Caribbean.

After that year, this fellow is better than I am. He told me that he is the first black man to be a franchise owner of a particular restaurant chain. Jerome recently released a book that became a best seller. I was able to help with that. Not too long ago, he showed me a letter saying that he would be receiving a grant for one million dollars. My joy is in his success. He is an associate in my environment. He is an example of how to train people to become better than you.

My greatest joy is when my mentee becomes greater than I am. This is why I work so hard. My greatest legacy is in the people who exceeded me. When my mentee becomes great and powerful, I can move on to something greater in this life or go on to my reward in heaven. I want to be just like my mentor, Jesus Christ.

Greater works shall you do. That is what mentoring is all about. It is about making you better, greater, more influential, and more powerful. It is about helping you to exceed your own expectations.

I would love to take the credit for that.

Points to remember:

Make others greater and take the credit.
Good leaders rejoice in the success of others.

Chapter 23

"Now You Go"

TRANSFER THE VISION

MY FIRST MENTOR was my father. He taught me how to love work as he provided for all of his eleven children. He demonstrated the manhood necessary to lead a home both spiritually and emotionally. He mentored me by letting me observe him as he prepared sermons. I watched him minister publicly to crowds. From my early teens, I watched how he dealt with stress. He even taught me how to be married to a woman, setting an example as he was married to my mother for fifty years until her death. For these and other reasons, he was my most important mentor as a man.

My mother was my second mentor. I was able to observe how she had a hunger for the word of God. My mother taught me how to read the Bible. My father taught me how to preach the Bible, but my mother taught me how to read it. She taught me how to love people. I do not think I ever have seen anyone who loved the poor as much as my mother did. While raising eleven children, she would practically take food off our table and give it to poor people. She mentored me in caring for people who are less fortunate.

Mother also mentored me in the act of prayer. I used to hear and watch her pray, even though she did not know I was observing her. This is true mentoring—when people can see the spiritual act of a person. Her example left a great mark on my life, and I pray daily as she did.

In addition to this great experience of my parents, I had two powerful mentors in college at Oral Roberts University. One was a professor in the school of theology who taught a class in New Testament studies, Dr. Jerry Horner. I took that class and instantly realized this man knew so much that I wanted to learn. I submitted myself to him. Today Dr. Horner is on my board of trustees and still is one of my chief mentors. He has been with me for more than thirty-five years. I have been able to observe him closely during the years, visit his home, and see his family. Jerry sleeps in my home every time he comes to the Bahamas to speak at one of our conferences. It is important to note that he is white, and I am of African descent. The people I mentor come from many different ethnic groups.

"Just as I received the gift of mentorship, I have a duty to pass it on."

Another great mentor of mine, Oral Roberts, died recently. I vividly recall one time I was on a television show as a student. As soon as I saw those cameras, I began to shake visibly as he was interviewing me. I was petrified because I had never been on television before. This commanding orator who had preached before thousands in live appearances and to the world through the airwaves acted instinctively to calm my fears. With one hand holding the microphone, he reached over with the other one and gently patted my knee as he was talking to me. His touch melted all the fear. He knew what he was doing. He was calming a frightened mentee, and I never forgot that. It has been more than thirty-five years since that day, but I can still remember the touch. The affirming power of a mentor's touch will last you a lifetime.

When I first came back to the Bahamas in 1980 after college and graduate school, I began this ministry. Some people said I was a cult. They would talk negatively about me on the radio and television, and ministers used to preach against me. I used to be sermon material. One of the highest compliments they ever paid me was, "He thinks he is Oral Roberts." That was flattery. At least I was not associated with some preacher who was not doing anything or who was misleading people. I was glad to be associated with somebody who was doing something.

Still another of my mentors, Dr. Fuchsia Pickett, taught me how to have a zeal for the things of God. She taught me how to pursue God with a passion, how to fast, and how to sacrifice for greatness. She also affirmed me in my desire to train leaders. She actually told me I should proceed with my global passion for developing leaders in Third-World countries.

As I matured as a leader, I had access to all of these people. I could call them at any time. They could rebuke me, correct me, or instruct me. Many times they would caution me in certain areas of my life. That was and still is important to me. I am still being mentored, even though I mentor thousands of people at a distance and hundreds of people directly.

Consider the Lion

In the introduction to this book, I talked about the lion. We consider this creature the most successful in the animal kingdom. The lion's effectiveness in survival and its ability to face down other creatures regardless of their size, weight, or power impresses us. The lion is a perfect example of a creature with the qualities necessary for effective leadership. That includes its courage, grace, and strength, but the most important is the way the lion mentors its offspring.

First, lions do not associate with any other animal. This is interesting because if you want to be a leader or maintain your leadership, you must first be mindful of the associations you form. You want to be with people who think as you do, people who walk and talk as leaders should, people who have leadership experience. You want to learn from them.

The second thing about the lion is that it travels in a pride. That is a family of lions who live, hunt and work together. In this way, lions have created an environment for mentoring their offspring.

That is what I find most interesting about the lion. At the beginning of the book, I spoke of our safari in South Africa, where I had the privilege of watching the lions hunt. I noticed little cubs around, and I saw the mother lion pick up the cubs by the back of the neck with her mouth, take them over to a shady bush near a tree, and drop them down one at a time. She came back, picked up another one, took him over to the tree, and left him there.

Then I saw something strange. She walked away, and they perked up looking at her but never moved. Four other female lions joined her. They all began to crouch toward their prey. The cubs never moved, and they watched their mothers. I was intrigued as I saw those lions strategize as they crept along in the grass, moving toward the target—one to the left, one to the right, one over to the side, and one stayed back. They were all in position, working toward the attack.

Still, the cubs never strayed, but they perked up, watching every move. Suddenly, I realized this was mentorship in action. This was an opportunity to preserve the future of the pride. Then I realized that the lioness had not just placed her young ones near the bush under a tree, but had set them up on a little mound where they had a perfect view of all the action. The mother chose a high place so that they could observe every move.

No wonder the lion is still the king of the jungle. The lion does not leave leadership training to experimentation. They do not risk mistakes or let the next generation learn by trial and error. They intentionally train.

What I also find interesting is that the lionesses are the real hunters in the lions' pride. In the lion kingdom, the father does not do the kill. The women go out and get the meat. Lionesses take the young ones with them on a hunt and find a safe place for them to observe how, when, where, and what to kill. The cubs can see the lionesses' movements, their strategies, their systems, their attack modes. This is mentorship by observation. This is the reason the lion is so successful. They continue to reproduce leadership.

You are responsible for creating a "pride of lions" mentality around you for those you mentor. Let them see how you do things. Many times leaders in our day hide what we do from the people around us. We do not want them to observe what we do because we are insecure. We believe that if they learn what we do, we will lose our position. However, we forget that the entire purpose for leadership is to reproduce leaders and that the greatest measure of success for a leader is to mentor a potential replacement. For this, the lions are a great inspiration.

Just as I received the gift of mentorship, I have a duty to pass it on. The greatest obligation of a true leader is to transfer a deposit into the next generation. As a leader you were given a gift, you developed a vision, and you carried it out to the best of your abilities during your tenure. Perhaps you exceeded your own expectations, or you did not finish. Either way, as part of the mentoring process, you have tried to instill your values and your vision into the next generation of leaders. If you have done things right, they "caught" your vision. Time is up. You must relinquish control, pass the baton, and trust that your successors will succeed.

Your successor will not always do things just as you might have done and may not think, "I wonder what he would have done now?" Even as a parent, you might have to accept that your children will not always think, "What would Mama or Daddy do?" Fifty years from now, your church members will not say, "Reverend Jones always said . . ."

Some of us do ask, "What would Jesus do?" as the popular saying goes. Often, however, we know very well what He would do because Scripture clearly outlines His vision for us. His parables prescribed what to do in many key situations that we can apply to what we do today. The principles, His rules for living and leading, tend to work whether you aspire to be a Christian or not, whether you are in the church or the boardroom or in the streets. Similarly, public leaders often like to read about their predecessors, and we encourage our youth to read about national heroes, hoping their lives hold clues for our own—that the vision will rub off.

The Advanced Class

The gospels leave us many clues about how Jesus mentored His disciples. I find it interesting that among the twelve trainees or students, He chose from among the group three to mentor at a different level. Peter, James, and John received more intimate mentoring than the other nine. You will observe that on many occasions in Scripture, Jesus would take those three to certain environments and leave the other nine out of it. He did it because He wanted them to experience certain things. Their knowledge of Him grew to a deeper level. Their leadership positions in the church in Jerusalem were at a higher level. Their work and teaching of doctrine was at a different level. Earlier, I emphasized that a mentor must devote time to the people he or she mentors. Jesus spent extra time with these three.

You will find that Jesus often chose to expose these three priority mentees to different events and did not take the other disciples. In one example, when He wanted to raise the little dead girl, Scripture says He left everyone outside except those three and proceeded to raise her from the dead. That was an opportunity Jesus provided for the three that He had singled out for close attention.

> **Luke 8:51–56** When he arrived at the house of Jairus, **he did not let anyone go in with him except Peter, John and James,** and the child's father and mother. Meanwhile, all the people were wailing and mourning for her. "Stop wailing," Jesus said. "She is not dead but asleep." They laughed at him, knowing that she was dead. But he took her by the hand and said, "My child, get up!" Her spirit returned, and at once she stood up. Then Jesus told them to give her something to eat. Her parents were astonished, but he ordered them not to tell anyone what had happened.

These same three were with Him at the Transfiguration.

> **Matthew 17:1** After six days **Jesus took with him Peter, James and John the brother of James**, and led them up a high mountain by themselves.

Only they were with Jesus as He prayed at Gethsemane on the eve of His death.

> **Mark 14:33 He took Peter, James and John** along with him, and he began to be deeply distressed and troubled.

These examples show how Jesus shared time and set the stage for transferring His knowledge and spirit to these three in particular. He would imply, "Look, I only want you three to come." What is Jesus doing? He is taking them into an environment in which He did not want the other nine. He wanted to mentor these three at a different level and allow them to see things He did not let others witness. He would tell them not to tell anyone what they had seen. He was testing them.

Jesus also exposed His vulnerabilities. Mentoring requires that you expose your vulnerabilities when the occasion calls for it so the mentee can understand your heart. When Jesus asked, "Could you not keep watch for one hour?" (Mark 14:37), He showed His fear or anxiety to those closest to Him. Do you have people in your organization you can take into some of the private parts in your heart?

You would normally entrust succession to those who know your strengths *and* your weaknesses. For the protégé to get past those obstructions in your life to understand your vision, you have to expose yourself. You have to convey your passion, and encourage the mentee to fall in love with what you love. Your successor must love you, your passion—what wakes you up in the morning. If the mentee never captures that, then he or she will never be successful as your successor.

Let Them All Prophesy

At times, Jesus shared lessons with all the disciples and He gave all of them His authority. When He sent them all out two by two to go into the whole world to bring the message of the kingdom, He was sharing an opportunity with them. The Bible says He gave them authority to go, which means Jesus wanted them to experience that environment, go out, and carry a message, dealing with people.

Moses transferred his spirit in a similar fashion. When God told Moses that he needed some help to do the work, He told him to call seventy people from the group so God could transfer Moses' spirit to them.

> **Numbers 11:16–17** The LORD said to Moses: "Bring me seventy of Israel's elders who are known to you as leaders and officials among the people. Have them come to the Tent of Meeting, that they may stand there with you. I will come down and speak with you there, and I will take of the Spirit that is on you and put the Spirit on them. They will help you carry the burden of the people so that you will not have to carry it alone."

The people who should be in your ministry or close to you in your business should be the people of your spirit. They should have the right attitude. They should think what you think, believe what you believe, and want what you want.

The Bible says that once these seventy got the spirit, they began to speak. The word the Scripture uses is "prophesied." They began to speak what Moses was speaking. In other words, they sounded just like Moses.

This transfer of the anointing of Moses also leaked over to people who were not even present. They were in the camp, and they too began to talk and sound like Moses. Joshua became a little nervous.

That was when he urged Moses to stop them. "They are all going to take your job!" That in a way was what he was saying. Look at the answer Moses gave. "But Moses replied, 'Are you jealous for my sake?'" (Num. 11:29). That is an important statement.

Again, the person who is jealous *for* you should succeed you.

Joshua was defending Moses. This is when Moses shows his leadership maturity, when he suggests in so many words, "I want everyone to be a leader. I want everybody to be a prophet."

Is that how you think? Do you wish everybody in the office could have your job? Are you saying, "I wish all of you could do this job. I am going to train all of you to have my abilities"?

True leaders are never married to a position. Leaders walk around with a debt they owe to humanity. "I am going to pay my debt and continue paying by mentoring and choosing the right successor." That is how I feel every day. I owe all of you what I am teaching. I have to do this. I owe you this. This is not a job for me. This is an obligation.

Moses was authentic. He was secure in his position—just as Joshua was secure in his. He was the servant, the aide—in other words, the one who was there to do anything and everything the leader needs. In fact, an aide outthinks you, always watches to see what you are thinking of doing next and does it for you. The aide thinks, "He is going to be thirsty, so let me get some water. He is going to need someone to rub his feet. He is tired. He is going to need someone to bring him food now. He is going to need someone to change his coat." The aide anticipates these needs and fills them. An aide is totally committed to the comfort of the leader. All Joshua wanted to do was to aid Moses since his youth, the Bible says. Joshua did not show up looking for power. He grew up serving. That is what qualified him to be Moses' successor.

If you are the boss, look around you. Who in your company, school, or church is like that? If you are a leader in training, are you a willing aide as Joshua was?

At the Eleventh Hour

Perhaps you have read this far in the book only to realize that you do not have a successor in mind. You have not mentored anyone. Time is running out, and no one is waiting in the wings fully prepared to succeed you. You need to go to work, make some changes, and find someone you can embrace as a potential successor while there is still a little time left.

If you are the CEO of a company or a manager of a department, your first responsibility to the board is to fulfill the mission and the expectation to the company. Your first obligation to yourself, even at this late hour, should be to identify an individual that you want to mentor to take your place. You might not have authority to choose your successor, but you want at least to mentor someone to take your place.

Given the circumstances, this does not have to be someone who loves you as I defined it earlier in this book. If you have not mentored anyone, chances are you have not attracted that kind of love or loyalty yet. Chances are that during the years you turned away those who pursued you, begging you to be their mentor. You never acknowledged how talented, eager, and willing they were. Many of them left for other opportunities. A few stayed, but you never groomed them for greater things, and most of them stalled or burned out. Now you have no one in the pipeline who is fully prepared, and your options are limited.

You will have to seek out someone you believe has great visionary potential, aspirations, or great intellectual capacity. Once you have identified the person, you might have to woo them. Initiate the discussion. Invite him or her into your office to explain your desire to mentor, and solicit that individual's interest. Say to them, "If you are willing to be developed, I am willing to develop you. I agree to help you. Do you agree to let me?"

People may be surprised when you approach them in this way, but the gesture will show that you care for them. I believe that very invitation to mentor them, the fact that you reached out, can be the basis of a caring relationship. Once the individual agrees, then proceed to mentor based on the principles outlined in this book. Eventually that can lead to the kind of "love" you need in a successor, or at least respect.

Yes, you may be mentoring late in the game, but now is better than never. Advise your superiors that you are mentoring this person. Now you are opening up the possibility of succession. If you answer to a board, they will respect you for thinking beyond your time with the company. The board will also feel secure in knowing that because you are mentoring someone, they will not need to go outside the organization to recruit a potential successor.

The board might even decide to pay you more for fear that you are planning to leave. The fact that you are being sensitive to the company's needs for succession makes you the kind of person they want to keep around for a while. As a manager, you have a win on all sides. You have someone in training to replace you, you have a board that might feel more committed to you, and you have an increase in salary. Just one act of demonstrating that you want to mentor can improve your relationship to the company, as well as your bank account.

Cast a Wide Net

If you are not the principal of the organization, you can mentor a successor for your position, but not necessarily for the whole organization. If you are the principal of the organization, you have more authority over mentoring and succession. Everyone can mentor someone, however. You do not need to be the president or owner. The minute you have a position of authority, your first act is to choose someone to mentor.

If possible, choose more than one individual to mentor and make them all aware that everyone will have the opportunity to advance and grow under the mentoring program. Let them know you are not responsible for the future, nor can you guarantee any position. You can promise that you will position them for any opportunity that will be available. This reduces the possibility of jealousy and infighting once your choice is clear.

I mentor hundreds of people from around the world. I also mentor twenty-two people within my organization. One of them is the one I chose as successor. Because I mentored all of them, none became jealous.

Jesus mentored twelve, but had three who were His favorites. Of course, we do have a record of James and John asking for a special place, and Jesus had to correct them that everyone has a spot (see Matt. 20:20–23 and Mark 10:40). I think this shows that His interest in mentoring all twelve of them reduced the tension and the spirit of competition among them.

Put your eyes on one individual who may be a potential successor, but open up mentorship to a broader circle to encourage development of all the gifts that are under your influence. Encourage those you mentor to mentor. It reduces the spirit of competition and anxiety when you require persons you are helping to help someone else. You will find that they all will develop a spirit of care and respect for one another.

The Greatest Failure

The worst mistake a leader can make is to mentor no one, choose no successor, and leave no legacy. The first example of this in the Scripture is the first created human, Adam. He died without any strong successor. The Bible does not indicate that he mentored anyone, not even his wife. He was so poor in his mentorship of her that his wife was subject to persuasion by a satanic force, and it destroyed his whole family. One son killed his own brother. This is the worst form of lack of mentorship.

The next one would be Joshua, who despite having had effective mentoring, appears to have left no strong successor. So Joshua failed as a leader. After the death of Joshua, the Bible says it happened that the children of Israel asked the Lord, "Who shall lead us now?"

> **Judges 1:1** After the death of Joshua, the Israelites asked the LORD, "Who will be the first to go up and fight for us against the Canaanites?"

The book of Joshua mentions no specific person he mentored—no aide to Joshua as he was to Moses. We ended up with a scattering of people with no organization. Israel never fully recovered.

If we do not mentor, we create chaos. Another example of weak mentoring is Solomon, who did not groom anyone to follow him. David mentored Solomon, but after Solomon died, the kingdom was divided and destroyed. In the New Testament, the trend continues. Jesus chose Peter, but Peter failed to appoint someone, so there was chaos. Paul appointed Timothy, but Timothy failed to appoint someone.

The constant principle flows through history that where there is no mentoring, there is no successor. Where there is no successor, there is no order. Where there is no order, there is chaos.

Whenever a void occurs in the succession of leadership, scattering and decentralization follow. God has to start all over again with the next generation, saying essentially, "Let me find someone who understands this." God has to find someone new who can start fresh, carry out the obligation to mentor, and choose a successor before time runs out.

Can you accept the challenge to lead as if the future depends on it? Are your successors in place, trained and ready to go? Then step back, give them full authority, and send them forth to do greater things. Your supervision is no longer needed here, and you too have better things to do.

You have conveyed your vision, you have produced leaders, and you have given them opportunities to apply their skills to practical situations, to practice the performance of miracles. Now trust that they will carry out—not necessarily your exact vision as you would have it—but a vision inspired by, shaped by, and formed from yours. You will have a legacy. This will be the ultimate test of your leadership. Can your successors perpetuate your purpose, carry on your vision, preserve your legacy, and go on to do greater things?

When it is time for you to go, you will be able to say, "I have transferred all I have, my grand vision, to my successors. I lived up to the mentoring agreement. I have trained them well. It is up to them to run on." Your segment of the relay race is over. It is finished.

The Apostle Paul put it this way:

> **2 Timothy 4:6–7** For I am already being poured out like a drink offering, and the time has come for my departure. I have fought the good fight, I have finished the race, I have kept the faith.

Points to remember:

The greatest obligation of a true leader is to transfer a deposit into the next generation.

The worst mistake a leader can make is to mentor no one, choose no successor, and leave no legacy.

Afterword

A Word to the Third World

Failure to mentor and produce successors in leadership is greater nowhere than in Third World or developing countries. We hear daily of government coups, political rivalries, battles over the spoils of power, and the realities of such disgraceful inhumane acts as ethnic cleansing, culture clashes, and religious wars. Tribal warfare and religious conflicts are pervasive in these dynamic environments and only add to the fragility of leadership in these emerging nations.

Why is it so difficult for leaders in these postcolonial nations to mentor others and consider the prospect of giving up power to succeeding leaders? Why is there such a temptation to hold on to power and even to go to extremes in some cases to annihilate any threat to one's leadership security? Why are leaders in these nations with such great potential willing to sacrifice and auction their people's future for the sake of keeping power? Is the problem psychological, social, economic, political, spiritual, or ethnic? Perhaps the answer is in the history of these peoples and the world that produced them.

Many social scientists and scholars are baffled over the plight of the leadership challenges in the developing world, and some have concluded that there must be a social or genetic defect in the psychological development of leaders in these regions. However, being a product of the social, economic, political, and spiritual history of this context myself, I can appreciate the unique perspective one gains after experiencing the environment of colonial oppression. The very terminology "Third World" that is used to describe the millions who live in these postcolonial territories and emerging nations has its detrimental consequences and renders one psychologically disadvantaged as it relates to a healthy self-concept, high self-esteem, and strong self-worth.

The Legacy of Colonization

Industrial states never have properly appreciated colonization's role in preventing the development of quality leadership in emerging and developing nations. Many of these industrial nations were the perpetrators of colonization. Colonization was the extension of the major European kingdoms of France, Portugal, Spain, Belgium, Holland, and Great Britain.

Colonization was mostly motivated by economic and territorial pursuits to exploit agriculture and extract natural resources as gold, silver, diamonds, other precious stones, oil, and wood. Theses interests led to the establishment of mass farming, mining, and timbering projects, which in turn led to the slave trade and indentured servitude. This resulted in the movement of peoples from their homelands, displacement of families, and destruction of historical and social bonds and infrastructures. These disruptions created grave emotional, social, and psychological disorientation for millions of people.

The reality was systematic oppression of human potential and the eradication of human dignity and self-worth. The system reduced humans to products, rather than recognizing them as persons. They were considered commodities, rather than creatures made in the image of God. These make up a large share of the people designated today as "Third World" people.

This historical backdrop provides the reference and context for many of the leaders that oversee the process of the developing nations. Many of these leaders struggle with fundamental issues that leaders in many industrial nations do not have to confront. Not only are the leaders challenged, but the people they lead are also. The social, psychological, and economic impact of colonization on its postcolonial territories is a very important component when considering the challenges related to the lack of mentoring and succession.

In many ways, colonization remains a reality. It is possible to assess some of the effects, such as lack of self-worth, low self-esteem, poor self-concept, and loss of a sense of history. These result in psychological disorientation, producing a sense of self-hatred, distrust, powerlessness, and a spirit of survival of the fittest among the people and the leadership.

One of the greatest tragedies is that the architects of colonization blocked the development of leadership among the peoples of the colonies. The purpose of colonization was to subjugate, not to educate, to overpower not to empower. The goals were to produce brainwashed followers, not leaders; to create servants, not stewards; and to have dependents, not independent thinkers.

When the territories and colonies eventually threw off the yoke of the colonial powers, the governing responsibilities often fell to unprepared, untrained, unskilled, and inexperienced leaders who were thrown into the seat of power by destiny. The psychological defects of poor self-concepts, low self-esteem, and lack of self-worth further crippled these leaders. The result is leaders who struggle not just with political, economic, and social issues in these emerging nations, but with impaired skills and knowledge.

Perhaps this is what the great king of Israel Solomon meant when he wrote, "Woe to you, O land whose king was a servant [slave]" (Eccl. 10:16).

In essence, the nation is in danger when the leadership has the mentality of a slave. It is unfair to judge these leaders by the same standards as those in the industrial nations who have had the advantage of hundreds of years of leadership legacy.

Hope for the Future

It is my hope that the leaders of emerging nations will overcome the mental and psychological damage of a history of oppression. If they dedicate themselves to investing in self-development and to freeing the people from the same mental damage that has held them hostage to their past, they will succeed.

The future of the Third World nations rests in the quality of leaders we identify, cultivate, train, mentor, and empower to serve their generation with humility and an awareness of their dispensability. May they be the new generation of leaders who love serving more than being served, empowering more than retaining power, giving authority more than taking authority, and producing leaders more than maintaining followers. May they be mentored and become mentors.